AN ECOLOGY OF

ENCHANTMENT

D0730952

DES KENNEDY

A YEAR IN THE
LIFE OF A GARDEN

An ECOLOGY of ENCHANTMENT

GREYSTONE BOOKS
Douglas & McIntyre Publishing Group
VANCOUVER/TORONTO/BERKELEY

Copyright © 1998 by Des Kennedy
Introduction copyright © 2008 by Des Kennedy

08 09 10 11 12   5 4 3 2 1

All rights reserved. No part of this book may be reproduced, stored in
a retrieval system or transmitted, in any form or by any means, without
the prior written consent of the publisher or a licence from The Canadian
Copyright Licensing Agency (Access Copyright). For a copyright licence,
visit www.accesscopyright.ca or call toll free to 1-800-893-5777.

Greystone Books
A division of Douglas & McIntyre Ltd.
2323 Quebec Street, Suite 201
Vancouver, British Columbia
Canada v5T 4s7
www.greystonebooks.com

Originally published in 1998 by HarperCollins Canada

Library and Archives Canada Cataloguing in Publication
Kennedy, Des
An ecology of enchantment : a year in the life of a garden /
Des Kennedy.—10th anniversary ed.

ISBN 978-1-55365-370-7

1. Gardening—British Columbia—Denman Island (Island)—Anecdotes. I. Title.

SB455.K46 2008   635.9   C2007-906842-1

Cover and text design by Naomi MacDougall
Cover photograph © Marion Brenner/First Light
Back cover photographs © Naomi MacDougall
Printed and bound in Canada by Friesens
Printed on acid-free paper that is forest friendly
(100% post-consumer recycled paper) and has
been processed chlorine free.
Distributed in the U.S. by Publishers Group West

We gratefully acknowledge the financial support of the Canada Council for
the Arts, the British Columbia Arts Council, the Province of British Columbia
through the Book Publishing Tax Credit, and the Government of Canada
through the Book Publishing Industry Development Program (BPIDP) for
our publishing activities.

For Sandy

CONTENTS

Acknowledgements · *xi*

Introduction to the Tenth-Anniversary Edition · *xiii*

Preface · *xxiii*

JANUARY

1 · Facing Janus *1*

2 · A Natural Pattern *7*

3 · Stone Angels *11*

4 · Born to Hedge *18*

FEBRUARY

5 · Ash Wednesday *27*

6 · St. Valentine's Day *34*

7 · The Accidental Orchardist *40*

8 · Stark Beauties *47*

MARCH

9 · Blood Sports *56*

10 · Spring Subtleties *64*

11 · Vernal Equinox *71*

12 · A Shed of Its Time *76*

APRIL

13 · All Fool's Day *82*

14 · Tiny Green Fingers *89*

15 · Dressing Down *95*

16 · Pest Asides *100*

MAY

17 · Lusty Tumescences *107*

18 · Beneath Blowzy Clouds *112*

19 · Seedling Dissension *119*

20 · At the Stake *124*

21 · Flights of Fancy *130*

JUNE

22 · Gooseberry Fools *136*

23 · Tour de Force *143*

24 · Summer Solstice *148*

25 · By Any Other Name *153*

26 · Ever So Blue *159*

JULY

27 · Fools for Fawning *165*

28 · Here Be Giants *170*

29 · Of Empires and Vampires *176*

30 · Poppycock *182*

31 · Armed and Dangerous *187*

AUGUST

32 · The Devil Finds Work *193*

33 · Others Don't Like It Hot *198*

34 · Night-Club Ladies *204*

35 · Mid-Life Crisis *209*

36 · Summer Whites *215*

SEPTEMBER

37 · Blighted Lives 221

38 · Amusing Oberon 227

39 · Autumnal Equinox 232

40 · High and Dry 237

OCTOBER

41 · Swelled Heads 244

42 · Thanksgiving 251

43 · Late Graces 256

44 · All Fall Down 262

NOVEMBER

45 · All Saints' Day 269

46 · Our Roots Go Down 274

47 · Vanity Fair 280

48 · Passages 285

DECEMBER

49 · Birch Barking 291

50 · The Permissive Gardener 296

51 · Winter Solstice 301

52 · Year's End 307

ACKNOWLEDGEMENTS

ORTIONS OF THESE essays originally appeared, in altered form, in my regular columns in *The Globe and Mail* and in *Gardens West* magazine, and one column in *Gardening Life* magazine. Thanks to my editors at each.

Thanks to *Better Homes and Gardens* Special Interest Publications for permission to reprint portions of chapter 15.

Very special thanks to Bernice Eisenstein for her help in getting the book underway at the outset.

INTRODUCTION

TO THE TENTH-ANNIVERSARY EDITION

*S*URELY ONE OF the great attractions of gardening is its endless interplay of continuity and change. In many ways the garden remains the same year after year—the precision with which a dragonfly alights on the floating leaf of a waterlily, the sweet nostalgia of honeysuckle scent on a midsummer evening, the resolute strength of stout oak limbs. Yet the place is never absolutely the same, even from moment to moment, as a sudden spill of petals changes everything, a hummingbird appears in an iridescent commotion, or the slant of light shifts to illuminate a corner in shadow moments earlier. In every garden timelessness and evanescence perpetually conspire.

Ten years have slipped past since this book of garden meditations first appeared. Back then we were hurtling towards the century's end with as much *Sturm und Drang* as the popular media could muster. But in retrospect that already seems a comparatively saner and gentler age, before 9/11 and the maelstrom of carnage and paranoia it unleashed. Despite the warnings of scientists and environmentalists, the monster of global climate change had not yet become real in public consciousness. Google and You-Tube were not on anybody's screen.

The mania for gardening was near its apogee as the century wound down. Gardening books were flying off bookstore shelves, big garden shows were jammed elbows-to-ribs with enthusiastic viewers, and nurseries bulged with new and exciting plant selections. Interest in organic methods, native plants and wildlife gardening was at an all-time high. You couldn't turn on a television without encountering a gardening guru in full plumage.

The gardening fever that swept through mainstream culture, as it seems to do every few decades, appears to have run its course. Busy professionals discovered to their dismay how much time and effort, not to mention cost, is involved in maintaining a trophy garden. Specialty plant societies and garden clubs complain of an aging membership and lack of young recruits. Some garden shows have shrunk or disappeared entirely. Publishers who ten years ago were baying like hounds in pursuit of gardening books now sniff, "We're not doing any gardening titles at present." Television producers now bend their attentions less to gardens than to home decor and outdoor living.

So, yes, there have been tectonic shifts and slips of all sorts since *An Ecology of Enchantment* was published as a modest celebration of one year in a garden on a small island off Canada's west coast. I wrote at the time that "this is not a book about how to garden—a highly site-specific matter—but about the passions and raptures, the heartache and melancholy of those who do." And, in this regard, *plus ça change!* Ten years, forty full seasons later, the passion abides, the raptures and sadnesses recur. An affair with a garden—the book's original U.S. title was *This Rambling Affair*—seldom grows stale. The garden of the heart holds charms that do not fade with age, but rather deepen and diversify.

A decade ago, our ornamental garden was ten years old and I was fifty-three. The photograph on the book's cover showed a springtime garden of narcissi and tulips and precious little else. Compared with this spring's display of maturing trees, shrubs and perennials, it looks an enthusiastic but rather paltry show. Nevertheless, I could write at the time: "Walking through the garden at dawn, and again in the late afternoon when sunlight seems to glow from inside the leaves themselves, you'd have to be a hopeless oaf not to feel, for all one's woes, a thrilling sense of a perfect world emerging." That very same tingling apprehension of perfection still occurs and I suspect will continue to occur ten springtimes from now, when we may glance back at today's garden as still very much a work in progress. And that's the great beauty of it, isn't it? That the garden remains an artistic exercise that's never finished but at every stage of its existence stirs with the excitements of the creative process.

We've added new arbours and new stone walls—for those who have it, the compulsion to pile up stones, like gardening itself, seems not to fade at all with time, although undeniably stones weigh far more now than they used to. In that earlier phase of the garden, plants could get away with a slaggardly performance without severe consequences, but we've gradually grown more ruthless in dealing with malingerers and underachievers. For example, a clump of lacecap hydrangeas of questionable provenance—not to be confused with the *bona fide* beauties celebrated in chapter 41—occupied a prime position for years, soaking up water and nutrients, sulking pitifully if neglected for a day or two, eventually producing a smattering of half-hearted blooms before declining into a long dormant season of unsightly twigs. Enough already! Up they came and rudely out they got booted, replaced by an undemanding installation of clipped yew and English boxwood that serves uncomplainingly every day of the year.

Several other impeachable specimens prematurely celebrated in these pages are no longer with us, most notoriously the giant cow parsnip recommended in chapter 28 as "a guaranteed show-stopper." This oversized thug has since been declared a noxious weed, and I expect at any moment a rapping on the door as the authorities show up to haul me away for gross intellectual indecency. I shall plead guilty as charged. Less dramatically, the evening primroses, those glamourous nightclub ladies swirling their skirts in chapter 34, are all but gone. Along with California poppies, mallows and foxgloves, these sun-loving self-seeders find fewer and fewer opportunities to put down roots in a garden so packed with plants there's scant spare space available.

Consigned to a winter wet/summer dry climatic regime, we've always leaned towards drought-tolerant and hardy plants, particularly natives. Ease of maintenance and all-season interest now play a larger role in the mix. We've brought in a lot more evergreen structure (although I'm beginning to question whether endless clipping and shearing truly qualifies as low maintenance) and far more ornamental grasses—stipas, fescues, *Miscanthus, Carex* and all the rest—undemanding plants that provide extended rewards in combination with shrubs and hardy perennials.

Up the hill, the vegetable garden remains a less giddy, more steady affair. The wisdom of organically growing as much of one's own food as possible has never been more self-evident. Issues of food security and the hidden environmental costs of long-distance agribusiness now clutter the popular media. Farmers' markets and regional cuisine are all the rage. And while dahlia societies and alpine plant clubs may be suffering a downturn in new members, Seedy Saturdays and other seed exchange programs along with community gardens seem to be seething with young characters devoted to growing their own healthy food.

But even in the potager there's continuous call for fine tuning. Neither a sentimental attachment to growing gooseberries nor apocryphal moaning over the devastation wrought on blighted tomatoes, as detailed in these pages, have survived the decade. With jars of unopened gooseberry jam piling up in the pantry, and the goose-berry bush in its dotage, we made the great life change away from gooseberries. Testosterone-laden tayberries now grow in their place. The great plague of tomato blight was permanently banished by growing all our tomatoes inside a pair of greenhouses.

But, as seasoned gardeners know, solving or avoid-ing one plague serves only to open up plague-space for another to encroach. Black slugs, the unlovely *Arion ater,* were the next to be visited upon us. An alien species intro-duced from Europe, these opportunistic gastropods are both voracious and exponentially reproductive. They were unknown on the island when we started gardening here thirty-six years ago. Then locals began reporting them and, like a monstrous slimy tide, they gradually flooded across island gardens. Having previously strutted upon the stage as a defender of plants and animals misguidedly labelled repulsive—and slugs were the poster boys/girls of this campaign—I found myself caught between the Scylla of public opinion and the Charybdis of having our gardens torn to tatters by marauding slugs. I resorted to soph-istry, touching upon the subtle distinctions between native and exotic species. We redoubled our kindnesses towards native banana slugs, but with the black invaders we were as implacable as Churchill on his beaches, dispatching many dozens of them every damp day. Eventually their population crashed, whether from natural causes or our interventions we don't know. But suddenly, marvellously, the hosta and ligularia and broccoli leaves were no longer perforated ruinations. The garden seemed saved and the world a better place.

Exeunt slugs; enter raccoons. Here again was a troublesome species, albeit a native one and thus beyond the casuistry that had justified the slug wars. Coons had been here many years ago, before our time, but had been wiped out, allegedly by distemper. For many years we lived and gardened in raccoonless bliss. But then began their gradual reoccupation of the island. Growers started experiencing overnight raids on fruit trees and vegetable gardens. We were among the last on the raccoons' list, but when they came, they came with a vengeance. Plum and pear trees and grape vines were entirely stripped of fruit, their branches torn and broken; snails were plucked out of our little pool, their crushed shells lying pitifully alongside the corpses of newts with their heads bitten off. I scurried about putting metal collars around fruit tree trunks and hanging all-night lights among the grapes and figs. But the figs and grapes proved indefensible. To see on a bright summer morning all one's juicy, near-ripe figs chewed to a stringy pulp—this is to know a rage and hatred such as fuels the interminable bloodbaths on view at every evening newscast. In the battle of wits being fought here, I fear I'm badly outmatched, reduced to fervent prayer for another outbreak of distemper.

Still, no raccoon can match certain humans for rapacity. Several years ago the 120-acre parcel behind our place was sold to an individual severely afflicted with avarice. He immediately clearcut the property, subjecting us to the noise and lights of a huge feller-buncher roaring all day and night. The scream of toppling trees replaced the haunting calls of owls. Within days a lovely woodland of frog-filled ponds and mossy glades, where for decades we'd picked sweet huckleberries in spring and wild chanterelle mushrooms in autumn, had become a wasteland of stumps and logging debris. Along our property line, big hemlocks, cedars and firs, now suddenly exposed to fierce southeast winds, were torn up by their roots and jumbled in treacherous tangles requiring endless hours of hard going with chainsaw and axe to get them cleaned up. Stripped naked, the logged land was flipped back onto the market.

This entire exercise was the complete antithesis of gardening. Plants, creatures, soil, water—nothing had value except insofar as it could be piled onto trucks and hauled away for profit. But there's always a cost with such profit. In this instance, the individual responsible seemed afflicted with a peculiar state of mind that rendered him miserable with self-pity. I've met others just like him. Indeed, their numbers are legion, and their combined pathologies contribute hugely to the mess our planet's in.

Successive years of summer drought are taking a further toll on our woodlands. Browning of needles and die-back of branches tell of trees under extraordinary stress. Another item in the global warming file: in the winter of 2006–07, our area was hammered by a series of murderous storms. The lighthouse off our island's southern tip clocked wind gusts up to 177 kilometres per hour. A hundred-metre-high water spout danced across the channel off our eastern shore. Trees and power poles snapped like brittle sticks. Big branches were hurled through the air and forest giants ripped from the earth. We lost dozens more large trees left vulnerable by the clearcut. Old-timers said they'd never before seen storms like these.

What with clearcut, blowdown and die-back, our place has over the space of a decade evolved from a small clearing in the woods to a far sunnier and semi-open prospect. We see far more blue sky and passing clouds. Unseen before, sunrise now comes pouring through the trees, casting long slabs of golden sunlight across the early morning garden. On clear nights, moon rise on the eastern horizon is now a visibly brilliant spectacle.

Through all of this change, and whatever perils lie ahead, the garden retains a well-grounded centrality in our lives. Its beauty and productivity increase year by year, as does its capacity to delight and soothe and inspire. In the latter part of life particularly, but not exclusively, it is appropriate to sit quietly in a place of great beauty and be at one with it. Not looking so much, nor thinking about it, but simply being within it. Somewhere over the last decade I have come to understand that the garden is not a simulacrum of the divine, not a mere backdrop against which lofty contemplations may occur. It is itself the divine. At its best—and there's the rub, this endless quest for its perfection—yes, at its best, the garden is one of those sacred places wherein the human spirit is set free.

PREFACE

$\mathcal{W}$ HILE TOURING in both Canada and the United States with my previous gardening book, *Crazy about Gardening* (a title one acerbic critic deplored as "ditzy"), I was frequently asked: "Is this book any good for someone who doesn't garden in British Columbia?" I answered for that book as I do in advance for this one, with a resounding Yes! It's true I have the good fortune to live and garden on one of the Gulf Islands off Canada's West Coast, a benign spot where both the gardening and the living are easy. But it's equally true that the sensations and emotions aroused by gardening readily transcend particularities of place and even of time. Those who are stirred by the love of plants know that theirs is a specialized view of life, a distinctive way of looking at and being in the world, no matter what part of it they hail from. We are people who walk hand in hand with green-fingered ancestors and soulmates from all over the place. Although written from my own garden-ing experiences, this is not a book about how to garden—a highly site-specific matter—but about the passions and raptures, the heartaches and melancholy of those who do.

I have written the book in fifty-two sections, one for each week of the year. We begin in the darkness of winter solstice, proceed through the soaring hopes of spring into the ecstatic interludes of summer, then tumble through the mournful brilliance of autumn back to the dark of mid-winter. I chose this format in part to celebrate the splendid circularity of the gardening year and in part because this marvellous dash between darknesses is such a tidy para-digm for the unfolding of a full life. In that sense, I dare to hope that the book may appeal even to readers who don't themselves garden. Because the moods and lofty medita-tions entertained at various points in the gardening year are at heart the pure stuff of being human.

All of which sounds terribly ponderous, in a way I pray to the heavens my writing is not. I've done my very best to avoid deliberate ditziness, but as every gardener knows, at a certain point in the journey all you can do is laugh.

Denman Island, British Columbia

AN ECOLOGY OF

ENCHANTMENT

JANUARY

WEEK 1: FACING JANUS

There's nothing I'd like better than to welcome you with open heart and cheerful disposition into our gardens, but I cannot. Not today. Today we're in something of a crisis brought on by brutal weather and are far from our normal buoyant selves. Instead, here we are plopped into a new year with renewed doubts as to whether gardening is a story that begins in disaster but ends in triumph or the other way around.

Gardeners are generally quite adept at surmounting everyday disasters, at picking up the pieces after some catastrophe or other, with only a minimum of grumbling. Here I mean events like the delphiniums toppling over despite assiduous staking, or the depredations of neighbourhood cats. Full-blown catastrophes are another matter altogether. Once-in-a-century floods or windstorms can wreck the work of decades and batter the stouthearted, so that everything is called into question, right down to one's faith in gardening itself.

Thus our year begins under ominous skies and melancholy reflections. We have just emerged, those of us who live in the Pacific Northwest, from what the commentators are calling "the snowstorm of the century." Between Christmas and New Year, clouds of snow came shoaling down like manna upon the Israelites, piling up hip-deep almost overnight. Looking out our kitchen window, I see the big native cedars, firs and hemlocks that surround our little clearing—normally plump and bushy trees—now stand as slender frosted spires, as though mimicking rugged spruce on some northern mountainside. The clearing itself lies transfigured into an undulating expanse across which Doctor Zhivago might come gliding any minute in a horse-drawn sleigh. Balalaikas might ring in the crisp cold air.

For normal mortals these could be hours of unsullied pleasure, snowbound with old John Greenleaf Whittier, an opportunity to ponder the transformative power of nature, and similar high-blown notions. But not for the gardener. The weather forecasters (having somehow failed to notice, or at least inform the rest of us, about the oncoming blizzard of the century) tried to recoup lost ground by predicting heavy freezing rain on top of the snow. Everywhere I looked, disaster loomed. The roofs of our owner-built outbuildings seemed to groan under the snow load. Prized saplings bent over and wept like the daughters of Zion. One power pole crashed down, a second leaned tipsily. This was no time for contemplation, but for action. We've spent the past two days wading through snowbanks as high as my diaphragm, barely moving at times against the depth of snow, doing what needed to be done if disaster were to be averted. For hours on end we pulled snow off the roofs and shook it from the smaller trees and shrubs, inflamed by that strange exhilaration disaster can excite. At times I felt like some demented Arctic explorer in his last desperate days before collapse.

That's January for you, named for Janus, the ancient Roman deity who protected doors and entranceways and so came to preside over the entrance into a new year. He's depicted with two faces, a normal one at the front and another on the back of his head, looking to both past and future, just as I'm doing now in my snowbound rounds.

Last winter, you see, ended with a freak late-winter snowstorm that wreaked more havoc at our place than anything else in the past twenty-five years. The typical heavy rain of March thickened to wet snow. The weather service issued a snow advisory for the area. Unconcerned, my companion, Sandy, and I stoked the woodstove and curled up cozily to watch a video of *Pride and Prejudice*. Before the movie was half done, the power went out. By then the snow lay ten centimetres deep with more still swirling down. A prudent gardener would at that point have gone out and shaken the shrubs and small trees to relieve them of their snow load. But with dozens of trees

3

and shrubs to worry about, we let the pull of comfort push prudence aside and instead snuggled into bed.

All night we heard the creaking and wailing of big trees around our place, the awful cracking of large limbs breaking and crashing to Earth. By morning the power was still out, the grounds mounded and heaped with fifty centimetres of snow and more still falling. The gardens and woodlands looked indescribably lovely, but also littered with disasters. I grabbed a broom and plunged out into snow well up over my knees—the kind of snow I remember from Lake Simcoe, back in Ontario in the fifties, the kind we're not supposed to get here in the Pacific Northwest.

Wet and heavy as well as deep, the snow had caused tremendous damage. Limbs as thick as a linebacker's thigh lay torn from big cedar trees and scattered on the snow. A young cascara tree seven or eight metres tall was bent completely to the ground. Adolescent red alders stood snapped in half. As battered as the natives were, our exotic specimens were worse. A large flowering plum tree was stripped of almost every branch. A twenty-year-old apple tree lay flat on the ground, entirely uprooted. The trunk of a young pseudoacacia, thicker than a broomstick, had snapped off completely. Shrub roses and rhododendrons splayed flattened under contoured mounds of snow.

We shook and brushed and disentangled what we could. Fearing the worst, I was sometimes relieved: a two-metre-tall cryptomeria lying prostrate in the snow bounced up once I had relieved it of its snow load. The same with various clumps of bamboo. None of the Japanese maples were damaged, though they'd bent their limbs grotesquely under the weight. The dogwoods had also bent but refused to break. Released from its snow load, Harry Lauder's walking stick seemed to shake itself back into shape, like a dog coming out of a pond, and proudly display its dangling yellow catkins.

The brittle woods fared worst. One flowering cherry that I'd carefully pruned to an open vase shape had lost about half its branches. A lovely little redbud had suffered severe breakage as well. Worst of all were the birches. The younger ones had bent down to the ground, just as Robert Frost described. The oldest tree in the grove, with a trunk as thick as a fencepost, had simply snapped in half.

Afterwards, in the grand tradition of gardeners everywhere, we looked to salvage some good from this desolation. The toppled apple tree, for example, was one of three transparents we've had growing for years, always producing far more apples than we could deal with. There's a quantifiable limit to how much applesauce any two people—even compulsive grow-your-owners like ourselves—can consume in a year. We'd often threatened to cut at least one of the trees out, but hesitated, reluctant to destroy a productive tree. Now nature, less given to liberal scruples, has culled one for us.

Same with birches. Robert Frost notwithstanding, birches don't do well on the coast. They're like prairie

5

people, or mountain people, needing hard weather to keep themselves true. Unsteady on their feet, repeatedly diseased, woebegone in appearance, ours had been an ongoing embarrassment, something outspoken visitors would look at and ask: "Why do you possibly keep those wretched things around?" But, again, we'd hesitated to root them out, like all soft-hearted gardeners forever willing to give the most decrepit specimens "another chance" to right themselves. Flattened and cracked beyond redemption by nature's harsher judgement, they were far easier to let go of. Perhaps best of all, we were able to take our place in the long line of gardeners who recognize that snow breakage can be conveniently blamed for causing distortions in trees and shrubs that were in fact caused by years of inept pruning. A killer snowstorm every once in a while is a real boon to bad pruners.

All this was last March, and having learned a priceless lesson from it, we weren't about to be caught flat-footed a second time. Thanks to diligent shaking and brushing during this Christmas storm, and to the bearable lightness of the snow itself, I think calamity has been averted. But staring out the window now, I realize it's hardly a triumph. Surely more of a holding action against the inevitable. We sit indoors these days, warmed by the woodstove and restless for new rains to wash the snow away, Janus-faced gardeners all of us, looking to both past and future, in a narrative finely balanced between jubilation and despair.

WEEK 2: A NATURAL PATTERN

Despite habitual fretting and occasional fits of melancholy, gardeners seem determined to take a favourable view of things over the long haul, to find good omens in the most unpromising entrails. Why else would one garden? We are utopians at heart.

Thus I've already developed a more cheerful attitude towards our record-setting snowfall. In this roseate mood I recognize that a great dump of snow has the distinct advantage of flattening most everything under it, and, once melted, affords a sparkling opportunity to study the garden in its most fundamental form, stripped, as it were, of its finery. The form of the garden we've created (or inherited, perhaps, from predecessors of truly fantastic tastes)—a form whose lines might be blurred amid the splendid superficialities of summer—now lies entirely exposed. We are down to the bones of our gardens.

Serious students of gardening (and I suppose we must have solemn plodders every bit as much as cheery day-dreamers, although both would do well to strike the happy balance you and I have achieved) argue that it is this skeletal outline, the ground-floor geography of a garden, that will ultimately determine whether it becomes an abode of enchantment or simply a place where a lot of plants, however charming in themselves, happen to grow.

Stripped this way of its adornments, the garden might appear no more alluring than we ourselves do when, our

7

summer colour and vitality faded, perhaps our paunches more than middling after Christmas nibbling, we stand before a full-length mirror modelling next summer's swimsuit. The inadequacies of our untutored stabs at landscape design (not to mention idiosyncratic features inherited) may be cruelly revealed.

This is not a time for panic, but rather for a period of relaxed contemplation of the wintertime landscape. Most gardeners have no formal training in landscape design (possibly not an entirely bad thing, considering some of the masterpieces created by persons blessed with such training). We do, however, I believe, have an innate sense of balance and proportion, what British gardening author Beth Chatto calls "a feeling for shape." The gardens of the nation attest to this. People concerned with earth respond instinctively to a pleasing configuration—perhaps a clever intersection of horizontal and vertical lines—if only we'll give ourselves unhurried time in which to have these perceptions arise. Gazing at our trees, walls, pathways, outbuildings and other large components of garden design, we come to recognize what parts of the whole are intrinsically well or ill balanced, and what remedial steps we might consider.

I was once taught by an entirely eccentric old English professor whose oft-repeated first commandment of composition, although hardly original, might readily apply to garden design: keep it simple, stupid. Simplicity suggests, among other things, that garden structures and features serve some useful purpose. I don't mean that we can't be

whimsical—whimsy is the lifeblood of ornamental gardening—but that we avoid the patently trivial and frivolous. I
know this is hard, cutting as it does against the grain of
our culture, but we should try anyway. A path that leads
nowhere, randomly placed statuary, waterfalls that gush
from aquatically impossible corners—none of these contribute to good form. They may provide a moment's
titillation, like the latest soap opera heartthrob, but their
destiny is to distract; by distracting, they undermine the
integrity of the whole.

And while simplicity counsels us to avoid the contrived,
it warns us as well to beware the heavy hand of artful impo-
sition. You know the sort of places I mean: grim precincts
where gardeners patrol in relentless pursuit of anything
wayward or improper, as though plants, unless kept under
stiff restraints, are predisposed to wander off aimlessly
like the offspring of certain acquaintances. "Symmetry is
wearying," wrote the old master Lien-Tschen, "and ennui
and disgust will soon be excited in a garden where every
part betrays constraint and art."

The subtle patterns of a landscape do create emotional
resonances, the less blatantly the better. Curves and undu-
lations generate a soft and leisurely ambience, perhaps a
whisper of romance. Zig-zag lines tend more to the herky-
jerky, provoking the imagination to dart forwards, like
water striders on a pond, expecting some excitement. Cir-
cular and spiral lines draw us into ourselves, calm us down
and suggest very gently that we might consider taking a
course in Zen Buddhism.

9

Winter lays bare these lines, revealing how the garden is structured and divided by solid masses and areas of open space. Do the solid elements provided by trees, shrubbery, fences and buildings serve to frame open areas and accentuate specimen plantings, or do they create a clutter of enclosures that prevents a flowing movement through the garden? Have we perhaps fallen prey to a misplaced mania for garden "rooms," dividing our landscape into the botanical equivalent of a furniture warehouse? Or is there too much open space, an ill-defined expanse without boundaries or break points, with no dominant features serving to link the garden to its surroundings and to bring scale and proportion to its plantings?

My own large country garden (well, Sandy's and mine) is a rambling and undisciplined affair, best referred to as an informal or, better still, natural garden, relying primarily on plant groupings to achieve spatial definition. To quote Lien-Tschen again: "The art of laying out gardens consists in an endeavour to combine cheerfulness of aspect, luxuriance of growth, shade, solitude and repose, in such a manner that the senses may be deluded by an imitation of rural nature." And that's really all there is to it. We've tried our mightiest to reflect a natural pattern of overstory trees, understory shrubs and herbaceous levels underneath. The idea, of course, is to achieve a harmonious composition by playing the vertical lines of trees against the rounded mounds of shrubs and spreading ground-level plants as nature herself would do. I have come to the conclusion that one completes this attempt, if at all, shortly before dying.

Perhaps the gravest threat to closure is what I call seasonal myopia—the temptation to tailor one's planning principles to fit fluctuating seasonal moods. In the mists and pallid sunlight of our coastal winters, when the horizon creeps forward like Birnham Wood towards Dunsinane and gloomy thoughts beset us, we're agitated by a seasonal hankering for openness, for clearing away the shadows and expanding the garden so it's free of restrictions and confinements. (Windswept flatlanders, I imagine, feel the opposite.) Deciduous trees are especially vulnerable in this state. We begin debating the questionable merits of several crabapples that are threatening to enclose us unduly. Tentative plans are made to move them out. By next August, when we're sweltering under blazing sunshine, grousing about ozone depletion and all the rest, we'll be equally determined to get more shade trees planted in the very spots that in midwinter seem already excessively treed.

Awareness of these contradictory seasonal demands can provide a wholesome incentive for the gardener to do nothing at all, lest it be done in haste and unwisely. Thus the bleak days of winter can be whiled away in trenchant analysis and stirring plans for action, the bulk of which can be abandoned with the onset of spring before any permanent damage is done.

WEEK 3: STONE ANGELS

Few aspects give me greater satisfaction in these dumpish January days than contemplating the stoneworks at our place, and while we're discussing the good or poor form of gardens as exposed by the rough handling of winter, we must certainly speak of stone.

I have over time arrived at the conclusion that people are either born to stone or they are not, in much the same unaccountable way that individuals seem destined to a fundamental happiness or sadness no matter what they do or fail to do with their lives. For those who have never felt its loving embrace, stone remains hard, cold and rough, metaphorically austere, obdurate and unfeeling. Hearts made of stone, they do not break.

But happy are those who are born to stone, who have heard the stone angels singing, for nothing contributes more to a well-grounded life. These are people whose idea of a grand vacation is to tramp for miles across moorlands in search of remote standing stones, megalithic tombs or the half-fallen walls of ancient masons. So too in a garden. Limestone or slate, cobblestones and flagstones, chalkstone or granite—stoneworks give the garden a lithic under-pinning that holds one's ground firm against the worst of winter's onslaughts, then carries the seasons of bloom to pinnacles of perfection scarcely otherwise achievable. There's nothing indeterminate or temporary about stone, nothing wishy-washy or apologetic, but a unified solidity, a strength of purpose within which whimsicality can be set free to fly.

12

I'm sure my own romance with stone began subconsciously in the old stone cottage in which I was born on the outskirts of Liverpool. There was a deep stone quarry nearby—a forbidden place of fascination and danger—from whose blocks many of the village buildings had been constructed long before. I spent my earliest years toddling around in haunts of ancient stone.

The love of stone lay quietly within me for several decades until I eventually washed ashore on this little island twenty-five years ago. At heart the island's just a heap of fractured sandstone and conglomerates, pushed and heaved up millennia ago as a great tectonic plate bashed into the west coast of the continent. Coincidentally, there's another old stone quarry, long abandoned, just up the road from our place. There, in the first years of the twentieth century, workers blasted out sandstone blocks to be shipped to the city for building. I now find myself at least halfway through a life that began, and promises to end, within a stone's throw of a quarry.

Shortly after arrival, following an instinct as fundamental as that of an ant gathering twigs for its colony, I set about heaping up all the sandstone I could lay my hands on. Sandy—still a prairie girl at heart, spiritually more given to grassy expanses and wide skies than to the intimacies of stone—had the good sense to tell me very early on that I possessed a remarkable "feeling for stone" that she didn't, so I'd best take over the stone work completely and make of it what I could.

This spousal blessing inspired a lapidarian binge that even I now marvel at in hindsight. Phase one involved an accumulative frenzy. Every spare moment I'd hop in our little truck and roar off to anyplace where fresh stone might

13

be gotten. Some I picked up along roadways, following the Highways Department grader for which no road, however wide, is ever wide enough. Some I pried with a steel bar out of stony banks, or gathered where new roads were being bulldozed. At the risk of self-congratulation, I'll tell you that these were not insignificant bits of stone, not chippy little cobbles or boulders—no, these were enormous great slabs of stone, the cumbrous bones of Mother Earth herself, some weighing hundreds of pounds apiece. I bullied them out of the bush and up onto the truck bed with a monolithic singleness of purpose and a brawny, muscular machismo. It's no mystery to veteran stone croppers how the great pyramids were put together, or Stonehenge, or all the rest, not with several thousand dullards like myself all juiced on testosterone for the moving of stone.

Nevertheless, those called to stone soon learn its hardest lesson: that what seems like enough never is. I hauled in truckload after truckload and heaped it up till it seemed I had enough to fashion a minor Matterhorn. But in no time at all it was gone, shrunken into a few miserable retaining walls. I repeated the exercise over and over, and by the end (oh, let there be an end!) I'd hauled in about seventy truck loads. You might wonder why a mindless, will-driven exploit like this can excite such satisfaction. It's because the moving of stone, in and of itself, is an aesthetic experience, as the Stonehenge rock rollers undoubtedly knew better than most.

Thick, flat slabs I bedded in sand as a surface for our pathways and patios, as they make a passable flagstone

14

paving. I bordered the raised flower beds with large, irregularly sized blocks. Smaller flat slabs I laid up as dry terracing walls along a gentle hillside, fancying ourselves in the Cotswolds or the olive groves of Corfu.

But the instinct to stone once roused is not to be satisfied with the practicalities of pathways and retaining walls. I soon found myself executing stoneworks of questionable necessity. We decided that we must have a rock garden of sorts even though, as Henry Mitchell writes, "Nothing in all gardening requires so much work for so little return as a rock garden."

I went further. Alongside the new rock garden, I excavated by grub hoe and shovel a large semicircle into the hillside and laid the whole thing up with stone blocks to a height of slightly more than two metres. It looks like some ancient ruin you'd stumble across in the back country of Macedonia, and serves no practical purpose at all, which doesn't prevent me from being inordinately proud of it. Further along, we created a flight of wide stone steps that connects three different garden levels in a rustic Canadiana version of the terraced gardens of the great Italian villas.

My enthusiasm perhaps makes this all sound a tad more grand than it really is. Compared, for example, with the stunning limestone rockeries of the Niagara escarpment region or the fieldstone walls of New England, my efforts, for all their brawny machismo, seem decidedly modest. In comparison with the meticulous placement of the guardian stone and the worshipping stone in a traditional Japanese hill garden, our laying up of stones looks inexcusably slapdash. Still, the rocks are a comfort, offering substantial rewards after all the back-cracking labour and mashed fingernails. On these wintry days, when most of the foliage is gone and incessant rains soak the earth, our exposed stone walls and paths glisten with a thrilling symmetry and solidity, a bulwark against muddy dissolution.

Stone's terrific for creating microclimates and special growing spots. Small stone alcoves and nooks that catch and hold the warmth of early springtime sunshine are perfect for encouraging some of the earliest bulbs. Dry zones along the tops of our retaining walls are where drought-loving plants like dianthus, euphorbias, nepeta and irises flourish. At the base of the walls other species thrive that prefer a cool and moist root run—summer phlox, delphiniums, Japanese anemones and hostas. The crevices and crannies in the dry stone walls provide cunning planting spots for cliff dwellers that droop and cling and form small tufts to accentuate the patterns of the wall. Various creeping thymes flourish along our stone pathways, available for a passing foot to crush them and release their fragrances. California poppies, wild bleeding hearts, foxgloves and feverfew are among the wildlings that seed themselves profusely around the stones.

Wildlife gardeners are among the loudest in singing the praise of stone. Warmed by spring sunshine, our sandstone provides important basking spots for entwined garter snakes assigned to patrol the grounds in search of slugs. I remember last spring watching two snakes coiled together in a copulation magnificent with serpentine loopings and lashings of tails and sinuous sexuality. Red-legged frogs and tree frogs enjoy sunbathing on the sandstone slabs which edge the small pool where they breed. Our lazy old border collie, Fen (now, alas, no longer with us) loved to stretch out on a summer evening on the still-warm stones, and I like to go barefoot on them too, feeling the sensual thrill of warm stone underfoot.

I have a pamphlet from a commercial "rock center" in Washington that boasts of importing rock supplies from the western mountains of Canada, the USA and Mexico. I have no quarrel with them, any more than with the quarrymen of my childhood, but I steadfastly maintain that it's far preferable to use local materials whenever possible. Apart from the lamentations of the hills from which they've been blasted, exotic rocks hauled in from the Sierra Madre are apt to sit uncomfortably in an alien landscape, like pale northerners on a tropical beach, making the garden evocative of certain pizza parlours with unfortunate faux rock facing. One of the great roles of stone is to pin our gardening compositions to the earth, so the bones of both are knit together. Exotic rocks, or any stones in a stoneless countryside, are hard pressed to anchor a garden to an ecosystem where they don't themselves belong.

Local stone, on the other hand, bears brilliant witness to the mighty forces that have shaped this place in time: collisions of huge tectonic plates, subductions and upliftings, volcanic eruptions and the relentless scraping

17

of glaciers. Sitting naturally on its landscape of origin, it brings to the garden a connectedness with forces and processes that shape our living planet. By its texture and age, stone helps impart a sense of timelessness that is at the heart of every fine garden, along with a marvellous solidity and unity. When things are at their bleakest, as they seem just now, sliding down the skid road of January, the bones are still there, reminding us of lovestruck snakes and the sweet scent of crushed herbs on warm sandstone in the carefree barefoot days of summer.

WEEK 4: BORN TO HEDGE

The hip-deep snow drifts of three weeks ago have disappeared, shrinking to a few remnant piles in cold shady corners, like ancient glaciers retreating into mountain fastnesses. All the rest got melted and pelted away by a "pineapple express," that great gush of moist, wild air that comes panting across the Pacific at us. We hunker down against the wind and slosh ahead. Sometimes, between storm fronts, the wind drops away and the sky clears to a stunning blue. These are outdoor days for sure, bracing and occasionally blissful when a whisper of spring flirts in the air.

I spend a good portion of clear winter afternoons on hedging. I do this every winter, digging holes and transplanting scores of young conifers. I dream of them one day forming pleasing green screens to provide background beauty and an enhanced sense of privacy. You know the sort of thing I have in mind: those enormous thick hedges of clipped yew or sheared cedar that one sees surrounding posh estates in the better parts of town. Beyond such marvellous hedges a different quality of life awaits, in which the tumult and pollution of the outer world are left behind, hushed to a calm and genteel seclusion.

This is what I too seek, this sense of clipped and leafy sanctuary. I know that examined closely it might seem a peculiar hankering, as we live on a quiet country lane, on eleven acres of woodlands that are already sequestered in a way some people would find oppressive. On a busy day two dozen vehicles might go rattling down the dirt road, a pedestrian or two, perhaps a few cyclists or riders on horseback. No logging trucks yet, but we can hear them coming. I can barely glimpse passersby through the trees, or they me. All this is beside the point. The installation of a hedge may, as in my own case, be unnecessary, even arguably ridiculous. This is not to say it should not be installed. For the hedge, as all true hedgers know, transcends simple considerations of practicality or even of taste.

Some people are born to hedging. Just why is something of a mystery, but there it is. The impulse, or should I say compulsion, to hedge arises from complex motives, perhaps foremost among them a profound instinct for enclosure. Who's to say in what dim ancestral past this impulse for boundary-marking bushes, protective hedgerows and bordering thickets was born? It is simply there, like one's eye colour, and for those who have it still, there can be no happiness without a hedge.

There may well be no happiness with one either, for destiny has arranged that there should, upon this mortal coil, be both brilliantly accomplished and tragically flawed hedge makers. Successful hedgers are a breed apart both literally and figuratively. I've known several over the years, and I think especially of a certain couple who live not far from us. Long after I'd commenced my own checkered hedging career, this pair of *arrivistes* trucked in enormous loads of hedging bushes, got them planted at the recommended eighteen-inch spacing and had them quickly form an impenetrable and precisely sheared hedge, both bushy and vigorous. They now live in enviably cloistered seclusion, fully screened from the prying eyes of the outer world. They could be romping naked on the lawns within, for all any of us know. Less gifted hedgers have been heard to mutter this, and worse, about them, for the air of easy accomplishment that clings to successful hedgers can inspire spite as much as envy.

Mortifying as it is to confess, I find myself numbered among the multitudes of failed hedgers. We're a pathetic bunch, really—fated by forces beyond our ken to never possess a satisfactory hedge, no matter how diligently we work at it. For no discernible reason at all, half the plants in one of our hedges will suddenly die, leaving a ragged pattern of gaps like a hockey player's teeth. Or every bush will drop all its interior needles, revealing scrawny trunks and blighted branches attempting to cover their nakedness with a pathetic greenish fringe of near-dead tips. Kids and dogs will push through these hedges brazenly, creating permanent trailways, so the individual bushes never meet, but stand forever apart like a line of strangers waiting for a bus. Empty beer cans and discarded condoms collect around the bare stems of the hedges and wind-blown scraps of plastic catch in them. Failed hedgers lack whatever vital gene it is that regulates how far you should plant your hedge from a neighbour's property line. The neighbour, quite properly maintaining the sacred rights of property, slashes his side of the encroaching hedge back to the line. The half-trimmed, half-slashed and (dare we say it) half-assed hedges of the nation bear inelegant witness to the plenitude of unsuccessful hedgers among us.

We are the playthings of fate, deserving neither blame nor scorn. How otherwise explain my own ineptitude? Like many a failed hedger before me, my undoing has been genuinely lame decision making made worse by questionable frugality. Our front property line runs several hundred feet along the road. It is lined by a stand of marvellous conifers, mostly big western red cedars. Not a great spot for a hedge, admittedly, given that hedges, like tomatoes, generally do far better in full sun. Still, the area required hedging, or, at least, I conceived would benefit from the addition of a hedge.

To begin with, I vacillated between a proper hedge and a less formal line of trees. Successful hedgers never vacillate. They first define what precise purpose the hedge is to serve, whether marking a property line, providing a backdrop for plantings, dividing the garden, creating a windbreak or screen. Then they select hedging material appropriate for that precise purpose. I, however, vacillated, eventually concluding that a colonnade of trees forming an unclipped screen might give a more natural appearance in our woodland setting than would a formal hedge.

Off to an equivocal start, I doubled my losses by poor plant selection. As the erstwhile thicket was intended to rise to our southwest, I reasoned that deciduous trees would offer the advantage of not further obscuring the low winter sun from what the conifers already do. Parsimony then pushed her pinched nose into the business, whispering in my ear that the numerous young bigleaf maples growing wild around our place would make an inexpensive but perfectly serviceable planting. I spent a good many hours digging up saplings and transplanting them to their new location. That was before I knew about bigleaf maples. They are what old-timers around here call a weed tree, by which they mean adventitious, aggressive and eventually problematic. A relatively short-lived species, they grow at an astonishing rate into enormous spreading trees, often of surpassing beauty, especially in deep forest, draped with mosses, lichens and licorice ferns. Tolkien kind of trees. In the wrong conditions they can be gangly and very careless about hanging on to their limbs. They give off toxins that prevent most anything else from growing under them. They pose an incredible menace to power lines. They are, in short, one of the least appropriate trees on Earth for hedging or screening purposes. But how was I to know this, knowing that beech, oak, sycamore, poplar, hawthorn and Norway maples are all used for deciduous

22

hedges. Why not bigleaf maples, I asked, and received no cogent reply.

Accomplished hedgers are somehow provided with the information that ideal hedge plants are ones that form branches from the ground to the tip of the plant. When buying nursery stock, they select conifers that are already densely branched from the ground up, then sheer them after planting. If buying deciduous trees that have been grown to a single trunk, they have the wherewithal to cut the plant back hard, to within a foot of ground level to force multiple branching. Unsuccessful hedgers, by comparison, cannot bring themselves to cut away several feet of a perfectly good specimen, especially when they've paid top dollar for taller stock! They prefer not to cut the newly planted hedge back, thus consigning themselves to a hedge that will forever sport bare legs for several feet off the ground. A grotesquely exaggerated case in point, our untrimmed maples now have bare trunks for thirty feet up and are entirely useless for screening, but very effective in lashing the power lines and in preventing anything else from growing.

Eventually receiving an answer to my question, why not bigleaf maples, through the dour headmaster of experience, I didn't miss a beat in realizing that a different approach was called for. This was about the time the ambitious new-comers I mentioned earlier were starting to hedge. Perhaps in part falling prey to an unseemly competitiveness, I began a secondary hedging effort by underplanting the ascendant maples with small conifers. Again dame frugality seduced

23

me into asking myself: Why should I throw good money away on hedging shrubs at a nursery when my woodlands are full of small conifers free for the transplanting and overcrowded where they are? Thus I set about digging out and replanting scores of young Douglas-fir, western red cedar and western hemlock. Unlike the compliant hedging trees acquired from nurseries by successful hedgers, native stock's got a mind of its own and ours have responded with something short of complete enthusiasm.

The little cedars, exposed to full view, are regularly cropped by our resident deer herds and now resemble very dense and tiny bonsai. The hemlocks, which I plant in the deepest shadows cast by the big cedars, either die outright or linger as skeletal specimens with scarcely any needles and no hedging effect at all. Trees of unquestioned merit in the forest ecosystem, western hemlocks don't like having their long roots torn from their natal earth. They may survive the move, but they'll carry its trauma for as long as they live.

The only arguable success I've enjoyed is with a stretch of young Douglas-fir, which are robust to a fault and at least as determined to make trees of themselves as I'm determined that they remain a hedge. Repeated shearing of their tops helps fill in the idle hours after transplanting more saplings to plug the perpetual gaps.

Trimming is a specific area in which the relative skills of successful and unsuccessful hedgers can be productively compared. Generally speaking, successfully engineered hedges are wider at the bottom than at the top, enabling light to reach the lower branches, stimulating bushy growth right to ground level. The school of second-rate hedging, however, prefers hedges that bulge above and wither below from lack of light and air, so that they rather resemble a certain type of older male carrying an enormous paunch on spindly legs.

Here again, clarity of purpose is useful, for those who have it, in determining when and how much to trim. You see competently shaped hedges being trimmed during the spring growing season to encourage bushier growth. Unsuccessful hedgers vacillate, again, trying to decide if their hedge should have an informal, graceful appearance or a closely clipped more formal look. Thus they dither until a hedge is unequivocally out of control, then dash out and slash the whole thing back with a vengeance. Most frequently this attack is launched in the summer, allowing the hedge just enough time to put out new growth that will not harden off before autumn, but be killed by early frosts, leaving further holes to accentuate the threadbare look of the whole.

Struggling wildlife gardeners like myself may get additional, if unsolicited, help with trimming. Recognizing the problems I was encountering with my native species, I thought to supplement them with that old tried-and-true exotic, English laurel. The classic laurel hedge is never quite a thing of beauty and a joy forever, but properly maintained it can be a hedge of unquestioned authority—dense, stout and completely uncompromising. I discovered early on that English laurels are laughably easy to propagate through softwood cuttings and so set about making great numbers of them. The early growth was phenomenal, so that I soon started planting them out as part of my grand hedge.

Now, looking at tough, shiny laurel leaves and smelling their pungent odour, you wouldn't suspect they'd be something deer would eat. Fools that you are: like English ivy, laurels are among deer's favourite winter browse. Consequently my laurels are now of two sorts: tiny specimens huddled inside wire cages, any wayward leaf of which is devoured overnight by the deer, along with a few much taller specimens that have outgrown the deer, leaving six feet of stripped bare stems below and a flounce of foliage high above the deer's reach. The combination is undeniably ridiculous.

Still, I'm far from dismayed. For one thing, my lacklustre semi-hedge doesn't require any of the meticulous shearing and shaping that preoccupies successful hedgers. Neither does my gap-toothed hedge obscure all view of the road, so I can still keep an eye on who's passing by. Nor does it expose us to the sort of ribald public speculation provoked by successful hedgers down the road. It is, in short, a cutting-edge hedge, a minimalist hedge, if you will, sufficient to satisfy the ancestral instinct for enclosure but not sufficiently so as to leave one cut off, out of the loop. It's what we failed hedgers, when pressed, refer to as hedging your bets.

26

$\mathcal{F}$EBRUARY

WEEK 5: ASH WEDNESDAY

There's been a lot of commotion in the popular media recently over what's being hailed as "simple living." Certain persons are sweeping through their homes—and, in the trend's most exalted form, through their lives—and tossing out whatever is superfluous, extravagant or immoderate. They are following in the footsteps of Gandhi, Thoreau and all the rest in clearing out the clutter and getting back to basics. Disciples of the trend are apt, whether encouraged or not, to quote Lao Tsu to you: "He who knows that enough is enough will always have enough," or "The sage wears rough clothing and hides the jewel in his heart."

Undoubtedly this trend will find most of its more ardent adherents among persons comfortably accustomed to having more than enough; it is not a fad likely to fire the imaginations of people consigned to life in public housing projects. Still, I applaud the "less is more" approach, and not solely because it could result in a windfall of discarded trinkets for those of us who cruise the thrift shop circuit. No, this fresh renouncing of materialism by renegades from the acquisitive classes very much speaks to my own proclivities, which once upon a time carried me to the rather extreme measure of entering a monastery and proclaiming a vow of holy poverty. Besides, the austerities of Lent begin today, a time when reflections on renouncing the things of this world are traditionally in order.

When I was a little chap growing up in post-war England, my brothers and I used to thrill to the pancake race that was held on Shrove Tuesday, or Pancake Tuesday as we called it. That was yesterday. The event featured an assortment of sturdy English housewives who would run down the main street of town, each holding out her frying pan in which lay a full-sized pancake that she would have to flip in the air and catch in her pan several times during the course of the race. This extravaganza was at the time the British working-class variation on the Mardi Gras carnival. For us, the six weeks that followed were shrouded in a penitential solemnity that forbade the eating of sweets or whatever else one had "given up" for Lent.

Looking back almost half a century, I realize that this was "simple living" of an entirely uncontrived sort. I'm remembering it this morning in part because at this time of year a mainstay of our diet is the lowly kale, and few vegetables are more closely associated with the simple life. My parents never grew it and I'm not sure if those able pancake flippers cooked it or not. But a lot of working-class people did for centuries. If aubergine is fit for a queen, kale is honest peasant food. One of its several names, borecole, derives from the Dutch for "peasant's cabbage." Elsewhere, less elegantly, it's "cow cabbage." Collards are a type of kale somehow fixed in my imagination as being eaten by abject sharecroppers in William Faulkner novels. An aura of rustic penury clings to kale and to those of us who grow it and consume it on these skinny winter days.

Like many West Coast gardeners, we pride ourselves on eating something fresh from the garden virtually every day of the year. In tough times, this may be only root crops—carrots, parsnips, rutabagas and Jerusalem artichokes—dug from freezing ground and grated for a slaw. In wet weather, chickweed's an abundant and healthy green. Kale—first Scotch, then, as winter wears on, Russian red—is the third leg of our fresh winter trinity.

Kale is an ancient and altogether honourable plant, among our race's first cultivated vegetables, ancestor of today's swell-headed cabbages and cauliflowers, easy to grow and a true nutritional superstar. But chronically underrated. Many gardeners don't bother to grow it at all. Horticultural reference books dismiss it as "of minor importance." Its specific name, *acephala,* means "headless cabbage," as though kale had, like Ross Perot, tried but failed to be something more than itself.

Still, its lineage is impeccable. Kale's a direct descendant of the wild cabbage, *Brassica oleracea*, described as a scraggly and emaciated-looking perennial native to the Mediterranean area. It is one of Europe's most ancient foods, from which a great number of cultivated plants were long ago developed. So we see Achilles, of the questionable heel, pictured in Homer's *Iliad* washing cabbages. All the wild cabbage descendants belong to a family traditionally called *Cruciferae*, literally meaning "cross-bearers," because their flowers have two separate petals and two sepals arranged in opposite pairs in the form of a Maltese cross.

Crucifixion might be pushing things a bit far, but there is an element of self-denial in kale cuisine, a certain gritty northern survivalism. The two most familiar types are Siberian and Scotch kale, both of them evocative of bleak and arduous environments. Very curled and crumpled, in both dwarf and tall varieties, Scotch kale (or kail) was once a mainstay of rural Scottish cuisine, at certain tough times the only cultivated green being eaten. The name also came to mean a broth in which kale was the principal vegetable. Thus Walter Scott has one of his stalwarts promise to do lunch: "I will be back here to my kail against ane o'clock." Because kale was by far the most prevalent vegetable in it, the cottage kitchen garden came to be called a kail-yard, as in the old lyric "There grows a bonnie brier bush in our kail-yard." This less-than-immortal line was penned by Ian Maclaren, one of a group of writers who came, in the 1890s, to be known as the Kailyard School from their depiction of humble life in Scotland, their dialogue laced with more extravagant brogue than an open bar at a Robbie Burns party. The kailyarders' rise to prominence a century ago leads me to wonder in passing if perhaps the celebration of simple living isn't specifically a *fin de siècle* phenomenon.

Frost tolerance commends the kale to those enduring an existence in rough and cold conditions. It's the hardiest of all the cole crops, surviving down to minus 10 degrees Celsius or colder. In fact, frost improves its flavour, meaning kale can be one of the last leafy greens picked fresh from the garden well into winter. Early European explorers carried kale seeds with them to the Americas for planting specifically to help them survive bitter winters.

Here on the West Coast, where winter rains assail the spirit more than numbing cold does, kale can usually be held over in the garden right through winter. Russian red kale is the cole of choice, being especially hardy. It forms a robust full plant about a metre tall. The branches and ribs of the leaves are a lovely purplish-red, the serrated and only slightly crumpled leaves a subtle grey-green, turning coppery red after heavy frosting. Although no great advocates of mixing edibles and ornamentals, we've taken to including these fulsome beauties in the mixed borders. They look absolutely smashing at times. Last August a splendid specimen positively put to shame a nearby cluster of half-hearted hostas.

Happiest, as all kales are, in moist and fertile loam on the alkaline side, this robust Russian is drought tolerant and will survive in pretty rough neighbourhoods—I've seen volunteers thriving in sand and seashell not far above the storm tide line, like the wild cabbages that flourish on certain British sea cliffs. Kales rate highly in disease resistance too. Our Russian reds are impervious to the clubroot that regularly decimates many of our other brassica plantings. Their only real pest is aphids, which appear to prefer Russian kale to any other plant we grow. This too can be turned to advantage. We keep several big kales in the veggie patch as sacrifice plants upon which aphids are encouraged to congregate, along with their natural predators. Looking through a magnifying glass at hordes of sticky aphids being systematically devoured by ladybird larvae brings a delicious sense that rough justice is in fact at work in an often unjust world.

Where they don't naturalize, winter kales are seeded in midsummer, which is when I plant our Scottish type, a particularly hardy variety called Winterbor. These we harvest, sweet and tender, after the first fall frosts. The Russian reds, surviving the winter, put out tender new growth right around now, as the earth begins to warm. Pretty soon, as we really get into spring, the mature plants will throw up vertical flowering stems with multiple pale yellow flowers, similar to broccoli in flower. These are easily harvested and excellent in salads or steamed greens. Certain prime plants we leave to self-seed wherever they will in the kail-yard. Thousands of offspring appear, most of which are pulled out and eaten over the summer, with a few dozen well-spaced specimens left to carry the cycle on through the following winter.

By now even the most forebearing reader may be asking: Why must this fellow persist about a single vegetable among so many? Why this fixation on kale? I do so for the simple reason that kale is absolutely one of the finest food-stuffs any of us can eat. This is a hefty claim, I realize, and one not easily substantiated. But kale is right up among the heavyweights and superstars, with soybeans and shiitake mushrooms, quinoa and amaranth. Its leaves are packed with iron, calcium and other minerals, throbbing with vitamin A, thiamine and absorbic acid, low in calories and sublime for roughage. Some enthusiasts claim it has ten times the nutritional value of other brassicas, that it is by far the most nutritious vegetable one can grow. Every mouthful seems to burst with healthfulness and vitality.

We mostly enjoy it raw, sliced fine into salads, or simmered in soups. It's excellent in stews, stir-fries and pasta dishes. As a steamed green, it needs only a touch of butter, pepper and lemon juice—or even just a splash of soy sauce and be done with it. Kale and potatoes combine in all sorts of healthy peasant dishes—and the whole exercise here, remember, is to stand in solidarity with the nouveau peasantry: Kale and potato soup, or steamed kale with boiled new potatoes in a cream sauce with dill, or that old Celtic favourite, "Colecannon," a mixture of creamy mashed potatoes with cooked chopped kale. Collards are traditionally cooked with salt pork or in a ham-based pea soup, wherein the smoky flavour of the meat is said to bring out the best in the vegetable, though this might not score all that high in the health food part of the competition.

There I am, trudging dutifully up the hill to our kail-yard on each of these wintry afternoons, bound to pick the evening's salad greens. I like to imagine myself as a bonnie Highlander or sturdy Siberian muzhik surviving the rigours of winter by pluck and wit alone. Of course, romanticized survivalism is a far more genteel affair on these benign Gulf Islands than it is, say, in northern Manitoba or wind-whipped Wisconsin. Nevertheless, in my books, the all-winter availability of fresh kale stands head and shoulders over the late-blooming roses and preternaturally early daffodils certain West Coast gardeners insist upon flaunting before every acquaintance in the rest of our ice-locked land. And certainly when the merits of simple living are discussed at an elegant dinner party, a spirited recounting of one's kail-yard career goes a good long way to carrying the day.

WEEK 6: ST. VALENTINE'S DAY

As dear as it must be to the hearts of florists and nursery-people, Valentine's Day is not a high feast in our household; as often as not, it comes and goes without notice. No red roses and certainly no chocolate hearts change hands. I don't mean that the *affaire du coeur* is a discounted item with us. Far from it. For love is a ravening beast prowling in the heart of every passionate gardener. Voltaire's description of love as "a canvas furnished by Nature and embroidered by imagination" must apply at least as powerfully to one's garden as to some of the personalities one

34

manages to fall in love with over the course of a lifetime. If we are indeed shaped and fashioned by what we love, how could gardeners be anything but beautiful people?

In slack moments I occasionally find myself reflecting on the old truism that maintaining a garden is quite like engaging in a relationship. Certainly there's no shortage of passion in a garden, nor of infatuation, intrigue, nor broken-heartedness. In truth, the great flood of emotions we normally associate with matters of the heart must ebb and flow at least as turbulently within the bosoms of gardeners as in those of other moonstruck mortals. The sexual excitement of the young—upon which, for good or ill, the future of the race depends—holds a pretty small candle against the blazing passion of a mad keen gardener champing to get down into the dirt this time of year. It's hard to imagine that Abelard ever fawned more devotedly over Heloise than some people do over their chrysanthemums. That Juliet was any more enamoured of fair Romeo than some of us are of our roses. Is the cattiest marital spat that much worse than repeated late blight on the tomato vines? Are separation and divorce all that much more painful than bidding a well-loved garden farewell?

Consider initial attractions to begin with—those tantalizing intervals of smouldering glances, aroused awareness and excessive glandular secretions. I ask you: Did ever a couple of lonesome singles gaze into one another's eyes with a lustier longing than that of a new gardener surveying a bit of earth awaiting the loving touch? Far busier than singles clubs, the garden shops and nurseries of the nation are aswarm with starry-eyed beginners billing and cooing over a newfound love of growing. You can see them fondly clutching plastic Grecian urns that they fully intend to plant with petunias. Perhaps as they wait at the checkout counter they're remembering romantic Keats celebrating in an ode that "Beauty is truth, truth beauty." They see, Lord love them, their gardens resplendent with truth and beauty.

Some of these darlings will enter gardening and find therein a lifetime of enchantment. They will rest in beds of petals, rise to rosy-fingered dawn with fair breezes wafting. They'll move in rapture through charmed seasons, and at last lie down with ease in goodly Elysian Fields.

Others in the crowd, however, may be persons more given to mad pursuits and temporary conquests than to long-term relationships. No matter that gardens are the work of decades, these enthusiasts are forever panting and forever young. They want it all and they want it now. They may buy it all, plant it all and leave it all behind for the next fad before the slow-but-steady types have even finished perusing the seed catalogues. I see the brassiest of them referred to in glossy magazines as "power gardeners," but I'm not impressed. I remember the line of a fine old gardener and writer out in our part of the world named John Norris. His garden is a thirty-year labour of love, from which he can tell us amiably, "The real pleasure of anything is in the making of it... I feel no envy towards people who can order palaces to be made for them overnight."

36

The next room over is the bridal suite where we hear the spectacular honeymooners going at it. These love-birds wing their way into the gardening life with reckless extravagance, the way foolhardy robins knock themselves senseless on our kitchen windows during the giddy flights of courtship. Their first weeks of gardening are all champagne and caviar, a dazzling breaking of new ground and amassing of exotic plants, fancy tools and ornate garden ornaments. Every day for them is a sweet May morning on which sunshine and showers coax entrancing new plants from the earth. But then they hit the glass. In no time at all, the bloom is off the rose. Like a tinseltown wedding, the glitter soon fades, their marvellous garden of the imagination collapses and the poor darlings find themselves in the weed patch of broken dreams. How did a vow to love and cherish so quickly curdle into a lifelong struggle against crabgrass? Where's the rapture in damping off? A corrupting disillusionment creeps into the relationship; the sweethearts begin to founder. Now their drooping spirits are easily seduced by the siren song of low maintenance landscaping, by the oily blandishments of condominium salespeople who tell you that everything outdoors will be done for you. Their grand passion was no more than a rapturous first love, what Shaw called only a little foolishness and a lot of curiosity.

Roving-eye gardeners are another matter altogether. More roguish than woebegone, these people are wholeheartedly committed to gardening as a way of life, determined to stick with it through good seasons and bad.

Hardship isn't their undoing, the charm of novelty is. They simply can't resist a wayward glance every so often, a weakness that frequently leads to indiscretions. One year they'll tear out the lawn to plant massed perennials. Then antique roses catch their eye, and soon it's farewell to half the perennials. Within a season or two they're beguiled by wildflower meadows, only to have them replaced in time by an alpine scree. Designed by what I think of as the serial monogamy approach to gardening, their yards are not without interest but seriously lacking in stability.

Even more prone to emotional tumult are the *ménage à trois* gardeners. However lovely it might be, however devoted they might be to it, the garden by itself is insufficient for them. They crave an excitement that the garden alone cannot supply. They take up bingo or skydiving or some other nonsense, thinking to divide their time between these trivial pursuits and the garden. Invariably, they come to a bad end.

Difficult as it is for us to admit, there are even outright philanderers in our company. I mean scoundrels who practise a deliberate deception. To all appearances, they are unconditionally devoted to their gardens. Apparently unstinting in their labours, tireless in garden maintenance, they'll speak with great enthusiasm about new gardening projects or a brilliant new cultivar they've just acquired from a research station in the Outer Hebrides. But inwardly their hearts are elsewhere. Hired help does their gardening while they take walking tours of Provence.

Secretly they dream of selling up altogether and spending the rest of their lives in a Winnebago.

Some gardening lives, like some marriages, simply go bad. Inclement weather, plagues of pests and diseases, impossible soil, floods and mudslides—all may play a part in the sad diminuendo. The daily routine becomes like living with a bully or a fool, and although love is the prerogative of the strong-hearted, to carry on this way would not be love but self-abuse. The fuchsias fail to fascinate. Black spot blights the heart and every plant appears to be a tormentosa. The dream, alas, is gone.

Sad indeed, sad and pathetic, as is the tragedy of those who never do break faith with their gardens, but in the end are rewarded for their loyalty with a broken heart. Like a mature person taking a spirited young lover, they find themselves unable to keep up. Their gardens outrun them, overwhelm them, exhaust them. The charm of the garden remains undiminished, Lord knows, and their spirit is still completely willing, but the flesh is weak. "Enough!" they cry at last, sitting by the lily pool and weeping that they are no longer young, that life in the end is so brief.

But like fools for love, gardeners will run the risk of bitter disappointment in quest of the ultimate prize: a long-term love affair with a garden moving through the seasons and the years in tender harmony. I've met many of these ardent gardeners over the years, and they are always a delight. They are what one wants in a lover—earnest, passionate, tender, devoted. Schooled in the lessons of the earth, they know that to live is to change, but their spirits aren't restless. Nobody knows better than they do the wild dance of passion that flares again each spring, the pipes and timbrels and mad ecstasy. But also the sweet repose of late summer, then the gradual decline in silence and slow time. They are content. Their lives and their gardens both are canvases furnished by Nature and embroidered by imagination to wonderful effect.

WEEK 7: THE ACCIDENTAL ORCHARDIST

I devote a good chunk of February to orchard maintenance, what with clean-up, dormant season spraying and pruning. The idea here is to get out into the fruit trees by climbing through the narrow window of opportunity that opens after the last real cold snap then slams shut when the trees break dormancy. Sometimes I come away from the exercise wondering why I bother.

Fate and Mother Nature have together amassed a formidable array of forces against our vulnerable orchard. Hercules, labouring to secure the golden apples of Hesperides, had it easy compared with us. Apart from a glut of transparent apples in August, we never realistically expect to harvest much in the way of fruit, seldom more than a handful of wormy scab-apples in November. Our orchard is more what an incurable optimist would call a learning experience.

But the very idea of oneself as an orchardist has tremendous psychological appeal. One pictures oneself strolling

40

beneath sturdy old apple trees garlanded in Maytime blossoms, later on gathered with rosy-cheeked children and
good-hearted friends wearing flannel shirts and designer
blue jeans to pluck bushelsful of ripe fruit in the shining
afternoons of autumn. One thinks of great cauldrons
of applesauce simmering on the woodstove and kegs of
robust cider fermenting in the basement.

These fruity visions are important, for they sustain the
star-crossed orchardist through what otherwise might
be an entirely dispiriting round of chores. We have about
eighteen fruit trees at our place, mostly semi-dwarf apples,
with a few peaches, pears and plums, a fig and several crabapples. During the off-season they require several full
workdays for clean-up, winter pruning and dormant oil/
lime sulphur spraying.

I never begrudge pruning; indeed, I find it inherently
satisfying, I think partly because, in a chaotic universe,
its purposes are so admirably straightforward. We may
not be certain whether we are the unwitting pawns of
grotesquely bloated transnational conglomerates, but we
know our pruning objectives: to maintain or enhance a
tree's shape, to eliminate dead and diseased wood and to
maximize fruit production by encouraging fruiting buds
and spurs on branches well exposed to sunshine and circu-
lating air. Simplicity itself.

And so to begin: I like broken, dead and diseased
branches because they can be eliminated without hesitation or misgiving by a few bold strokes. But after that,
things get a bit more challenging. Beginners may be

41

immobilized at this point by fear of making radical amputations that might set the tree back years or kill it outright. The stakes are very high, for as old Canon Henry Ellacombe put it: "[I]n nothing is the gardener's skill more shown than in the judicious use of the pruning-knife."

My own experience has been that pruning—like landscape painting or auto mechanics—is something best learned by doing rather than by reading about it in a manual. For people new to the business, I think the most useful thing to do is either take a course in pruning or tag along behind someone who knows what they're doing. I studied manuals and handbooks for a good many seasons, but never quite "got" pruning until I spent a session wandering around a Vancouver botanical garden with a master pruner who has created a display garden of fabulous espaliers, fans and cordons. Watching him at work, hearing him explain why he was cutting at a certain point and how the tree would likely respond, cast a clear light onto what before had been at best obscure. Successful orchardry, I sensed, was at last within my grasp.

Certain principles can be usefully articulated, even on paper. The first of these is the principle of arm's length overview, which bids us occasionally to pause in the midst of pruning and stand back to survey our handiwork from different angles, the way a sculptor does, to ensure that the overall shape we're developing is properly balanced. It is a source of considerable amazement to me that, although following this prescript religiously, I have still managed to create several trees with no more sense of balance than the last tippler out of the pub late Saturday night.

We want also to prevent branches, as with children, from developing in contrary directions. After eliminating damaged and diseased wood, I go after crossing and transverse branches. You don't want twigs or branches that cross or rub against one another, like certain long-married couples, nor branches that grow back towards the centre of the tree. All should be spreading outward, vaguely Buddhist in feeling, leaving the centre open for the free passage of sunlight and air.

As earnestly as the next person, I try to follow the fruit tree precepts: That the long leader at the end of a branch should be cut back by at least a third, and that the side shoots growing off the branch should be cut back by two-thirds. That the nearer to horizontal you can get fruit-bearing growth the better, because sap is more evenly distributed along a horizontal branch, producing more uniform fruit. That lateral shoots growing up or down from a branch will be weak and unproductive and are best eliminated. Why it is that the overwhelming majority of shoots insist upon growing this way is something of a mystery. Where possible, I bend vertical shoots onto a horizontal plane so that they'll become fruit-bearing laterals. In the past I embarrassed myself by using plastic bags filled with sand for this purpose. No more. I now have concrete weights cast in old styrofoam coffee cups, with a hooked piece of coated wire embedded in the concrete. Dangling

43

from the fruit trees, if nothing else, these help create the impression that one knows what one is about.

I remember, early in my pruning career, reading a handbook on the topic by a curmudgeonly old expert who wrote that anyone who couldn't distinguish a fruiting bud from a growth bud was a damned fool who had no business in an orchard. Perhaps I should have taken the hint. Fruit buds are the plump ones, often growing in clusters on fruiting spurs. It is these one wants to maximize, in part by cutting unwanted shoots back in the summer. Growth buds, from which foliage, not fruit, will ensue, are smaller than fruit buds. This much I absorbed completely. If a shoot is cut back to a growth bud in the dormant season, I know, the tree will respond by throwing out a new shoot in the direction the bud is pointing. Thus the overall shape of the tree can be directed by pruning to a bud that is facing in the direction—normally outward and slightly upward—in which you want the new branch to develop.

By pruning judiciously, and observing closely how a tree responds to pruning cuts, the amateur arborist begins to develop a "feel" for the tree. Trust it. Implicitly. It is one's surest guide—I know this more from conviction than actual experience. In time, what was a daunting chore becomes an exciting collaboration with the tree, a tantalizing tango, where you're responding to the beautiful logic of its growth patterns and it's responding to your judicious prunings.

I've come to think of pruning, much like art for art's sake, as being for its own sake, something in which one

44

takes delight for the process itself, rather than in anticipation of any product. The same cannot be said for its seasonal workmate, dormant oil spraying. I hesitate to dwell on the irregularities of spraying, except perhaps to wonder why it is that human ingenuity can hurl astronauts into outer space and bring them safely back but cannot devise a simple hand sprayer that works for more than thirty seconds at a time. What with plugged nozzles, inadequate air pressure and cantankerous trigger mechanisms, my spraying days feature more work stoppages than a Polish shipyard.

Lime sulphur/dormant oil is a clean-up insecticidal spray, thankfully accepted as an organic treatment, that's intended to destroy harmful insect eggs and fungal spores on fruit trees and berry canes—the blights, scabs, rots, scale, mites, aphids et al. that do so especially well in our moist, mild climate. I spray all the fruit trees as well as the raspberries, strawberries and gooseberries and weakling roses. Ideally you want to get three separate sprayings done between leaf drop and bud break, but the application days must be windless, above freezing and with no rain having fallen, falling or forecast. Never mind that our winters seldom present three such days. Typically, after a long session struggling with a sprayer hissing and spitting like an amorous tomcat, at about the moment when the last tree is done, torrential rains begin washing off the spray before it can take effect. Discouraged, one neglects to thoroughly clean out the sprayer before storing it away and thus new clogging agents are left to coagulate and subsequently bedevil the next outing.

Unchecked by ineffectual spraying, various blights, scales, scabs, rots, mites and aphids infest the trees. Thus the idle hours of spring and summer will be whiled away in applying tanglefoot paste to the tree trunks and wondering whether to spray insecticidal soap on burgeoning aphid populations, or optimistically await legions of aphid predators. I take particular delight in observing the ingenuity of ants in circumventing the tanglefoot collars. After several days of initial bewilderment, and a few dozen sacrificial ants stuck to the paste, the colony devises some ingenious scheme or other—perhaps just hopscotching across on the corpses of their dead forerunners to get back up the tree to resume tending their aphid ranches.

Our oldest fruit tree, a gnarled sugar plum, features every year a magnificent display of scale, whose lumpy excrescences on the twigs are bigger than the plums, along with a reliable infestation of smut. I used to think smut referred to naughty pictures and dirty talk, but its sooty contamination of our old plum is obscene enough to make Hugh Hefner blush. Leaf rollers, peach leaf curl, coddling moths—all of them have a go at our trees. When things get dull, the neighbourhood sapsuckers set about drilling multiple holes in the trunks.

But it's not really until harvest time that one gets a full appreciation of the forces arrayed against us. Two years ago, we had a marvellous crop of peaches ripening on the peach tree I keep meticulously clipped under the eaves of the house, out of the rain and the peach leaf curl it encourages. Just to see the fuzzy fruits ripening to a succulent gold gives a thrill of satisfaction. False, of course, false and foolish, for when we went to test them for ripeness, this particular time, we found the peaches had almost all been hollowed out from the back side by cunning mice who'd scrambled up the trellis against the house wall. We were left with a scattering of bitter pits.

Our meagre apple crop we divide fairly evenly between the deer and the woodpeckers. Before the late apples are fully ripe, big pileated woodpeckers assemble in the trees and attack the fruit with their chiselling bills, chipping a sizeable hole in each apple. Those that get knocked from the trees are quickly gobbled by the deer. Their appetites whetted, the deer devote themselves to reaching any remaining apples on the trees. A favourite ploy involves balancing on their hind legs like laughable ballerinas on their points. They scratch and scar the tree trunks in the process. Repeated over a couple of weeks, this succeeds in breaking and scraping chunks of bark off the trees and exposing the cambium layer to additional insect and disease infestations. All this just in time for a new round of remedial pruning and spraying, and thus the year's work is brought full circle.

47

WEEK 8: STARK BEAUTIES

"I have three crocuses and a snowdrop in bloom," a friend announced at a small gathering last evening. A dear and unfailingly modest soul, she seemed uncharacteristically aglow with self-satisfaction at having kick-started the gardening season so forehandedly. The rest of us feigned admiration while doing our best to conceal any alarm we were feeling at having already fallen behind in the "beating the seasons" sweepstakes.

Our garden occupies one of the colder sites on the island, lying in a small gully on an eastern slope, hemmed in by tall conifers. We cannot hope to match the microclimatic miracles commonplace on south-facing slopes at sea level. So we don't. Like climatically challenged gardeners everywhere, we instead place our faith in "all-season gardening" and become adept at insinuating, without giving offence, that a garden which retains its charms throughout the year is far preferable to a smattering of early blooming bulbs.

The woods are really the place to be this time of year—they're brilliant with vivid mosses and the glistening leaves of native broadleaf shrubs. But out in the clearings, beautiful things happen too. I remember a couple of winters ago a particular combination of cold air and atmospheric moisture sheathed every surface in a thick furze of ice crystals, transforming the garden by sunlight and starlight into a landscape of brilliantly glistening skeletons. The stark beauty of the scene spoke to the dramatic possibilities offered by the winter silhouettes of deciduous trees. I would think a garden of almost any size or style might be enhanced in the off-season by the careful selection and placement of such austere beauties. If I were to be asked, which I'm not, I'd highly recommend brisk winter walks through municipal parks and older neighbourhoods to study the intricacies traced by bare tree limbs against the sky.

Among the larger pyramidal trees with excellent winter skeletons, none comes more highly recommended than the American sweet gum. A native of eastern U.S. woodlands, valued chiefly for its brilliant autumn foliage, the sweet gum, or liquidamber, once established, is reputed to be virtually trouble-free. We've planted several of them at our place, and although they're still scrubby little customers imprisoned in wire cages, our hopes are running high for them. Liquidambers grow at a moderate rate—always reassuring to learn, when one's own specimens aren't growing at all—eventually reaching up to forty metres, with a branching pattern of exquisite symmetry. Their furrowed bark and spiny little fruits add to winter interest.

We've also introduced a European native, the little-leaf linden, likewise prized for its tightly pyramidal and appealingly proportioned crown. Another slow grower, ours got badly mauled by this year's heavy snowfall. Barring further misfortune, it should eventually grow to thirty metres. The sight of mature specimens outlined in the parks and boulevards of wintertime Europe is enough to excite in even lukewarm tree lovers a burning lust for lindens.

Deciduous trees with a horizontal branching pattern can be especially splendid in winter, none more so than the oaks with their stout and elegantly sinuous limbs, their gnarled twigs and corrugated bark. The only native oak out in these parts, the Garry oak, makes an intriguing winter pattern. It's hard not to like an oak and, if you've got the room, to grow one. There's an agedness, a solemnity and sacredness about them that seems even more obvious in winter. One almost anticipates a venerable procession of Druids intent upon ritual business emerging from the oak grove. Among the several we have growing, one given to us by a friend traces its lineage back to a mighty oak at Westminster Abbey.

Dogwoods, of course, are terrific for horizontal branching patterns too. They have a particular knack for catching powdery snowflakes among their twigs. Our favourite is the Japanese or Korean dogwood, *Cornus kousa*, of which we have several growing.

Deciduous trees with pendulous branches weeping towards the earth can etch very effective outlines, especially when seen against a dependable background of snow. Weeping pears, willows, birches, crabapples, cherries and beeches all have outstanding winter applications. "Red Jade" is a particularly fine weeping crab that seems happy enough at our place. Would that the same might be said for our weeping silver pear! Planted many years ago in a gravelly patch on a hill, it's supposed to provide a silvery foil against which a grouping of pink-flowering roses will show to stunning effect. But the wretched tree refuses to grow either up or down. It hangs around, year after year, indifferent to our ministrations, disinclined to do much more than maintain itself in its current wizened state, a skeleton for all seasons. We've done much better with the familiar contorted hazel called Harry Lauder's walking stick. Not particularly choice when in leaf, it's outstanding in bare form when its peculiar serpentine branching pattern can be seen to full effect. This time of year it's covered with handsome little dangling yellowish catkins.

With any of these skeletal stars, location, as they say, is everything. Crowded plantings or a cluttered and busy background will obscure the effect entirely, especially with the smaller weeping trees. In enclosed spaces, a solid background of contrasting hue—provided by evergreen plantings, the wall of a building or a fence—helps showcase the bony framework of a featured tree. Night lighting of smaller trees will do the same. If you can get it, naturally, open sky is optimal, and the silhouette of a handsome tree backlit by the rising winter sun, by moonlight on a clear cold night or by the glow of winter sunset in the west can be as marvellous in its bare beauty as anything a garden has to offer.

I don't think variegated broadleaf evergreens conjure up much in the way of mystical imagery, but they do provide a way of livening up the winter landscape. A little bit of variegated foliage goes a long way in a garden, and some people would as soon have variegated plants in their yard as slugs in the spinach. No question, the *variegatas* can be prima donnas, subject to unsteady tendencies. At their worst they can become gaudy and boisterous, like certain swashbuckling males doomed to permanent adolescence. Still, now that we're down to the dregs of winter, we're perhaps inclined to look more kindly on them.

Thanks to the fertile imaginations of the hybridizers, one can get variegated foliage on everything from ground covers to trees, bearing splashes, stripes, flecks, and margins of gold, silver and white. They are an excitable-looking bunch, but not necessarily vigorous, and they may require some extra care. I've purposely not thought too much about the ethics of variegation, which is achieved by reducing or eliminating chlorophyll in the non-green portion of the leaves; the less chlorophyll present, the closer the variegation is to white. Because of their reduced chlorophyll, we know, most variegated plants prefer not to be exposed to blazing sunshine. They may also grow more slowly and be more susceptible to cold than if their leaves were fully green.

Nevertheless, they have a way of working themselves into gardens, and ours is no exception. We have a somewhat faint-hearted variegated box elder, also a "Drummondii" Norway maple whose leaves are edged in a striking silvery white, and a pack of dogwoods, all of which are useful and reasonably discreet in their variegations. Throwing caution to the winds, we've recently added two evergreen euonymus to the collection. Widely used as landscape structure plants, variegated euonymus are hailed as "cast-iron shrubs" that will tolerate poor soil and maintain their variegation even in full sun in hot-weather climates. *Euonymous japonica* is a standby in

mild winter zones such as the West Coast. Our new additions are called "Silver King," whose green leaves have
elegant margins of creamy gold, and "Aureo-marginata,"
whose bold gold margins bleed into the leaf, threatening
to overrun the green entirely. If it ever achieves its prom-
ised height of three metres and spread of two metres, this
character will be a leading contender for gaudiest plant
in the place. The discreet white margins on "Pearl Edge"
might have been a more prudent selection. In colder zones,
gardeners rely on E. *fortunei,* which is among the hardiest
broadleaf evergreens and comes in a number of useful and
attractive variegated forms, as both a vine and a shrub.

Rounding out the show at our place is one of my favourites, a golden-edged English holly, "Aureo-marginata." For
those lucky enough to have it, this holly bush is a splendid
winter performer. It has immensely attractive glossy green
leaves bearing a thin margin of creamy yellow. New leaves
are yellowish with a marvellous mauve blush. The English
holly comes in several hundred varieties, many of them
outstanding, but is hardy only in mild winter zones. Slow
to grow, happy to be sheared and easy to propagate by layering, our variegated holly makes a splendid bright cone of
light in the pale sunshine of late winter.

53

Evergreen conifers are, of course, the real workhorses
of northern winter gardens, though it may take novice
gardeners a little while to appreciate their true worth. I
remember scarcely giving them a thought, early on, thinking them dull and stodgy-looking. The bleakness of winter
soon taught us better. The range of types available at local

nurseries is both thrilling and daunting: conical, ovoid, columnar and globose, prostrate and spreading, in blues and greens and greys and striking gold—there's a conifer perfect for every condition.

Frankly, my dears, I don't give a damn how many shopping malls have mugho pines plunked forlornly along their faceless walls—I still like these shrubby little natives of the eastern Alps and Balkans, and never more so than a month or two from now when I get to clip down their new candles of growth to help them bush out. (Oh, that wilderness-rich scent of pine! The cry of the loon, the plash of canoe paddles on a glassy lake!) The same goes for the overplanted dwarf Alberta spruce with its soft, moss-green needles forming a compact and classically pyramidal Christmas tree.

Last year we acquired a "Hoopsi" blue spruce as a more demonstratively blue companion to a Colorado blue spruce a friend had given us from seed. We've planted these blue-grey beauties as backdrops to the garden and as transitional plants between the garden and surrounding forest. I admire all spruce for their bristly, bottle-brush needles and stiff rectitude. They play so handsomely against the softly drooping fronds of our native western red cedars and hemlock. Another pleasing blue-grey performer that came our way combines the drooping languor of cedar with the bristliness of spruce. One of the many varieties of deodora cedar, this eccentric "glauca" trails its stiff branches along the ground like a dispirited chimney sweep.

To my mind—but not to Sandy's—one of the most beautiful of winter conifers is the plume cryptomeria, which forms a billow of soft green through the growing season, then turns a rich, tawny ochre throughout the winter. I think of the shrub as having a wonderfully warm glow; to Sandy it appears near dead. I concede that it's terribly ready to topple over in the least breeze or snowfall but still love it unconditionally.

The positioning of conifers for maximum wintertime effect can, as with deciduous skeletons, be a tricky business. Many of the dwarf specimens appropriate for small gardens seem to show best when grouped in little colonies. This was the motivation for our attempting a small winter garden of conifers and heathers that would be visible from the kitchen windows to lift our sinking spirits around this time of year. We gathered a motley collection of sale-priced dwarf conifers and winter-flowering heathers, along with some miscellaneous grasses and plopped them into the bed willy-nilly. There they all now sit like a pack of mongrel dogs at the pound, waiting for something exciting to happen. Perhaps a few broadleafed variegated evergreens would help them along? Perhaps a deciduous winter skeleton—although they already have a dogwood looming disapprovingly above them. Plus we've just read someone-or-other ridiculing the whole misbegotten notion of conifer and heather gardens. I suspect that's right. But if one isn't to have the first bulbs blooming among acquaintances, something must be done, and for now, this is it.

$\mathcal{M}$ARCH

WEEK 9: BLOOD SPORTS

I staggered into the general store the other morning. "Good Lord!" exclaimed one of the regulars behind the counter. "What have you done to yourself?" I realized I was dripping blood on her countertop.

"Oh, that?" I replied, putting a finger gingerly to the swelling lump on my forehead. "I just clobbered myself with a steel bar."

I'd spent the better part of the morning digging out a truculent bigleaf maple stump, in the process dinging myself badly with my long steel pry bar. It was the sort of injury that would bring everything to at least a temporary halt in the off-season, but by now the frenzy of pre-planting's upon us and there's no spare time for nursing minor wounds. This is how it is with gardeners. No matter how frail the body, nor how grievous the injury, when there's work to be done in the yard there's no place for moaning over discomforts. As much as they might grouse about inclement weather or contrary plants, gardeners have an astonishing capacity to suffer cuts and bruises, slashes and gashes without a word of complaint. They'll emerge from a pruning session in the shrubbery lacerated in a way that would send nongardeners dashing to the emergency ward. Gardeners seem scarcely to notice.

I remember last spring having sharpened my secateurs to a lethal edge before tackling the strawberry beds. We all know that there are few jobs more boring than clearing off all the old dead leaves and delinquent runners that strawberries insist upon producing. I snipped away methodically, but after a while my mind began to wander. Next thing I knew—crunch—I'd caught my middle finger between the snipping secateurs and cut myself deeply. I tried to keep on working, being as the damn strawberries should have been cleaned up last fall, leaving me already four months behind schedule, but blood kept gushing freely, making a mess of everything.

"Oh, hell!" I said to myself, far more annoyed that my work had been interrupted than that the tip of my finger was hanging by a thread. Naturally the medicine chest is always bare at a time like this, so I eventually staunched the flow of blood by wrapping my finger in a paper towel and masking tape. Then scurried back to the strawberries.

A few days later, when I proudly displayed my mutilated finger—by then wrapped in fresh masking tape—to an audience of gardeners at VanDusen Botanical Gardens in Vancouver, they all laughed knowingly, presumably because most of them had at one time or another sliced a finger in the same moronic way.

Rock gardeners, of course, prefer their fingertips squashed rather than slashed. Few pains are more excruciating than the agony of having one's fingers scrunched between large boulders. Even so, the hurt is never sufficient to deter enthusiasts from the thrilling business of piling up rocks on top of one another.

Thorny roses offer a particularly bloody challenge. We grow a number of big rugosas that maintain a combative attitude towards any attempts at pruning them. One of the snarliest is Sarah Van Fleet, who blooms with exquisitely fragrant soft pink flowers, but beneath which lurk thick and thorny arms. I always emerge from a pruning engagement with her far more badly lacerated than she ever is. Equally pugnacious, rambling Albertine throws her huge thorny arms around the puny pruner like a malignant giant squid, stabbing and gashing awfully.

The simple truth of the matter is that gardening's a bloody war. Those who believe it a genteel pastime carried on in summer whites with a chilled spritzer in hand are sorely deluded. I tell you it's a blood sport engaged in by horticultural warriors of tremendous valour. My grasp of this simple truth was refreshed just a few days ago when, scarcely recovered from the beating the maple root had given me, I decided to take on a knot of Himalayan blackberries that have been encroaching on the vegetable patch for several years. Himalayan blackberries are the botanical equivalent of Ronald Reagan's "evil empire." An introduced species, they have taken to life in the Pacific Northwest with terrifying aggression, putting down roots that are all but impossible to tear out, and stretching long thorny arms that you tangle with at your peril. To reclaim a patch of ground from them, as I proposed to do, is to engage in hand-to-hand combat of the bloodiest and most ferocious sort.

I chose a rainy afternoon for best effect. I dressed, much as a mediaeval knight might in his suit of armour, in heavy clothes, thick gloves and safety goggles. I carried a machete in one hand and my grub hoe in the other, wielding it like the great battle axe of a B-movie warrior chieftain. With a fierce cry I threw myself at the blackberry copse (fierce cries being absolutely essential to eventual success). I slashed through its great thorny arms with the machete. They lashed me back dreadfully, curling around my legs like vicious pythons, impaling me with cruel thorns. But I had them out, I did! One by one I tore them loose and cast them onto a bonfire where they smoked and writhed like Lucifer's scions.

Down to the roots now, I lay my machete aside and took up the grub hoe. I don't mind admitting that my heart was full of malice. I tasted the sweet nectar of vengeance as I went after those malignant roots. I swung the grub hoe viciously, crunching it into roots and rocks. With each mortal blow I cried a loud "Hai!" as I imagined a samurai warrior might do as he lopped off a head. Whenever a great knot of roots refused to come loose, clinging to the earth with fierce tenacity, I shouted curses of the most appalling sort. Make no mistake—this was war in all its mindless bloodthirstiness. When it was done, as the last of the monsters lay smouldering on the fire, I shouldered my weapons and trudged home, drenched with sweat and rain, bleeding from several bad gashes, weary now that my violence was spent, and painfully aware that this was only one brief skirmish in a lifelong war.

Most true gardeners are familiar with this battleground; they have their equivalent of our delinquent blackberries, whether it be horsetail, kudzu or other barbarous invaders. Some of these creep insidiously along the earth; others send subversive suckers snaking underground in spiteful directions; still others broadcast seeds with a perfidious knack for finding cracks and crannies from which their malignant offspring are impossible to extricate.

Perhaps the worst of them are plants that we ourselves have introduced to our gardens, unknowingly, naively, only to have them turn on us, returning our care with treachery. Their numbers are legion, and many a gardener can tell a woeful tale of having been blindsided by what at first seemed a charming addition. Running bamboos are notorious in this regard, and more than one unwary plantsperson has been run right off their place by bamboos running riot. English ivy has been known to infest not just small gardens but entire forests, covering the forest floor and twining a hundred feet or more up trees, suffocating them as it goes. Scotch broom, introduced to these parts by unwary Scottish settlers, has claimed vast tracts of what were once perfectly lovely meadows. But I also remember a friend gardening in moist ground who was brought near to her wit's end by creeping Jenny. A pretty little ground cover in the proper place, with crisp green leaves and charming yellow flowers, this little creeper loses all sense of perspective in rich, moist and shady conditions, running rampant over perennials and even small shrubs.

Suckering plants offer particular challenges. Early in our gardening career, Sandy and I introduced a Japanese angelica tree whose menacingly thorny limbs we were willing to overlook for the elegance of its large leaves and its cloudlike clusters of ivory flowers. But within a year or two this angelic customer produced vigorous suckers, some running several metres from the mother plant, that were hellish to root out. After a fierce skirmish, they've all been banned to a remote and wild corner of the garden.

With comfrey the prognosis is less positive. It's incredibly useful stuff for medicinal purposes and for activating compost heaps and sweetening the compost privy. I can't say I regret having been swept up in the comfrey mania of early back-to-the-land days, but this is not an innocuous plant. It's deep-rooted and indefatigable in seeding. One of our bibles, *The Sunset Western Garden Book*, sounds a sensible alarm: "Although comfrey has a long history as food and as a folk remedy, think hard before establishing it in your garden. Plants spread freely from roots and are difficult to eradicate." Tell me about it. Once established, comfrey, like the poor, are always with us. They're all over our veggie patch now, and I think the best we can hope for is a policy of containment, whacking them down repeatedly before they set seed—meaning that one dare not leave home overnight during comfrey seeding season.

Two other useful and time-honoured plants, lemon balm and Sweet Cicely, have their menacing sides as well. Our first-ever lemon balm seemed like a gift from the gods, so tasty were its lemony leaves in drinks, salads and fruit cups, so pungent in sachets and potpourris. But talk about a prolific seeder! We've got them everywhere now, and there's no balm to be had from these lemony breeders. Sweet Cicely's cut from the same cloth. Oh, her ferny leaves and umbrels of fragrant creamy flowers are sweet enough in rhubarb pies and salads, but let her seed and you'll regret it. Like comfrey and blackberries and so many of these adversaries, she sends her white fleshy taproots deep into the earth, and if in trying to dig out an unwanted plant you leave even a scrap of root behind, back it comes even stronger than before.

62   Nevertheless, the suckering and self-sowing monsters are child's play compared with the sinister spreaders that send roots and rhizomes and rooting branches in all directions. We have several of these menacing our place, and I fear they're destined to claim it all in the end. Ground ivy is one. We have a patch of it in the old goat pasture. I'm fully prepared to blame former neighbours for its intro-

duction. Each year the patch expands, inexorably, like a cancerous suburban sprawl nothing can contain.

Perched as we are on the edge of some lovely native woodlands, I'm occasionally assailed by guilt that we've ignorantly introduced exotic invaders that will eventually overrun all local flora, leaving the ecosystem ruined and our names besmirched in local legend, like the geniuses who imported rabbits to Australia. Then I look around at other plants we've got—giant cow parsnip, spurge, Saint John's wort, lily of the valley, Japanese anemones, even hellebores. All of them show alarming expansionist tendencies. In especially weak moments I begin reconsidering the relative merits of 2,4-D.

For in the end, the battle goes to the strong, and over time one feels one's manly vigour begin to falter. Arthritic joints creak like old wooden buildings in a wind. Tendonitis and carpal tunnel syndrome weaken once-mighty arms. Back spasms perhaps are the worst. Trouble may start with just the slightest twinge, as a malignant root refuses to let go. It progresses to a pinch, swells to a dull ache and eventually culminates in full vertebral gridlock. I vividly remember the time my back gave out halfway through spading the vegetable garden one spring. There I lay, flat on my aching back on the fresh-turned earth, staring up into a brilliantly blue April sky. I could hear voracious earthworms and centipedes closing in on me. Is this how it all comes to an end? I asked myself, lying there, a fallen soldier in the war of the roses, yet strangely at peace and

63

altogether uncomplaining over the bloody passage of life and death through the garden.

WEEK 10: SPRING SUBTLETIES

Spring is bustling through the garden now like a practical nurse, insistently cheerful, though the gloomy days remain cool with sharp winds and rain. Shoots break from the earth, leaves unfurl auspiciously and peacockeries of colour—dashing golds, purples and whites—illuminate the grounds. Although we're still shivering against winter's hoary bosom, our spirits swell with fresh unfoldings: the first splashes of white arabis break like wave froth in moonlight over cold stones. Waxen hyacinths, stiffly erect, tumescent, perhaps a little indecent, cast scents that are apt to affect the head. Wild violets huddled in warm corners whisper small secrets overheard at woodland trysts. And everywhere buds swell tremendously as Mother Earth bulges with green birthings.

There are places, we know, where spring bolts from the grip of winter and blossoms almost overnight into pre-summer ripeness. Plants emerge and bloom in time-lapse video. This is not how it is with us on the coast. Here spring tiptoes in somewhere during February, retreats, teases from a distance, returns, then flees again, carrying on like an intemperate flirt, often well into June. Those of us who garden here consider ourselves connoisseurs of spring, like feverish poets fattening their slim chapbooks on the season's charms. We are familiar with its subtle-

ties, just as true northerners know the many ways of snow.
Some coastal locals succumb entirely to the seductions of
the season, creating spring gardens jubilant with stunning
rhododendrons, azaleas, flowering cherries and all the
rest, achieving pinnacles of splendour that condemn the
remainder of the gardening year to plodding anticlimax.

Spring does not enter our gardens quite this way, like
the Queen of Sheba, mostly because our rhodos and azaleas haven't been quite up to the challenge. Instead we
dwell at the other end of spring's wide spectrum, where
she dangles before us smaller and more modest charms. I
especially like the tiny bulbs and corms that bloom early
on, putting up brave flowers that seem too delicate to survive the rough going of late winter. Like certain friends,
they are attractive to us because they combine extreme
hardiness with a tender appearance, embodying the possibility of small beauties in a rough and tumble world.

First to show themselves at our place comes a scattering of little winter aconites. After only a day or two of
warming sunshine—perhaps as early as late February—
they open their flowers, each small golden globe balanced
beautifully above the cold earth on an Elizabethan ruff of
finely cut leaves. They're *Eranthis hyemalis*, literally "flower
of spring," members of the buttercup family and even now
their bravely radiant little blooms have that same golden
cheerfulness scooped from a warm summer afternoon.
Although miniature and sweetly delicate in appearance,
these are tough little nuts, growing from peculiar small
tuberous roots planted shallow. "From my experience,"

65

wrote Englishman Beverley Nichols, "[a winter aconite] would come up if you planted it on an iceberg." If snow and sleet and hail assail them during blooming, they calmly fold up their petals, shut out the cruel blasts and wait until things improve. Excessive heat will do them far more mischief than cold will, and they need protection from warm afternoon sun. Growers blessed with a sheltered southern exposure can expect a splendid early aconite show, provided the soil's rich in humus, and there's plenty of deciduous cover to keep them shaded later on. During warm spells, Nichols wrote, "They open very wide, and one sees how essentially innocent and childlike they are, which makes their courage and endurance all the more remarkable." We find it's wise to mulch them generously with grass clippings after blooming to prevent a careless heel from crushing them in the rush later on.

Close by the aconites, and only a few days later, the snowdrops, another familiar old favourite, reveal their white flowers, dangling towards the ground, it strikes me in a poetic moment, like the pearly earrings of a small green goddess. "The fair maids of February," they were called. Their shining whites gleam appealingly alongside the glowing gold of the aconites, and their cultural requirements are almost identical. If anything, snowdrops are even more sensitive to warm sunshine—deciduous woodlands are where they do best. Last week we saw a splendid show of them in an old garden in Victoria, massed under derelict fruit trees, snowdrops packed in so tightly they formed a thrilling white drift of blossom many years in the making. Until such perfection is achieved, their pearl white blooms will show far better against low evergreen ground cover—blue-grey dianthus leaves are excellent— than against bare earth, where they're apt to be splashed with mud. On the same trip to the city I saw how not to plant snowdrops: forlorn little clumps of them stranded in raised concrete planters, in bare earth, fully exposed to wind and sun and the disgruntlements of roaring traffic.

The old cottage garden snowdrop produces a single flower on each stem, with pure white outer petals surrounding a centre delicately etched with green. They come in double- and larger-flowered forms as well, but the old standby retains its popularity. Individually snowdrops give the appearance of frail plants, but nobody's fooled: they're tough as ironwood. Like aconites, they'll simply wait out a return of wintry weather and resume blooming once conditions improve. They are, however, fussy in their own way. They take their time getting established. Some locations they simply won't abide, no matter what, and they thoroughly dislike being dug up, moved around or in other ways put upon by improvers.

A third pioneer cut from the same rough cloth is the delightful little rock garden iris, *I. reticulata*. This exotic beauty produces exquisite flowers in purple, blue or yellow, each of its three lower petals etched with an intricate small tattoo in white and gold. Perhaps even more than aconites and snowdrops, these miniature irises appear too dainty for the dirty going of late winter. After a dump of snow or sleet, they can look awfully bedraggled. But they are natives of the mountains of Turkey and Iran, and remarkably hardy. In severely cold conditions, they'll benefit from a protective winter mulch. Unlike the other two, they enjoy as much sunshine as they can get, and prefer light and well-drained soil. I think they're happiest facing due south, tucked into protective nooks and crannies, as they would be in their mountain home, where their intricate blossoms show to better advantage against a background of sheltering stone.

Like the aconites and snowdrops, they're beginning to naturalize all over our gardens, whether from self-sowing or inadvertent moving of their bulbs, or a bit of both. What luck, for no flowers of the entire growing season are more timely, more necessary for sustaining hope. As American author Bebe Miles writes of *Iris reticulata* in *The Wonderful World of Bulbs:* "Blooming steadily through wind and sleet, they are worth planting every year just for their jewel-like presence on one of those days when it seems winter will never leave."

After the aconites have faded, but while the snowdrops and irises still linger, the earliest crocuses begin to splash the gardens with their bold shows of gold, purple, orange, mauve and cream. Within days they've taken over the whole garden, like an old-time travelling circus come to the village green. "The spendthrift crocus, bursting through the mould / Naked and shivering, with his cup of gold."

The old lines from an anonymous poet catch the crocus spirit, for these flowers hold nothing back, their vibrant colours splashed together shout with a great strong sense of purpose, almost a swaggering cockiness. No modest hanging of heads in shady corners for these partygoers—they're out in full sun, flowers held upright, announcing to the greeny world that old man winter's on his knees.

We walk among them on fine mornings as they open to the warming sunshine. Perhaps a dozen different sorts have now naturalized at our place, some the little species types, others big Dutch hybrids. The names of most are buried somewhere in the archives, but it seems scarcely to matter, for there is a great abundance of good crocuses and I've yet to see one I didn't like. Here, for example, is a little species type, its white petals turning to a soft green-gold at their base, framing the brilliant yellow stigmata at its centre. Three outer petals wear a large purplish patch on their outsides. Nearby another bears small white flowers with a faint blush of lilac, again turning to vivid greenish gold at its heart. Yet a third is a delicious buttery yellow throughout, its little flowers set well down among the thin spears of spiked leaves. Usually the Dutch hybrids produce their larger flowers slightly later than the species types, but this year they've all come bursting out around the same time.

All the crocus colours seem compatible—I don't believe they'd let us growers make a mess of things no matter how we tried—but I think they show best in drifts of a single colour. We prefer a predominance of whites

69

winding through and binding together bold splashes of purple, mauve or gold. Perhaps the only glaring error one can make with crocuses is trying to confine them to straight lines and prim formality. Crocuses will have none of it; they're vagabonds at heart, free spirits from the wild mountains of Europe and Asia Minor and they won't sit in disciplined rows minding their manners no matter who demands it of them.

One looks down directly into the hearts of the flowers. In full sunshine they stretch their petals apart, swelling with welcoming cheerfulness, a gladsome open-heartedness. Crocuses seem always ready for a party, especially when they're massed together, crowding in at different heights so that some flowers are higher than others, creating an effect of multiple miniature layers of bloom. Here's another beauty bearing large flowers with delicate lilac etchings against a white background. Five soft stripes of lilac emerge from a centre point at the base of each petal, fanning slightly outwards and upwards, with finer lilac lines angling away from the main lines in a fanlike pattern that reflects the splaying out of the leaves. Nearby, another is a soft mauve with a white sheen shimmering through the petals, recalling Coventry Patmore's "The crocus while the days are dark / Unfolds its saffron sheen." Dozens of wild bees, bumblebees and flies work giddily inside the flowers, the bigger bees dusted all over with golden pollen. I grow giddy looking into them too, seeing their jubilant profusion, their brassy trumpeting of spring's arrival.

WEEK 11: VERNAL EQUINOX

Last night I slept outdoors for the first time this year. At the far end of the garden, perched on a little hill overlooking the grounds, we have a small summer house that once upon a time served as our goat shed. Many was the winter night we crouched in the bedding straw of the shed, lit by the pale glow of a kerosene lamp, while one of our lovely does laboured to give birth. The goats are no more, but their shed, after several undignified years as a junk collection depot, is now reborn as a summer house. We gutted it last spring, knocking out two walls and replacing them with screening, painting the bare interior white and adding a deck. From the queen-size bed inside, one has a panoramic view of the gardens, lawns and woodlands beyond.

What you don't have is any source of heat beyond yourself. Although night temperatures are still near freezing, I decided last evening to wait no longer; I was bound to sleep out. Sandy, nursing a rare cold, went off to her own snug bed indoors. I packed a second goose-down comforter up the hill, paused on the deck to look up into a clear night sky brilliant with stars, threw off my clothes and slithered between cold sheets.

I long ago accepted the premise that mortification of the flesh produces rich spiritual reward, and thus it was as I lay shivering in the dark a great truth was confirmed: spring is, first of all, a season of sound. Pacific tree frogs massed around the garden pools sang lustily as I drifted towards sleep, a croaking version of "The Anvil Chorus." Suddenly, abruptly, in perfect unison, their singing would stop, leaving a silence ringing through the dark. Dimly I could hear the creek gurgling and plashing on the far side of the clearing. Then an introductory croak or two from a froggy choirmaster would set the whole chorus off again. I floated away to sleep serenaded by the rapturous songs of frog love.

Once in the depths of the night I heard a hooting of owls in the woods—wild, Dionysian cries, songs of love as well, but a fierce love from darkened haunts. I snuggled under the comforters, aware of the cold night air. Sometime later I heard the thud of deer bounding across the clearing.

I awoke to a pale light shining through the woodlands off to the east, and all around me birdsong bloomed in the air—trillings and chirpings, intermittent cries and whistles, warblings and pipings, plaintive single notes and elegant arpeggios, swelling together in a chorus that lifted my spirit I can't tell you how high. I lay there for a while, propped up on pillows, watching the pale light intensify behind the trees, exulting in birdsong.

72

Eventually I leapt from my cozy bed into the cold morning air. A white sheen of ground frost silvered every surface. Walking through the garden back to the house, I noticed the spring flowers, so jaunty by day, huddled closed against the cold. I struck a fire in the woodstove right away, then was startled to see the time was 5:30 AM. No doubt about it: notwithstanding the frost, spring has broken.

"Make me over, Mother April," Bliss Carman once wrote, as the season is all promise and expectation, cleansing and renewal. Which brings me to the redemptive possibilities of leafy greens, the spring tonics that have purified and restored our temperate ancestors for millennia. Of all the marvellous salads plucked from the vegetable patch in the course of a year, none is more wholesome, none excites greater cheerfulness, than the first fresh greens of the season. A salad bowl heaped with these early risers offers at once a delectable freshness, a purifying tonic and exhilarating promises of things yet to come. Every evening now, as close upon the supper hour as practical, I take my colander and scissors and set off for the garden to see what's on offer. Dependable Russian red kale and chickweed—two nutritional superstars about which I've already gushed enough—may still form the backbone of the earliest spring salads, but now they're joined by a half-dozen other early starters boasting a more cosmopolitan range of tastes.

Chervil is one of our most reliable early herbs, and a more delightful plant you'd be hard pressed to find. A cool season annual, it self-seeds freely at our place and, depending upon the severity of the winter, is often ready for cutting in February. Tough as nails in its own way, this low-growing plant bears sprigs of delicate ferny leaves, like a parsley that's gone to art school. Aficionados call it "gourmet's parsley"—but the shopworn "gourmet" here means that chervil is hard to find in a supermarket because it so quickly perishes after cutting. Freshly cut, its leaves impart a fine hint of anise and a subtle something else—as the English writer John Evelyn put it three hundred years ago: "The tender tips of chervil should never be wanting in our sallets, being exceedingly wholesome and cheering of the spirits."

In a small separate bed at the edge of our vegetable patch we grow chives and sorrel, both of them amongst the earliest shoots of spring. The first small sorrel leaves add a delightful crisp freshness and that lovely lemony acidic tang. The first spears of chives are the same, their familiar taste enlivened by a sweet heartiness. The trick here is to have the plants cleaned of old stalks and winter debris in order to simplify cutting the tiny new spears. For eagerness, reliability and indestructibility, it's hard to surpass perennial sorrel and chives.

The same may be said of Sweet Cicely, which breaks from the earth only a few days after the others. Used in moderation its ferny new leaf-tips add a distinctive sweet licorice taste. Within weeks this rather assertive herb will be a metre tall. We grow it primarily as an ornamental— its soft grey-green foliage and massed umbrels of white flowers billow handsomely beneath a red Japanese maple. For now it's a wholesome and flavourful contributor to the salad bowl, though perhaps a touch fuzzy for particular palates.

Overwintered parsley is also ready for cutting. We grow both the curly and flat-leaved, or Italian, types. Their springtime sprigs are especially rich in minerals and vitamins, particularly A and C ("three times the amount contained in oranges!" enthuses one of our manuals, although the comparison may be even less fruitful than the time-worn apples and oranges). A biennial, parsley's stubbornly slow to grow from seed; the plants that do best at our place are often self-seeders that find an out-of-the-way corner and develop contentedly without any help from us.

Corn salad also springs into action at the first hint of spring warm-up. For us, seeds sown in August or September produce small rosettes that shiver through winter, then put out abundant new leaves in spring. They also self-sow, popping up in densely packed small colonies that can be sheared with scissors. The little leaves have a sweetly distinctive taste. Corn salad too labours under the "gourmet" label, popular varieties having chichi names like Verte de Cambrai.

Just when we gourmands may becoming a tad jaded by the unrelieved green of these seasonal openers, another old favourite comes to the rescue. The massed white flowers of Arabis, or rockcress, are a familiar spring sight in rockeries and lolling over walls. Its edible flowers have a slight peppery taste and make a bright addition when sprinkled across tossed greens. I dream of the days when I'll have enough spare time on my hands to get a similar effect plucking, one by one, the tiny flowers of wild violets.

Like the nightly rites of sleeping out amid the love songs of frogs and birds, the daily ritual of gathering the salad greens, even on the chilliest afternoons of early spring, brings one into an intense and intimate connection with the stunning surge of growth erupting from the earth. Returning to the kitchen carrying a colander brimming with succulent and wholesome shoots, one feels John Evelyn's "cheering of the spirits" and a sense that, for all its wrongs, for the moment all's right with the world.

WEEK 12: A SHED OF ITS TIME

Raptures over the rites of spring are all very well and good, but I'm not sure they can compare with the sublime state of bliss brought on by having just completed a new shed. No plant, however lovely, no arrangement of plants, however comely, can quite compete in certain gardeners' affections with a spanking new shed. This, after all, is the heart and soul of one's estate, at once a storehouse of fine implements and oddments, a place of sanctuary during domestic squalls, and an outpost in the noble work of making a better world.

Indeed, zeal for all the good things sheds have to offer can lead some people to have more than one. They'll have a tool shed for tools, a storage shed for storage and a potting shed for potting. Sheds, in short, are infectious. Every so often you come upon a property entirely given over to sheds, a complex rabbit warren of Dickensian outbuildings all leaning tipsily against one another with tortuous little paths running among them. This is shedding elevated to an art form, offering the distinct advantage of there being no ground left over for non-shedding functions such as gardens, lawns and pools. The compleat shedder—usually an older bachelor and often a trifle mad—can wander contentedly from shed to shed, storing and rearranging treasures with no further care in the world.

While many of us might long for such an arrangement for ourselves, the realities of lot size as well as the legitimate expectations of neighbours, spouses and offspring normally confine us to a single shed or two. More's the pity, for this is where trouble as often as not begins. Shed space is very much like garden space in that there is never quite enough of it. Even the most spacious, the most intelligently engineered shed is destined to eventually fill up and become insufficient.

For some of us, like myself, inadequacy may stalk the shed from its inception. I think of my jerry-built sheds in the same way as trees in an ancient forest, growing to an enormous fullness and complexity, then eventually collapsing to be replaced by a new generation.

My latest shed, and finest one yet, may linger a little longer in usable form than some of its precursors. It came into being because of undeniable shortcomings in its immediate predecessor. Siting can be a problem with some sheds, but that was not the case with my old shed. Indeed, it had been cunningly located within quick reach from the back door of the house, as though a Feng Shui master had long studied the site to determine just where the flow of *chi* might have a well-placed shed arise. No, the problem was in roofing, specifically in my decision to install a sod roof.

In hindsight, I recognize that a sod roof, for all its splendid correctness in a prairie setting, is at best a questionable choice for a region that features four feet of rainfall per year. But sod roofs have a certain frisson that enticed me into a miscalculation that has been the undoing of many an unsuccessful shedder: namely, dragging aesthetic considerations into the shed, where they have no right to be. Sheds are above all practical places; function informs the shed. Leaded glass, fancy barge boards and gambrels, curtains and cornices, and certainly sod roofs in a rain forest—all of these are repugnant to the true blue-collar shed. A battered old couch in the corner is permissible. So is a derelict television set for keeping an eye on the Stanley Cup playoffs while performing small miracles at the workbench. But adornments and embellishments, decorative touches and ornamentations are anathema.

This is what my sod roof was, a wandering from the straight and narrow path of practicality, and it has cost me dearly. Built on the cheap, from recycled metal roofing and swaths of plastic sheeting under the sod, it is something short of watertight. Once the rains begin, leaks start dripping all over my precious stuff. After the deluge I find cans of perfectly reusable nails, only needing a bit of straightening, full of rusty water, the nails themselves like gobs of drowned worms. Seeking its own level, groundwater rises like the Red River through the shed's earthen floor, forming small pools in which my valuable equipment would sit like hippos in a mud hole. Delighting in the moisture, renegade slugs rasped the labels off paint cans and other containers, so one wouldn't know what was in them. Stored bags of cement hardened to concrete. In heavy weather the sodden roof groaned with threats of collapse. After a few years of this, the shed began to lose its point; its contents might just as well have been outdoors for all the protection they were getting. And so the solemn decision was made to build a new and better shed nearby.

Once one has decided to shed an old shed and move to a new one, the experience is equal parts exhilaration and challenge. The newfound spaciousness is marvellous, of course, and one takes delight in arranging tools so that rakes, spades, forks and all the rest hang in orderly rows against a wall—something they steadfastly refused to do in the old place. This unaccustomed orderliness in turn triggers other elevated impulses, for example a determination to treat one's tools better. In my old waterlogged shed it seemed perfectly appropriate at the end of a slogging work day to simply lean spade, rake, manure fork or whatever against the wall and hasten indoors for a well-deserved glass of wine. A new shed frowns upon such carelessness. It reminds one that competent gardeners clean their tools thoroughly after each use before putting them away. Spades, forks and trowels are washed in warm soapy water. Rust spots are scrubbed with steel wool. The tools are dried and then polished with an oily rag to protect against rust. Shears and other cutting implements are sharpened and spades given a good sharpening with a file, during which one recalls the old adage that a sharp spade is half the work of digging. Cleaned, dried, oiled and sharpened,

79

the tools are then arranged in their allotted spots, allowing one to proceed indoors for a refreshing glass of carrot juice while basking in the warm glow of a well-regulated life.

But there's pain here too, for the move to a new shed may involve suggestions from interveners and other parties that certain old treasures be disposed of. An ancient lawnmower that might be put to useful purpose some day; coils of wire that might eventually be needed for the raspberries; old rake handles that could make passable dibbles; rusting spade blades that only need a new handle. The list is endless. One hears suggestions that it all be thrown out, but you know the rubric as well as I do. You can keep a piece of junk for twenty years and never need it until the day after you've thrown it away.

This brings up the disquieting question of what to do with the old shed. Perhaps a clean break is best. I remember one time felling a large red cedar tree which, in the way of top-heavy cedars, swung about contrarily and crashed down in the wrong direction, completely flattening an old tin-roofed shed that had long been an embarrassment to own. Good riddance to bad rubbish, as my old mum used to put it.

Other sheds, like certain house guests, have a habit of hanging around indefinitely. There is a certain advantage here, in that the junk that has accumulated inside them—and here I'm talking about bona fide rubbish, not the marvellous artifacts germane to all well-operated sheds—this undeniable junk can simply be left inside and the whole business abandoned to rot back into earth. We have just such a shed at our place and have decided to cover it with a rambling rose and think of it as a folly. This is one of the genuine benefits of an acreage over a small lot, that one can simply walk away from sheds that have run their course, replicating them with new ones. It might be convincingly argued that a scattering of decomposing sheds across the landscape enhances biodiversity. And, in a pinch, one can always nip back into an abandoned shed to unearth something useful, something that will shed a whole new light on things.

$\mathscr{A}$PRIL

WEEK 13: ALL FOOL'S DAY

I wandered today through the woodlands that make up most of our property, following a footpath that meanders alongside the creek. I came upon a splendid sight: dozens of skunk cabbages in full bloom, shining like brilliant yellow beacons. What beauties they are, I thought, almost tropical in their jungly lushness, able to transform even the most dismal-looking swamp or bog into a glamorous wetland. One's spirit lifts at just a glimpse of them, spring-time harbingers, messengers of hope, marvellous for their brave hardiness.

Yet we call them skunk cabbage, even polecat weed in certain backwaters. It is perhaps the most chronically underrated of our wild flowers. As one writer put it, in discussing the relative merits of the earliest spring wild flowers: "Comparing the Dwarf Trillium with Skunk

Cabbage is like comparing a Ruby-throated Hummingbird with a Turkey Buzzard."

The stench of skunk spray clings to the plant, at least in popular imagination. Personally I find their odour not so much offensive as pungent, redolent of the swampy ooze in which the plants so often grow. It is perhaps disagreeable to some people in the same way as the bracing scent of barnyard manure fresh spread on farm fields. In any event, the smell is insufficient evidence to ostracize one of our finest wildlings.

We Canadians are blessed with not just one, but two quite distinct skunk cabbages. The western plant bearing the name is *Lysichiton americanum,* a native of the Pacific Northwest more happily also known as swamp lantern or yellow arum. It is these that flourish in a merry yellow ribbon along our creek. Their stout fleshy rhizomes plunge down through the streambed silt, and you'd wonder how they survive the creek's wintertime fury, but they do. The runoff from winter storms has hardly subsided before they send up through the cold running water their large clear yellow flowering parts, followed by enormous green elephant-ear leaves.

The smaller eastern version, *Symplocarpus foetidus,* is native from Quebec to Manitoba. Its spring colours are more varied, pleasingly mottled with purplish browns and greenish yellows. Even more than its western counterpart, this is a hard-nosed harbinger of spring. While other plants hold back, protecting themselves against late winter's killer instincts, the skunk cabbage pushes its tightly furled fist of growth through half-frozen earth or derelict snow-banks. Those who know its ways say it generates internal heat to assist it in breaking through icy ground. Overnight, dreary late-winter marshes and wetlands are illuminated by blooms lush and lovely enough for the tropics.

Despite their brilliant show, skunk cabbages bear really inconspicuous little flowers. These cluster on a small stem shaped like a Keystone Cops billy club which is sheathed in a hoodlike bract called a spathe. The bright colours are produced on the spathe, not by the small flowers within. The colours and scent of the plant attract pollinating insects, carrion flies and beetles and pollen-seeking bees.

Something like an underdeveloped urban myth surrounds the alleged delights of skunk cabbage cuisine. Tales are told of indigenous peoples boiling the roots or leaves for food. But Euell Gibbons, that insatiable stalker of wild plants, found the leaves "thick, heavy and foul" even after repeated boilings in successive pots of fresh water. He eventually struck on a passable recipe for an herb-meat-cabbage pudding, but its preparation involved more time and work than amending the Canadian Constitution. The plants do, however, provide food for squirrels and deer, and the roots are said to be a favourite of foraging bears. I remember more desperate times when we harvested great bundles of the enormous leaves to spread as summer mulch on the parched vegetable patch. Nowadays we leave them for big banana slugs to feed on, and by summer's end the slugs have rasped the thick leaves to tatters.

Notwithstanding its inelegant name and alleged stench, the skunk cabbage is enjoying a renaissance of sorts. It is now photographed growing alongside perfect ponds in impressive estate gardens. Gardening experts sing its praises. In *The Concise Encyclopedia of Favourite Wild Flowers,* Marjorie Dietz writes that *Symplocarpus foetidus* is "well worth planting in rich, moist or wet woods and beside large pools or ponds (either man-made or natural) for its early appearance in spring and later for the striking accent value of its large foliage." American plantsperson Judy Glattstein praises it as "premier among swamp plants." British authority Penelope Hobhouse features *L. americanum* for its "striking arum-like spathes, followed by massive glossy green foliage." Many wild flower nurseries now carry the plants, which are easily transplanted.

This transformation from lowly commoner to international garden star is not a new story for native plants, nor is the frenzy for native plant gardening now afoot on the land. While plant geneticists are busy fiddling with the building blocks of life, wild gardens are springing up in the most respectable of neighbourhoods. We've witnessed a burst of entrepreneurial zeal that has leapt from attractively packaged wildflower seeds to wild meadows in a can, to wildflower mixes in pre-seeded mats that one rolls out like a carpet and trims to fit irregularly shaped beds, all the way to wildflower "sod" with already-growing wildflowers in it: you just plop the sod down and water it! Deep-rooted skunk cabbages, of course, hardly lend themselves to this couch-potato approach to native plant gardening.

Even more disconcerting, I recently read an account of *The Mania for Native Plants in Nazi Germany* by garden historian Joachim Wolschke-Buhlman. One leading promoter of native plants in that demented time wanted to ban from the Fatherland "all that until now has pleased the heart of a gardener: everything high-bred, overfed, conspicuous, foreign." In 1941, German landscape architects—focusing brilliantly on the fundamental issues of the day—proposed passage of legislation outlawing the use of non-native plants in German landscapes. The use of indigenous plants became identified with doctrines of racial purity, with driving out foreigners—a mindset the author claims still contaminates certain discussions of native plant gardening today, particularly the segregation into "good" and "bad" plants on the basis of place of origin. This backlash chatter isn't exactly what you need to be hearing just as you're getting your native plant garden underway.

The Garry oak meadows of southwestern British Columbia offer an illuminating tale about the fine line we humans walk in dealing with native plants and naturalist plantings. Open parklands dotted with elegant oaks, these meadows in springtime display successive flushes of wild flowers blooming in a profuse and splendid harmony of colours. Acres of blue camas, white Easter lily and yellow western buttercup create a perfect interplay of colours, an impeccability of design any gardener might spend a lifetime trying to emulate. Shooting star and little monkey-flower, chocolate lily and satin flower, literally dozens of spring ephemerals bloom in their turns, sustaining a springtime show that can last for three months. When Captain George Vancouver first spotted the meadows on the southeastern tip of Vancouver Island, near present-day Victoria, he was astonished to see "an extensive lawn covered with luxuriant grass and diversified with an abundance of flowers" creating "a landscape almost as enchantingly beautiful as the most elegantly finished pleasure grounds in Europe."

But even in the captain's day, the landscape was not entirely the work of nature. The meadows were gardens of a sort, expertly tended by the native inhabitants of the region who valued the open grasslands as hunting grounds for deer and elk, as well as for the abundance of edible bulbs and herbs, especially camas bulbs. Fire was the native gardener's principal tool here, and the meadows were regularly burned to prevent shrubs and conifers from overrunning the grasslands.

That was just the appropriate level of human interference to maintain this extraordinary ecosystem. Today the meadows are in extreme peril, reduced to fragmentary remnants, for they occur on some of the choicest real estate on the continent, a thin band stretching from southern Vancouver Island to central California. Rapid urban development, notably in the Victoria area, has destroyed many of the finest meadows. Some estimates place the loss as high as 95 per cent. Only a few small ecological reserves offer permanent protection. In areas not yet urbanized, overgrazing by domestic livestock has taken a toll. Suppression of wildfires has allowed non-native plants, particularly

Scotch broom, to invade the meadows and displace native species. A number of rare plants, birds and butterflies are disappearing along with the meadows.

This is where the gardeners come in. The Victoria-based Garry Oak Meadow Preservation Society began promoting a "backyard biodiversity" program that urged landowners to keep their remaining oaks, plant acorns, and return their thirsty lawns to natural wildflower meadows. Forestry Canada helped out with "Project Acorn" by growing and distributing thousands of oak seedlings for planting in yards and along roadways. A specialty nursery on nearby Saltspring Island carries many of the three hundred vascular plants that thrive in the meadows. Meanwhile crews of robust preservationists are volunteering to assist in supervised work bees to remove Scotch broom from meadows where it has become invasive. Other groups are lobbying to protect oak groves and have the meadows recognized as a heritage landscape. Provincial authorities are scrambling to map and evaluate the remaining Garry oak communities, with an eye to rare and endangered species and plant communities. Municipal councils are belatedly enacting tree preservation bylaws that will include Garry oaks, and are at least beginning to exercise closer scrutiny of development proposals. Whether all this activity will be enough to save this threatened ecosystem time will tell. Similar initiatives are underway all over the continent as gardeners and other volunteers work to preserve or restore plant communities that typify the genius of their region.

88

Whether that's a Garry oak meadow, a tall grass prairie or a swamp made brilliant by arum lilies, I say "Bravo!"

WEEK 14: TINY GREEN FINGERS

The bold chorus of the crocus show has already faded; the garden gives way to a softer, more serene colour scheme. Vivid blue ribbons of grape hyacinths wind through emerging mounds of green foliage, and in several spots a tumult of red tulips has broken out. But the overall impression is more of pale golds and creams, colours that complement the subtle shadings of green in emerging leaves.

On certain shining spring mornings, sunlight spilling through the garden seems itself a mix of green and gold, the distilled essence of spring. This springtime light—at least where I live—is not the honeyed golden glow of September; rather it has a clarity and lucidity about it, a sprightly sense of fresh unfolding. It is an unmistakably vernal green from which the blue has been washed, so that it gleams of yellow. Walking through the garden at dawn, and again in the late afternoon when sunlight seems to glow from inside the leaves themselves, you'd have to be a hopeless oaf not to feel, for all one's woes, a thrilling sense of a perfect world emerging.

Three white-flowering crabapples grow in our garden, each a tree that in full bloom would bring the tender-hearted to tears with its beauty. But even now, well before their blossoms begin to break, their new leaves, barely emergent, create lovely clouds of pale green tinted golden in the sunshine. Wild elderberry bushes at the edge of the woods have the same shining yellow-green quality in their new leaves, soon enhanced by candles of creamy flowers. The grasses of the lawns have it too, this shining virides-cence, and the hazy weeping willow across the pond.

This brief epiphany of tiny green fingers unfurling is among the most precious of the year, and the gardener's challenge for the moment—I'm not sure just why gar-deners must, like questing knights, be always facing challenges, but there you are—the challenge is to develop planting schemes that reflect something of nature's green-gold virtuosity.

Daffodils, of course, ride the crest of the wave, seeming almost to embody this distillation of spring. Shakespeare hailed the daffodils "That come before the swallow dares, and take / The winds of March with beauty..." I think the most frequently seen big yellow trumpet types work best at a distance where they're free to excite the romantic poet's imagination from half a mile away without yellow-ing us to death. We've moved most of the big King Alfreds and his cohorts out of the garden and scattered them in drifts across the yard where they're free to be as unabash-edly yellow as they want. Inside the garden the subtleties of spring light are better reflected by the softer coloured sorts, of which there are dozens in white, cream, pale gold and apricot. Among my favourites are elegant cream-white "Thalia"; "Ice Follies" with a hint of yellow inside a crown surrounded by a paler perianth; shining icy white "Mount Hood"; and jaunty little "Cheerfulness" with a soft apricot centre inside its small double crown. Drifts of these pale beauties wandering across the gardens create an impression that is, as one observer put it, "serene and softly exciting."

Cream and pale yellow tulips pick up and extend the motif. We have clusters of one lovely tulip that blooms faithfully year after year, whose name has for the moment fled. No matter, for its blooms are exceptional—a rich creamy white, blushed with hints of green and yellow. When afternoon sunlight shines through them, they give the impression of holding a translucent green-gold elixir in their chalices. The little species tulip, *Tulipa tarda*, is nowhere near so spectacular, but has its own small stratagems for combining spring colours: each of its six slender petals is a soft yellow at the centre, fading to pale cream at its tips. What the species types may lack in grandeur they more than compensate for with steadiness; they may be counted upon to return each year in a way that certain other bulbs—and most certainly certain other tulips—cannot. Last year, for example, Sandy achieved an exemplary small composition made up of hybrid tulips that bloomed a lovely soft green, intermingled with pure white waxen hyacinths. This year neither is quite what they were a year ago. Another year or two they'll be only a memory. April's really too early in the year for regrets, though regrets there already are that the first ephemerals have fled.

On the subject of steadfastness and a charm that never disappoints, consider old English primroses whose buttery yellow flowers tucked in amongst crinkly green leaves seem to embody the ancient spirit of spring. Keats caught that sense of "primroses gathered at midnight / By chilly finger'd spring." They're at their loveliest just now, nestled under shrub roses and in other shady spots, so old-fashioned in a goodhearted way, looking as though they're thriving in a hedgerow past which Jude the Obscure or Jane Eyre might wander at any moment. Other primulas add a more contemporary touch: we have one with larger white blooms vivid with strong orange-yellow markings at their centres, another with tiny double flowers coloured rich gold brushed with orange. I admire them all, and fully understand why there are primula people out there every bit as rabid as rose or rhododendron people, but if I had to select just one, I'd choose the old English standby with all its passing ghosts.

Right down at ground level, a patch of golden marjoram gleams between sandstone blocks, its opposite pairs of golden heart-shaped leaves washed with pale green. Emerging clumps of that old Victorian favourite, feverfew—which self-seed perhaps a touch more enthusiastically than necessary at our place—have a fresh lime green-yellow cast to them that nicely complements the other tints crowded into this part of the spectrum. There's also a subtle hint of yellow in the new foliage of lady's mantle and the aquilegias. The nubs of emerging variegated hostas hold their creams and greens scrolled together like the colours of furled flags.

Several of the euphorbias are especially fine at creating a wash of bright yellow-green in spring. We first developed an affection for euphorbias seeing them growing wild on the Mani peninsula in the Peloponnesus. Hiking through a gloriously warm winter afternoon, we came upon an especially lovely group of them growing along a stony roadway. An enormous sow with her litter of tiny piglets shambled among them. One of the best for us is the cushion spurge which forms a golden mound suffused with pale green, from the clear yellow bracts surrounding its small flowers. Right in front of our kitchen, Mrs. Robb's bonnet creates an equally lovely and long-lasting massed effect from its lime-green bracts. It's particularly useful in dry shade, leaving one to wonder who Mrs. Robb was and how euphorbias took her bonnet for their namesake.

You'll notice I'm not mentioning forsythia here, not because its paler-flowered forms aren't precisely the type of soft yellows we're after just now, but because the several forsythia shrubs we possess have been moved from spot to spot around the property on an almost yearly basis, being pruned back with each move, so that they've never enjoyed an opportunity to show their true colours. Other people's forsythias are quite splendid, but I'm not about to sing the praises of any species that can't settle down and be splendid for us as well.

As hellebores do, for example. Now there's a group of plants about which one can get enthusiastic this time of year. Hellebores are stoutly Christian perennials. Legend has it that the Christmas rose bloomed outside the manger

93

on the first Christmas Eve. The Lenten rose earned its name by always being in bloom for Easter. There's even a Saint Patrick's rose whose greenish flowers appear for the saint's March feast day. Like all good Christians, hellebores are never difficult, remain steadfast in the face of adversity, and display their considerable charms with an agreeable humility.

Two that contribute handsomely to the green-gold motif are the Lenten rose and the bearsfoot (or Stinking) hellebore. The second, a native of western Europe, grows like a small shrub, with several thick green stems almost a metre tall sparsely draped with leathery deep-cut leaves. Although evergreen, it has a forlorn and world-weary look about it in the depths of winter. But come the first hints of warmth in February, it brightens up appreciably, eventually producing massed clusters of flowers in peculiar little pale green globes. The flowers and subsequent seed heads last for several months—by mid-May they're bleached a stunning green—and the plants remain structurally handsome well into late summer. A little gangly-looking in winter if stuck out in the open on its own, it shows best in groupings set against a wall or shrub background and is excellent among naturalized daffodils. It self-sows freely at our place, a trait I appreciate so long as it's done in moderation.

By early March the Lenten roses have broken into bloom, quickly becoming undisputed stars of the early spring garden. Their blooms in variable colours are borne on short waxy stems. We have a white variety tucked on the north side of a moss-covered cedar stump, the white blooms showing exquisitely against the vivid greens of the mossy stump. Close by, other Lenten roses bear flowers of purple, rose, claret and a delicious chocolate red, many of them flecked with maroon. The clustered heads bow towards the earth, evocative of meditating Buddhist nuns. The blooms last for many weeks—far longer than the bold spring bulbs that hellebores complement so well—often with subtle changes in colour. Whether white or coloured to begin with, the flowers gradually turn soft green and, as they do so, raise their heads skyward. It's a lovely transformation that makes one cherish these modest beauties even more.

The combined effect of all these plantings—complemented by the whites of flowering cherries, arabis and all the rest—is a shining lightness, a glimmering and pure clarity that somehow, like spring itself, evokes hopefulness and a bracing sense of well-being.

WEEK 15: DRESSING DOWN

Recently I came across an article on "power gardening" in an American magazine. "An earthy hobby has been transformed into a status game by boomers with plenty of money," the piece declared. I wasn't unduly confounded by the article's breathy disclosures of nouveau gardeners spending $585 (us) for a pair of leather-handled rose shears from Hermes or $950 for the "first clear yellow clivia" from White Flower Farm in Connecticut. No, what really unnerved me was the article's pronouncement that "the garden is no longer a private refuge: it is a fashion statement." Great. As if it weren't sufficient that we be bedevilled by tumultuous weather, unscrupulous nurserypeople and problematic colour clashes, we're now also expected to concern ourselves with stylish gardening attire.

Glancing through the magazines and catalogues, one realizes that expectations are running rampant that we romp about our gardens in twill caps and khaki vests, designer pants and kid-leather gloves posh enough for an audience with the Queen. Gum boots are no longer good enough—one should have English wellies. The whole idea seems to be not so much that one actually goes out and mucks around doing dirty work, but rather that one is fashionably attired in such a way as to suggest that brute physical labour is altogether possible.

All very well for dabblers, I suppose, but this insistence upon horticultural haute couture runs smack up against the ancient and inalienable right of gardeners to dress in rags. The time-honoured dress code, as we know, is to wear while gardening those clothes that have become too shabby to be worn anywhere else. Comfort, familiarity and a certain devil-may-care insouciance far outweigh considerations of prevailing taste.

Stylish footwear is not a specialty of the average plantsperson, for whom practicality is of the essence. One is in and out of doors so frequently, ease of slipping footwear off and on is crucial. This is best accomplished with battered runners or dress shoes that have seen better days. Laces are eventually discarded or permanently knotted, and the backs of the shoes are flattened under impatient heels so that one ends up flapping around the patio garden in unprepossessing flip-flops. Not long ago I was given a pair of fancy French rubber clogs that can be quickly slipped off and on, like cut-off gum boots—just the sort of thing with which to at least begin one's fashion statement. But, needless to say, these are far too tony to be torn to pieces working in the garden, so I carry on in my decrepit old runners, while saving my fancy French bootlets for when I step out for an evening.

There is no compelling reason I can think of that while pruning the roses one's socks should match.

I suppose a favourable impression might be created in the neighbourhood if one could flounce about the yard wearing designer blue jeans or those $75 pliant cotton canvas pants modelled on the Japanese farmer style, with tagua-button flap closures and rubber knee pads. But really, for people so frequently down on hands and knees, appearance is the least consideration to be applied to trousers. Splitting resistance is everything. Among the finest work pants I ever owned was a pair of unsuccessful casual slacks acquired for a pittance from the Sally Ann thrift shop. Made of 100 per cent polyester, miraculously stretchy and hideously yellow, they resisted tearing and fraying for what seemed like decades. Baggy old soccer pants are good too, except that they often lack sufficient pocketing. Pockets are indispensable for holding entangled scraps of twine, small tools, markers from newly planted specimens whose names one fully intends to write down somewhere, and the seed heads of pernicious weeds or blighted leaves seized in passing. Muddy and/or torn knees are de rigueur in pants and there's certainly no reason to be ashamed of a fly zipper that has lost its zip. When seams do eventually split, particularly in sensitive areas, they can be closed with strategically placed safety pins, a standard, if hazardous, accessory in the retro-grunge gardener's ensemble.

Torn T-shirts, unravelling woollen sweaters and dress shirts with irredeemable ring-around-the-collar are all appropriate. Colour coordination is not necessarily a consideration. In cool weather I'm partial to an ancient down vest that exudes through multiple tears and punctures tiny puffs of goose down whenever I move.

I shan't dwell long on gloves, as one of each pair is so quickly lost among the compost heaps and leaf mold piles, mixed pairs are as common as in tennis. Every so often I come upon an old glove lying in some unlikely corner of the garden, like the hand of an old friend waving in greeting, perhaps a bit the worse for wear from a few months of rain and the preliminary gnawings of decomposer organisms. As often as not, all the glove needs is a bit of a shake and a good drying out and it can be cycled back into the revolving collection of gloves about which the only real mystery is why one ends up with multiples that fit one hand and none for the other.

Hats, however, are an essential element. In cold weather I rely upon a battered baseball cap with foam rubber lining that keeps my bald patch warm. I've always used an old straw hat to keep the summer sun off, straw hats customarily being to gardeners what hard hats are to construction workers. But I was shocked to learn not long ago that straw hats are hopelessly ineffective at blocking harmful ultraviolet radiation. Then by happy chance I was given a fancy new cap designed to block uv. Practical to a fault, it sports a large bill and neck-protecting flap, all of it a brilliant luminescent red. Wearing it, I'm advised by acquaintances, I rather resemble an oversized pileated woodpecker.

The combined effect of these arrangements is a gardening ensemble that many a gardener might mistake for their own, but one guaranteed to incite dismay in an up-and-coming power gardener. Every so often a party of immaculately attired strangers will wander into our place, uninvited and unannounced, only to behold Sandy and me smeared in dirt and perspiration, resplendent in our tattered outfits that no self-respecting knight of the road would sleep under a bridge in. The looks of shocked dismay on our visitors' faces are well worth the bother of the work stoppage.

But there's the point: the keeping up of appearances is simply not on, no matter what we're told by elegant editors. Gardeners have an inalienable right to dress in rags, and I'm fully confident that this ancient and venerable tradition will survive the temporary aberration of power gardening arrivistes posing in some beau-monde vogue for horticultural fashion statements.

WEEK 16: PEST ASIDES

We were strolling the gardens the other evening when I saw a dreadful thing: our little purple-leaved sand cherry, barely past blooming, stood entirely defoliated. The mood of a tranquil evening stroll destroyed in a stroke, I hustled over to see what had caused this calamity. A moment's inspection revealed the agent of mischief: a tent caterpillar nest cunningly nestled among the lower twigs of the little shrub. Platoons of small caterpillars were wriggling their way down the branches, returning to the nest for the night. The sense was of a plague, like the ones wrathful Jehovah inflicted upon the stiff-necked Egyptians.

It's been a banner year for tent caterpillars at our place; I've probably destroyed two dozen nests already. The optimists among us maintain that we're at or near the high point in a population cycle whose peaks nature eventually brings level. This assurance that a "natural crash" in populations is imminent wears thinner as it's repeated year after year, like the half-baked predictions of New Year's futurists. Meanwhile, the silken nests, seething with scores of small hairy caterpillars and fouled with their vile excrement, are undeniably repulsive. One's reminded of a corpse teeming with maggots. I remember first encountering them years ago as a young gardener, then going to extraordinary lengths to destroy them without actually touching any of the filthy things. At one point I went so far as scorching the caterpillars in their nests with the flame of a small butane torch. Just recently I fell into conversation with a formidable gardener who still employs the flamethrower approach; she seemed transported with joy describing to me how she roasted her caterpillars with a fierce flame.

I take an equally perverse satisfaction in using the more traditional hands-on approach. Crouched by the defoliated sand cherry, I didn't hesitate to reach in, scoop out the nest and squeeze its squishy inmates in my hand. Then I followed along each branch systematically squeezing caterpillars between thumb and forefinger, so that their innards burst outwards like squeezed pimples, until there wasn't a sole survivor. This technique is what's known as manual control in its purest form.

Tent caterpillars are the gregarious larvae of a moth called *clisiocampa,* a member of the genus *Bombyx,* which includes the silkworm moth—our repulsive pests are only the tiniest twist of DNA away from the untold wealth of the silk trade. In autumn the moth lays her eggs on the branches of selected plants that will feed her hatched offspring the following year. Around here native red alders are a favourite host tree, while in our gardens, the moths are drawn mostly to apple, cherry and plum trees. Mountain ash, wild cherry and hawthorn are also preferred host trees. Careful observation during the dormant season might reveal clusters of eggs like tiny rings of hammered pewter encircling certain branch tips. The eggs can be scraped away, or the branches may be pruned off and burned, or sprayed with dormant oil and lime sulphur. My experience has been that no matter what preventive measures are taken, in a bumper year you're going to get tent caterpillars.

Egg clusters that elude control hatch in spring into colonies often containing many dozens of larvae. They collectively spin the telltale cobweb-like tents that offer them protection from bad weather and predators. In poor weather, a colony might extend its tent along the entire length of a side branch, enclosing the leaves for easier access. Voracious eaters, the dozens of larvae in each tent can quickly defoliate small shrubs or whole branches of trees.

When a major outbreak occurs, as we've had this spring, prompt response is of the essence. Even for those of us who like our gardens au naturel, when it comes to tent caterpillars, a zero-tolerance policy is best. Some experts recommend spraying with insecticides, but manual control, if at all feasible, is both a wiser and psychologically more gratifying approach. Nests are best assailed while the caterpillars are inside—on a cold day, or early morning or late evening. For nests located high on the tips of tree branches, I take my pole pruner and snip off the twig just below the nest. When it falls to the ground, roiling with excited larvae, I grind it underfoot and there's an end to it. When a nest is located in such a way that pruning off the infected branch is not realistic, one resorts to the hands-on approach. Alternatively, one can take a small stick and twirl it gently to gather up most of the nest in the same way carnival venders gather cotton candy on a stick. Some nests are very hard to spot, and it's prudent to check host trees from different sides and angles to be sure there isn't an extra nest tucked in somewhere. Twice this year I'd thought I'd eliminated every single nest, only to spot new ones several days later. Constant vigilance is the order of the day.

You'd think these plump larvae would make appealing food for predators, but they carry on largely unmolested, thanks in part to their defensive nests. Toads are said to feed on them, but I doubt many toads could make it to the highest tips of fruit trees where nests are frequently located. More promisingly, certain parasitic wasps and tachinid flies prey on them—close inspection may reveal tiny larvae attached to the caterpillar's body, already sucking the life from their host. Equally gratifying, ichneumonid wasps use their threadlike ovipositor to inject their eggs into the caterpillar, so the developing wasp larvae devour their host from the inside out.

These parasitics are among the high-profile beneficial insects, a class of creeping, crawling and flying creatures that are coming into prominence in better gardens everywhere. They are inspiring a paradigm shift in how gardeners feel about bugs, reminding us that pest insects like the tent caterpillar—or infuriating aphids and cutworms, whiteflies and cabbage moths—are a rogue minority, far outnumbered by beneficial species. Some beneficials help out by pollinating flowers or breaking down organic matter, but the gardener maintains a special affection for bugs that prey on pests. Their numbers and their strategies are legion, and their identities sometimes surprising. Lacewings, for example, are delicate creatures that float on gossamer wings in the glow of cottage porch lights on warm summer nights. They look more like ballet dancers than back-alley bruisers, yet their larvae are called "aphid lions," so ferocious are they in devouring aphids as well as spider mites, thrips and other pests. Same with hover flies, those little wasp-like creatures that hover and dart about in straight lines like miniature helicopters. After much nuptial hovering, the adult female lays her eggs directly into an aphid colony. Hatched out, her voracious offspring set to gorging themselves on nearby aphids. Lady beetle larvae, which resemble tiny alligators, and aphid midge larvae, which look like miniature orange maggots, are so effective at eating aphids, they're sold through commercial insectaries, with sales boosted by salient facts such as that a common ladybird beetle may consume more than two thousand aphids in its short life.

My handbook tells me there's a beetle that attacks tent caterpillars, reinventing the butane-flamethrower motif because it goes by the marvellous name of "fiery searcher." Beetles generally offer the bug-conscious gardener a particular challenge because there are so many thousands of species, some like the fiery searcher a beneficial, others like the Japanese beetle a real pest. Even within a generally benign beetle clan like the ladybeetles, you find a black sheep: the nefarious Mexican bean beetle. On the other hand, rove beetles and ground beetles are great at suppressing pests. Rove beetles come with elongated bodies that allow them to move swiftly through soil in search of root maggots and grubs. You can often spot a ground beetle in the garden, large and stocky with a shiny black back, living under a rock or board and quick to scurry for shelter if disturbed. They hunt by night, preying on root maggots, slug eggs, cutworms and other undesirables.

Murderous assassin bugs, pirate bugs, ambush bugs and scores of others—a healthy garden swarms with beneficials, all of which need the gardener's cooperation if they're to do their deadly work. Attracting and maintaining their populations is serious business—you can buy all the cartons of ladybirds you want, but they'll soon fly away home if conditions aren't right. Insecticides, of course, are *verboten*. Shelter, food and water are essential. Some of the plants most necessary for beneficials are real commoners— stinging nettle, Queen Anne's lace, goldenrod, dandelion and wild mustard. A "wild patch" in a hidden corner of the yard, or even a brazen display of beautiful wildlings like Queen Anne's lace, will help enormously. Herbs like dill, parsley, catnip and thyme produce small flowers ideally suited for tiny nectar and pollen feeders. Alyssum, candytuft and other small-flowered annuals are good too. Coneflowers, yarrows and daisies are among the recommended perennials. Water must be available at wet spots, or with stones or plants in shallow bowls, so that tiny beneficials can alight to drink without drowning. Plants that catch and hold moisture in small droplets on their leaves— lady's mantle is one of the best—are invaluable.

105

Gardening with beneficials is full of gratification but never instant. These legions of diminutive allies take time to do their lethal work. But with patience and foresight, the bug-smart gardener will eventually reap the rewards of a garden buzzing and humming with congenial insects, perhaps even allowing for an evening stroll uninterrupted by the dreadful spectacle of tent caterpillar defoliation.

$\mathcal{M}$AY

WEEK 17: LUSTY TUMESCENCES

Great excitement this morning: overnight a portentous fissure opened up in one of the mixed borders. The soil was heaved upwards a couple of centimetres and cracked open as though this were the epicentre of a minuscule earthquake. I was cheered immensely because I knew instantly that the subterranean force causing this eruption was the great desert candle that had flowered in the very spot for the first time last June. Our pride in it the previous year had been tempered by apprehension after being told by a gardener vastly more accomplished than myself that she cannot get desert candles to survive the winter. Another nearby acquaintance has them not only survive but bloom magnificently. So you understand the great psychological freight being carried on the reappearance of our desert candle.

Two years ago, we'd spotted a single naked root at an end-of-season nursery sale and bought it on a whimsical impulse of the sort that sound garden planning frowns upon. We were far from confident that it would survive at our place. The root was a flaccid and desiccated-looking thing that rather resembled a dead sunstar on a beach. We planted it in a well-drained spot—soggy earth being the bane of desert candles—and sat back to await results. The following spring it produced a pathetic little basal rosette of straplike leaves, like a yucca that lacked the courage of its convictions. Then, miraculously, two magnificent flowering stalks shot up more than two metres high and by mid-June flared like blazing torches massed with gorgeous small salmon-pink flowers. They were the talk of the town and for a few brief weeks our place partook of the beauty of desert candles blooming wild on the hillsides of their native Middle East. Afterwards, calmed down, we suspected the plant had exhausted itself in this singular manifestation and would never be seen again. But here it comes, heaving the earth in its path, the great desert candle (or foxtail lily or giant asphodel) back for another season.

The subtleties of springtime emergences, although lost on casual passersby, thrill a gardener because they verify the survival of what might have been lost in a killing winter, but also because it is through these tiny cracks and fissures we glimpse the golden days of summer still to come. Nobody does emergences better than the lily family, to which the desert candle belongs. They're like charismatic personalities at whose entrance into a crowded room all heads turn. Although the lily has since ancient days symbolized purity and motherhood as well as the joyful resurrection of Easter, its insistent thrusting from the soil in springtime has undeniably sensuous associations. Gazing intimately at the erect stems of emerging royal lilies, their thick little protrusions red at the tip and a hairy green beneath, I sometimes wonder if repeated readings of *Lady Chatterly's Lover* at a tender age haven't done me permanent damage.

Blooming earlier and now long disappeared, the hyacinth, another member of the clan, is unabashedly lascivious in how it bursts from the earth. These beauties, of course, spring from the blood of Hyacinthus, the beautiful youth loved but accidentally killed by the sun-god Apollo. The ancient festival of Hyacinthia celebrated the springtime resurrection of vegetation previously withered by scorching sun and wind, and there's an instant party atmosphere when the hyacinths come bulging urgently up through the cold spring soil.

Solomon's seal is yet another lily relative that breaks from the ground beautifully. This denizen of shady woodlands grows from densely packed underground rhizomes. Their crowded shoots appear as smooth blue-grey nubs, curved downwards like the crook of a bishop's crozier. Within days they straighten into slender lancets, pale green at the base with a pointed cap of a marvellous blue-grey.

Emerging simultaneously with the Solomon's seal— and perfect shady companions through all stages of their

109

growth—come the hostas, or plantain lilies. Their true glory is in their foliage, not their flowers, and begins the moment they push through the soil in tightly furled spirals of fresh leaves. Straight away they show themselves in gorgeous greens and blues and saucy variegations, the variegated wavy-leafed plantain, *Hosta undulata,* making a particularly giddy entrance.

The ornamental onions, also members of the lily tribe, share the family's penchant for dramatic eruptions. And their timing is impeccable for Canadian gardens, as they burst onto the stage just as the glory days of the springtime bulbs are fading. Most of the desirable types are neither expensive to acquire nor difficult to cultivate. They have an extended season of bloom, come in a variety of sizes, and vary in their presentations from the subtle to the stupendous. One of the first to appear at our place, *Allium aflatunense* is a hardy native of central China that produces flowering stalks a metre or more high. At the tip of each stalk a flower head swells inside a tightly wrapped sack that appears to be made of pale green rice paper. Within days this bulging spathe splits open, releasing a gorgeous big globe composed of multiple small lilac flowers. Within a few days the Turkestan onion executes a similar emergence, but much closer to the earth. A stout little chap with a low centre of gravity, it has appealingly broad blue-grey leaves that arch out to the ground and a globose flower head coloured like lavender faded to a ghostly grey. By late May the truly astonishing Stars of

Persia are in bloom. The flowering stalks rise to about knee-height, each holding aloft a galactic explosion of six-pointed lilac flowers that together form a perfect globe. Each tiny, shining flower is held on a stiff thread, creating an effect of gleaming stars exploding outwards through space. Thus alliums give a double thrill, both when they first break from the earth and then when their flower heads burst open.

Arguably the most splendid of all emergent Liliaceae—and one we don't have at our place—the crown imperial fritillaria shoots from a bulb the size of a grapefruit, sending up a stout and fleshy stem. Ontario garden writer Patrick Lima describes the emergence of this exotic Persian: "Early in spring, fat pointed noses, bronzed and polished, push aside the earth in a determined reach for light." Combining lusty tumescence with impeccable good taste, asparagus is yet another of the Liliaceae well worth close examination in its earliest stages of growth.

All these plants are useful and beautiful in their later stages, but at this time of year their robust explosions into growth provide just the sort of provocative tonic the gardener needs after a long winter. Plus they provide a timely reminder to slow down a bit, to allow ourselves the luxury of really looking closely in order to appreciate the small miracles that are happening, day by day, in our gardens. Already those other wildling lilies, the erythroniums and trilliums, have faded away. So will they all, too soon. Best to savour them today, while we may. It pleases me to think of fellow gardeners across the nation now down on their hands and knees, revelling in the luscious lasciviousness of erupting fissures and fat noses pressing up into the light.

WEEK 18: BENEATH BLOWZY CLOUDS

As I've said, azaleas and rhododendrons are not every-thing they could be at our place, not yet anyway, and we've resigned ourselves—as one resigns oneself to a bald patch or double chins—that they will never be for us what they are in some gardens hereabouts. So after the splendour of late-spring bulbs we enter something of a floral quiescence. Lots of green, in other words. But the garden is far from in a funk, because everywhere you look there are small won-ders of the green world occurring, marvellous textures of unfurling leaves and great buds trembling, trembling then breaking open. Besides, I think we gardeners are too unduly harried in the matter of maintaining an unfalter-ing sequence of colourful shows with never a dull moment between. We dread the down times, the drop zones and black holes, those awful non-events that cause us to berate ourselves for failing to keep up appearances, chastise ourselves that we're not standing ready to dash out from the greenhouse with a new battery of bedding plants the moment their predecessors fade. Far saner, it seems to me, to appreciate the yin and yang of gardens, the inhaling and exhaling, the green silences against which pure notes of colour sound so sweet.

112

I can afford such high-flown reflections this week because, no matter how little bloom is evident elsewhere in the garden, the crabapples are at a pinnacle of perfection. Over time I've learned that a life well lived includes spending at least a few minutes each spring beneath their blowzy clouds of fragrant blossoms, that to miss crabapples in full bloom is to live a year at less than perfect pitch. Crabs share with other members of the rose family (to which they belong) an extravagance of bloom that seems to surrender everything to the glory of blossoming. Like comely youths not yet conscious of their beauty, they exude a lovely sort of purity, an old-fashioned innocence that can conjure scenes of idealized rustic delight. Bustling around the yard these days I stop every once in a while and stand transported by their beauty.

By some standards we may have gone a bit overboard for crabs—we have a dozen or more scattered about, five of them in the front garden where they're easy enough to plant under. Outside the fences we have about half a dozen of the old standby Japanese crab, *Malus floribunda*. Ours are still young, but should eventually reach about ten metres with gracefully arching branches. Later blooming than many, their carmine buds open to a pale blush pink, creating a sumptuously fragrant, hazy gauze that gradually pales to white. Their small yellowish fruits are showy until autumn, when they're eaten by foraging birds.

Most ornamental crab species originated in Asia and were introduced to North America only about a century ago, but they've become one of our most widely adapted spring-flowering trees, with more than six hundred species and varieties available, ranging from shoulder-high shrubs to medium-sized trees. They come in columnar, upright and weeping forms, some with dense foliage, others light and airy, coloured from soft green to purple.

The line dividing crabapples from regular apples is about as subjective as the one dividing sane people from crazy ones. It's a simple matter of measurement. Trees bearing fruits less than five centimetres in diameter are crabs; those more than five centimetres are not. Of our collection, several produce useable fruit. The steadiest of them is another old variety called Dolgo, a tough old customer of Russian descent that produces abundant white aromatic flowers and large red crabapples that are excellent for jelly. It tends to fruit heavily only on alternate years, a habit shared with other older types, and not altogether a bad thing. The making of crabapple jelly, while undeniably admirable, is seldom convenient. Usually we end up casting the crabapples into the freezer and hauling them back out in the depths of winter when the crush of chores has lightened slightly. Jelly making is the sort of thing one really wants a handy grandfather or helpful great-aunt around to do.

Crabapples are loosely divided into white-flowering and rosy-bloom varieties, the latter including flowers that range through rose, pink, magenta and red. Some of the rosy-blooms can border on the brassy, as though blushed with a touch too much rouge. Two of the five in our front garden are of this persuasion, beautiful and seductive, certainly, but not what one would call distinguished. The prettier of the two, bearing lipstick-pink blooms on weeping branches, has the unfortunate habit of holding on to its fruits for too long—many of last year's dark and wizened little apples are still on the tree as the spring blooms break, creating a slightly bizarre juxtaposition of aged decay and youthful beauty. When we can remember to do so, we go out before bud break and knock the old fruits off with a broom.

But things could be worse, and they have been. Experiencing their transcendent beauty at this time of year, an enthusiast might be tempted to dash to a garden centre to acquire a crab, any crab, at any cost. This is an impulse to be resisted because, as one observer puts it, "There is still no shortage of poor performers in the trade." Some varieties, including many old favourites, are highly susceptible to a rogue's gallery of diseases: apple scab, cedar apple rust, mildew and fire blight. These can ravage entire plantings, reducing spring beauties to defoliated disasters by midsummer. The wise buyer checks a variety's resistance to disease as well as its growth form before selecting a tree.

Several years ago, for absolutely no sound reason at all, we acquired a purple-leafed crab growing in a large pot. It looked perfectly healthy, and I was fool enough to ignore the small alarm bells tinkling in the back of my brain. Ask not for whom they tolled—it was against that pervasive inclination in certain gardeners to acquire plants with purplish foliage. No matter how frequently reminded of the insidiousness of this predilection, no matter how stoutly well intentioned they remain in the normal course of things—suddenly, for no discernible reason, they'll veer off and acquire a purple-leafed something-or-other. One wants to implore them, as callow youths are so frequently urged concerning illegal drugs, to "just say no" to purple urges. But they cannot, poor things, and so a plague of purple sweeps across the landscape. Municipal authorities seem especially vulnerable to landscapers given to purple perversions. There are certain boulevards in Vancouver, for example, that are planted mile after unrelenting mile in purple-leafed ornamental plums, which must be brutal on nearby property values.

I don't scoff at these displays, as purists might, for our place is no better. Our descent began years ago with a couple of those same plums, whose screaming-pink blooming period is like a child's teething, painful but mercifully soon over. We planted them off to the east, down near the creek. Not far away we added a purple-leafed filbert to carry the motif across the yard. Our three Japanese maples of purple persuasion I would fight to the end to retain, especially one on the hill that, when backlit by the westering sun this time of year, glows like a bowl of illuminated rubies. Farther along the hill three purple-leafed smoke bushes aspire to a similar effect, and might be quite brilliant if they weren't backstopped by a Norway maple whose plummy-red leaves lurch towards purple, and by a copper beech for good measure. The overall effect reminds me of Lent in my childhood, when every statue in church was shrouded under a sombre purple cover while one beat one's breast in penitence and sorrow. This, I think we can generally agree, is not the preferred ambience in a successful garden.

Not that our newly added *Malus purpurea* was unrelievedly sombre—far from it. At blooming time, we discovered the following spring, the little purple wretch broke out into an unfortunate display of rosy magenta flowers which seemed somehow reminiscent of one's worst attacks of adolescent acne. By midsummer the little tree was ailing from a withering blight and continued to cast a dismal pall across its section of the garden for the rest of the summer. In the dormant season it was discreetly removed to a quiet corner out of sight, like Mr. Rochester's mad wife, where the following year it concluded its short time among us, stricken again by a blight it no longer had the heart to fight. In crabapples, as in mates, one wants to be careful with initial choices lest years of heartache ensue.

Two of our more recent acquisitions have justified the judiciousness of cautious middle age. One is the weeping "Red Jade," a smallish, white-flowering variety. Its deep pink buds open to white flowers that show stunningly against its emerging glossy green foliage. Mature specimens create a gorgeous effect, like a fountain weeping with flowers. The second is the highly recommended "Red Jewel." Also smallish, growing to about five metres, but with a pleasing horizontal branching pattern, this is

117

recommended as a tough and hardy tree. Its pale pink buds open to pure white, set against richly dark green leaves. It gets its name from the small, bright, cherry-red fruits that remain through the winter, providing excellent colour. Persistence and colour of fruits for winter interest, along with enhanced fall foliage and disease resistance, have been the main improvements with the new cultivars. Generally speaking, white-flowering varieties produce more brilliantly coloured fruit than the rosy-bloom types. When their fruits have ripened in September, our trees are alive with foraging birds.

Our oldest and finest crab is a white-flowering beauty whose name we don't know, growing in the centre of the garden. She is almost perfectly vase shaped, a condition I'm willing to attribute as much to my astute pruning as to her natural growth habit. Hydrangeas and azaleas grow contentedly beneath her billowing skirts. The flower buds are brushed with a rose-pink patina, then open a heart-breakingly pure white. Today her branches wave like great wands of white, entirely swathed in flowers. Her blooming is so effusive, so exorbitant, there's scarcely any leaf to be seen. Within a few days, shining new green leaves will emerge, giving the whole tree a striking effect of dappled green and white. New leafy tips will emerge like elegant fingers beyond the thick sleeves of bloom. Then, too soon, after maybe ten days of transcendent bloom, the petals will come cascading down in showers of white; crabapple season will be over, fled like the fleeting seasons of youth. But not today. Today the blooms are perfect still.

WEEK 19: SEEDLING DISSENSION

Come what may, May's always a mad month in the gardens, much of the hubbub involving transplanting. The seeds and schemes of February are now made flesh as dozens of germination trays stand jammed with bedding plants, daily growing more leggy, their roots more inextricably intertwined. They resemble your poor, your tired, your huddled masses of immigrants gazing towards the torch of liberty that illuminates a new and spacious land vibrant with optimism and opportunity. Meanwhile the gardener, plainly in far too deep in plants, goes quietly mad in the potting shed.

This is just my position at the moment. With victimization so in vogue these days, I'm pleased to see myself as a victim of excessive germination. I suppose a privileged minority do manage to germinate just the right number of plants for their purposes, but the majority plainly do not. As befits the times, excess is the order of the day—wallowing in your own superfluous seedlings, you're also required to do a lot of fancy footwork to avoid having colleagues fob off their extra plants on you. Just the other day, before I knew quite what was happening, I found myself gratefully accepting three anemic-looking fenugreek seedlings. I'm not sure I even know what fenugreek is, and have certainly never longed for any, but here I was, putting my own several thousand essential seedlings on hold in order to transplant fenugreek. Mercifully these came from a friend of understanding disposition—but woe betides a gift of seedlings from some taskmaster who'll keep a sharp eye on their progress for the rest of the year.

Busy with a book tour and a heavy schedule of speaking engagements, I decided last spring to skip the whole germination stage by purchasing vegetable seedlings from a nursery. The results were mixed at best—butternut squash plants hampered by an irrational fear of the outdoors; celery seedlings that bolted to seed like a premature ejaculation. This year we've reverted to the devil-you-know of growing our own.

I nurture a deep and pleasing fantasy of one day possessing a state-of-the-art germination chamber, with computer-controlled misters and grow-lites, that will allow us extended winter holidays in balmy latitudes while the young plants begin their lives in a warm, supportive environment. I know people who have set-ups like this; at times I find their air of accomplished enthusiasm just the tiniest bit grating, but I would like to be one of them. For the moment, our household makes up for what we lack in techno-wizardry with a certain rustic low cunning.

For germination pots, I lean towards the small plastic trays in which we buy our tofu, with a few (usually too few) drainage holes punched through the bottom. Seeded, I enclose these in old plastic bread bags and arrange them artistically around the house in warm locations. Once the real crush begins, I also haul indoors a plastic tent that we discovered some years ago during an especially rewarding foray to the local Sally Ann thrift shop. Fashioned from thick plastic, it's a collapsible affair with rigid wire ribs that fold down like those of an umbrella, originally— and, I believe, unsuccessfully—marketed for enclosing house plants while one is away, so that they require no watering. Inside the tent, I supply bottom heat through an antique electric bed warmer that my dear old dad used in his dotage and which I suspect will one day burn the house down. Squatting in a corner of the kitchen, this set- up, although something less than tastefully ornamental, is amazingly efficient.

Too efficient, truth to tell, for somewhere back in March or April, while we were romping about amid the saffron sheen of crocuses et al., we were also being overrun with far more seedlings than we knew what to do with. Pushed aside by new generations on the rise, the older ones go out into the unheated greenhouse where they huddle uncom- fortably through too-hot days and too-cool nights. This is the Tough Love approach to plants, a time of tempering their spirits, much as my own were tempered years ago as a monastic seminarian in whom a succession of humour- less spiritual directors thought they detected unsuitable tendencies.

Some days ago we visited friends on the island, good- hearted types who'd never inflict such a spartan regime on their seedlings. Instead they lovingly transport multiple trays of seedlings out to a glass room each morning and back into their warm kitchen each evening. Twice the size of ours, their fulsome plants spoke unarguably of great promise. But are they better equipped than our tough runts for the long run down the mean streets of an extended growing season? Ah, there's the great imponderable.

Just as there's a time to plant and a time to reap, there's a proper time to transplant. In our vicinity, this truth is traditionally borne home when the first May heat wave ignites a blazing mad panic because we've left things too late. An overcast day is naturally preferable for putting plants out, which is, after all, the rough equivalent of open-heart surgery. Withering sunshine and desiccating winds are the last thing defenceless transplants need. But, you ask yourself, will there be another overcast day between now and October? Or should we, as the running-shoe moguls urge, just do it?

Some people are far more blasé than others in the crucial question of sun scorch. Not long ago, we wheeled into the parking lot of a large nursery and beheld a ghastly sight: a bare-root fruit tree sprawled on the asphalt beside a car, with the warm spring sun beating on the tree's exposed roots. Some enthusiast had, apparently, purchased the sapling, then nonchalantly laid it down and gone back inside to shop some more. I felt as one does seeing a harried parent give their kid a slap in the supermarket. Most plants, like oysters, are designed to remain in one place, and those of us who presume to move them about owe them at least the courtesy of proceeding with due care.

Advancing wisely within this ethic, practised transplanters first prepare the area into which plants will be moved, coaxing the receiving medium into a splendid readiness, so that the interval between lifting the plant from its natal bed and firming it into its final resting place is pared to almost nothing. Seedlings are hardened off in a cold frame or similar set-up before going outdoors. Their soil is well-soaked so that no roots are damaged being torn from dry earth. They are lifted gently by their leaves, rather than having tender stalks squeezed between rough fingers. Roots are spread lovingly, and care taken when firming in, to avoid scrunching roots or snapping stems. In short, the seasoned transplanter proceeds with a dexterous precision only the very best organ transplant surgeons achieve.

Certain gardeners prefer to use an implement in their microsurgery, while others find that fingers are finest. Some lift small blocks of seedlings with a fork or knife blade, then disentangle their roots by hand. Left overlong, roots may form a finely interwoven mat that can be sliced up with a knife or spatula as one would a tray of date squares. I prefer to probe the earth with a finger or two and gently lift out either a clump of tiny seedlings or an individual.

Some plants naturally take more readily than others to the trauma of transplanting. Tomatoes are especially cooperative and a real pleasure to work with. I move ours from small trays to individual pots somewhere around the end of April, then fatten them up for putting out in the last week of May. Handling the plants gives rise to that distinctive scent of tomato leaves and the promise of juicy fruits by August. Other characters—squashes, melons and cucumbers come to mind—really object to the disruptions of transplanting. I go the extra mile for these fuss-budgets,

123

germinating them in individual pots, then slipping them out of their pots and into the ground, smooth as a cucumber, before they know what's happening. I enjoy doing celery too. These are plants that never take happily to life in a pot. I start ours indoors in February, and try to have them into their trench by April. They seem grateful to be emancipated from the confining pot, in which they only reluctantly produce tiny little tops perched on long thread-like roots. I spread the roots tenderly in their composty trench and, like a city kid set free in the country, the plants quickly adapt to life outdoors.

Watered gently, sheltered from direct sunlight, whispered encouragement and generally pampered for a day or two, little weaklings soon grow accustomed to their new surroundings. Their great lust for life—combined with the gardener's tender dexterity in transplanting—assures complete recovery and eventual great success. The gardener, meanwhile, with most of the annual flowers and vegetables now well situated, turns with a brave heart to face several thousand tiny perennials crowding their trays, straightens shoulders staunchly, and begins anew.

WEEK 20: AT THE STAKE

I've been busy this week staking perennials and vegetables, reflecting as I puttered along with sticks and twine how everywhere you go nowadays you run into stakeholders. These are people with a vested interest in some particular issue or dispute; I have nothing against them except that their ebullient holding of stakes tends to eclipse the really significant work of true stakeholders who are, of course, gardeners. Nobody knows more than the home gardener about the refinements and perils of staking. Persons who believe that the uncomplicated cultivation of plants is our sole, or even primary, preoccupation, have plainly never witnessed the peculiar spectacle of a gardener at the stake.

"Staking individual plants like delphiniums, lilies and dahlias is simple," declares one of our trusty reference books, no doubt attempting to alleviate the anxieties novice stakers may be attached to. "One should know the approximate height of the staking required and the strength needed." This is all well and good, but rather like advising people that they should know the meaning of life. How is it that the approximate height of delphiniums can be so elusive? The heft of herbaceous peony heads so treacherously unpredictable?

For delphiniums, which grow in great clumps at our place, I use one-inch-square cedar stakes stained green. I prefer the OK Corral Principle for group staking: a palisade of stout stakes around the perimeter, bound together by encircling twine to keep the foliage massed together and discourage the flowering stalks from flopping over. In placing the stakes, I bear in mind my manual's admonition that "the stakes should not be prominent and certainly should not reach above the plants." This is where so many gardeners get burned at the stake, attempting to determine that precise and capricious height at which stake and twine will hold the glorious spires securely aloft while not themselves appearing too prominently.

"Curse, Miscreant, when thou comest to the stake," Shakespeare fulminates, and cursing there is aplenty when the sumptuous delphinium heads come tottering over in the wind, victimized by staking of perhaps quite proper improminence but insufficient height. Mere millimetres lower than necessary, the high twine serves like a trip-wire over which the wind-whipped stalks perform a ghastly jackknife. Nor is it just us backyard muddlers who suffer these indignities. I once visited one of our internationally renowned show gardens and was mortified to see groups of blooming delphiniums lashed rudely to coarse stakes that towered far higher than the flower heads themselves. Obviously the handiwork of a deranged gardener baited too cruelly at the stake, the effect created was of horticultural bondage of the most crudely explicit sort.

Herbaceous peonies are every bit as problematic in my experience, as they will not send consistent messages from year to year as to how many flower heads they intend to produce and to what size they're inclined to produce them. Last year we tried using wire cages on the least cooperative of them but I really didn't care for the sense of metallic entrapment the cages created. Too frequently the foliage, crowded within, withered from blight. I do admire the look of those handy snap-on adjustable peony collars one sees on the market, but not sufficiently so to fork over the cash required to properly collar our several dozen peonies.

We've settled instead on bamboo and twine as the staking mode that best combines the high principles of thrift, aesthetics and use of organic materials. I drive four slender bamboo culms into the earth around the root perimeter, carefully avoiding the roots themselves. Two dozen peonies at four stakes apiece comes to roughly one hundred stakes, which is convenient for calculating the percentage of them that manage to locate an underground stone to block their downward plunge. Stakes are withdrawn and pushed in again a few inches over, much the way an inept physician repeatedly plunges an intravenous needle in search of a vein. Once in, the stakes serve as a framework for twine running around and through the thick foliage. But when the great double blooms unfold, they go nodding down on their slender stems like the heads of schoolkids on a warm June afternoon, bending the tensile bamboo as they go. Thereafter, most of the blooming season is squandered fiddling with supplementary stakes and laughable bits of twine added in a futile attempt to keep the enlarged heads upright through the traditional June monsoons.

I've been up in the vegetable patch as well this week, staking peas and broad beans, neither of which offers quite the challenge of a peony or delphinium. I'm just not sure why peas, snow peas especially, while plainly in need of support, consistently refuse to accept it, like doddering oldsters insisting "Oh, I'm all right; don't worry about me." You put in perfectly respectable stakes and several miles of twine; you hook the young vines onto the twine, guide their little tendrils to it; you just about hold their hands until they get a grip. Then, once your back's turned, they all let go and flop down on the ground again as though being deliberately difficult. Or they'll end up clinging to one another in a hopeless tangle of tendrils. Always in a mad rush this time of year, one is goaded into saying cruel and hateful things to them, which is perhaps why they fail to produce the bounteous crops other growers achieve.

Big clematis vines can be difficult too, but their obstinacy takes the form, not of refusing to cling, but of clinging indiscriminately to every toehold in sight, like certain New Ageish acquaintances given to unbridled hugging. I train, or attempt to train, big viticella clematis—rampant climbers that are cut back to the ground each winter—up rough wooden tripods with pretensions towards becoming obelisks. Growing by leaps and bounds this time of year, the vines have unsteady tendencies to reach out and touch other plants, or fencing, or whatever. Once they've taken hold, they refuse to let go, and if I didn't get after them repeatedly, forcing them skywards, they'd leave the peaks of my poor person's obelisks rudely exposed to ridicule for the remainder of the summer.

128

But where the gardener's reputation is really at stake is in the supporting of tree saplings. We know there is a postmodern school of thought out there that maintains it's unnecessary, indeed counterproductive, to stake a young tree, because all one is doing thereby is creating dependency, rather than encouraging a self-reliant sapling to stand on its own one foot. This theory sounds suspiciously as though it's derived from the neoconservative cant that blames poor people for having too much money, thereby depriving rich people from having enough. A more balanced approach recognizes that certain trees in certain situations need a bit of support. One sees this done well in some places—two stout poles on opposite sides of a sapling, with twin hoops of coated wire holding its trunk firmly in place.

Personally I prefer a slightly less rigid arrangement featuring a single stake and whatever scrap of wire or twine comes to hand. One of the fundamental principles I've discovered here is that deviant young trees invariably require staking for a slightly longer period of time than any wooden stake can remain in the ground without rotting. The premature letting go of the stake and consequent flopping down of the tree can be quite a spectacle, enlivening the neighbourhood with a welcome levity.

I have to believe that more than a few gardeners are guilty of choking a tree to death by fastening a loop of wire too tightly around its trunk. I narrowly missed conviction on this charge myself when I staked a weeping willow with a genetic predisposition for toppling into the pond. I used plastic-sheathed clothesline for the job, foolishly reckoning it wouldn't cut into the tree. Growing at an astounding rate while I was preoccupied elsewhere with the state of the world, the willow's bark entirely engulfed the encircling wire. Miraculously, the tree did not succumb to strangulation, instead developing an unhealthy-looking lump girdling that part of its bole, rather like the huge goiters on people's necks pictured in old medical texts. A tell-tale trail of clothesline still dangles from the swollen lump, like a remnant fallopian tube. We discreetly steer visiting friends away from this arboreal wonder, and now always make a point of sheathing tree wire in bits of old hose pipe.

As I putter about these days, driving stakes and spinning twine as a spider spins her cunning silk, my thoughts wander to all the other stakeholders out there, perhaps preoccupied in besieging numbskull politicians, or stuck in mind-numbing board meetings, with no true stake to hold. I still find myself numbered among them on occasion, but mostly I give thanks to have real stakes and real twine in my hands, a clump of flowering wands to be held aloft by artful staking that conceals its art, a whistling wind as nemesis, and elemental triumph or disaster hanging in the balance.

WEEK 21: FLIGHTS OF FANCY

Just the other day I stood entranced on our garden path as two large swallowtail butterflies came fluttering across the flower tops in an elegant nuptial dance. Whirling and spiralling around one another, the two black-and-yellow beauties swept past me, like enraptured lovers oblivious to all but their own passionate affairs.

Now's the season for all sorts of giddy flights across the garden, as insects, bats and birds flit about. We have two nest boxes, spaced far apart, in which violet-green swallows are nesting. Brilliant with iridescent green backs and wings that flash in the sunlight, the swallows swoop and glide across the clearing with freewheeling grace. They're only with us for the brief nesting season—arriving in a noisy party some weeks ago, squabbling over who gets what houses and who doesn't, courting and mating, nest building, laying and incubating, which is what they're up to now. Soon we'll have a few frantic weeks of feeding the hatchlings, a day or two for fledging, and then they're gone for another year, graceful gliders off to greener pastures.

Lower down, little rufous hummingbirds are all over the yard, zipping this way and that, hovering and darting and chasing one another with bossy twitterings. These days they're feeding mostly on wild columbines and foxgloves and on the first flowers of honeysuckle. Every so often one will perch on a horizontal twig of a huckleberry bush or the redbud tree by the deck, but not for long: motion is their metier. They're drawn to running water, often hovering above our little cascade, sometimes alighting at one special spot where water spills over a flat stone, to splash themselves with their wings, twittering the hummingbird equivalent of singing in the shower. Then off again on another mad dash. Only once have I seen a nest, a cunning, tiny demitasse of moss and grass, suspended in the fronds of a hemlock tree deep in the woods.

Squadrons of big dragonflies are out as well, criss-crossing the garden methodically across their cluttered flight paths. Fierce-looking fliers, each forms a clever net with its legs in which to trap small insects on the wing. When the crabapples were in full bloom, I noticed clouds of tiny flies whirling in nuptial flight above the trees while dragonflies repeatedly sliced through the seething cloud netting prey on each pass. Every so often a dragonfly gets trapped in the greenhouse, rattling against the glass, betrayed by an instinct towards light that is blind to open windows behind it. I gently take the captive's wings between my fingers— shimmering, transparent wings, finely veined—in order to release it. Seeing the big insect up close, with bulging compound eyes and devil's-darning-needle body, I'm reminded that these are prehistoric creatures, survivors from the time of dinosaurs when their enormous ancestors had wings that spread nearly a metre wide.

Of all the wild fliers about on these warming days, none surpasses the butterflies in enchantment. They are the perfect garden creature, floating flowers, elegant and ethereal, flitting erratically, changing course in mid-flight with sudden pirouettes and darting in new directions. Their grace is like that of the three mythical sister goddesses, combining brilliance, joy and bloom. For the gardener—even at one's most flamboyant, a drab plodder by comparison—few sights are more pleasing and appropriate than hosts of multicoloured butterflies fluttering among the flowers.

In many urban and suburban gardens, that sight is depressingly rare. Partly because of the toll pesticides have taken, of course, but also because many of the plants that gardeners prize most highly—our splendid irises, hydrangeas and begonias—are not particularly appealing to butterflies. Perhaps most damaging of all is the continued eradication of plants crucial to butterfly larvae. Some butterfly species are fastidiously particular about what plants they feed upon, especially in their caterpillar stage. The magnificent monarchs—which, alas, don't inhabit our gardens, but which I remember vividly from my boyhood in Toronto—are singularly fussy. Their rather grotesque-looking caterpillars feed exclusively on *Asclepias,* milkweed or butterfly weed. Weed's the operative word, for these plants and many others upon which butterfly larvae depend—wildlings like Queen Anne's lace, nettles, thistles, clovers and dogbane—are weeds by any other name. When gardeners and municipal workers set about eradicating weed patches, too often they succeed in eliminating butterflies as well.

The country gardener has the advantage here, for there's usually enough wild land about to support butterfly populations. Where that's not the case, where all wild patches have been eradicated from a region, the butterfly gardener is left no alternative but to create a personal weed patch, neighbourhood opinion be damned. Controversy may be minimized by selecting an out-of-the-way corner of the yard where the soil can be roughed up each year, allowing pioneering herbaceous weeds to thrive as a nursery bed for butterflies.

Providing food plants for the adults that emerge in spring and summer is easier and more socially acceptable.

133

Successful butterfly gardens are sunny places, since the adults spend a fair bit of time sunning themselves, and sheltered from strong winds. Butterflies also need moisture and trace minerals which can be provided at a wet spot or through a sunken container of mud or sand. Some species will sip only nectar from a few specialized plants. Others, like the big monarchs and swallowtails, will drink from a wider range. They seem to be attracted by both scent and colour, with richly scented plants more attractive to them, as are flowers coloured red, orange, purple, lavender, yellow or white. The flower must have a rim upon which the insect can perch while it feeds. A mix of annuals, biennials and perennials—many of those most abundant with accessible nectar are old-fashioned types with small single flowers—can provide a seasonal progression of butterfly feeders.

Again, some of the very best candidates are weedy plants—goldenrod, clover, yarrow, pearly everlasting, teasels, burdock, milkweed and dogbane. Three weedy characters blooming in our gardens just now, and included for both their carefree beauty and their attractiveness to butterflies, are oxeye daisies, common foxgloves and sweet rocket. The swallowtails particularly love sweet rocket, or dame's rocket, a weedy phlox introduced from Europe. Its clusters of fragrant white, mauve or purplish flowers wander happily among the Siberian iris and delphiniums, continuing to bloom well into summer. Earlier on, lilacs, creeping phlox and arabis were useful. Sweet mock orange will be good in a week or two, and dianthus

134

and delphiniums. Later on, butterfly bush and coneflower, goldenrod, yarrow, globe thistle, fennel and the forever-linked parsley, sage, rosemary and thyme are all valuable. With the tremendous recent surge of interest in butterfly gardening, there are now good sources of information available about what native and exotic plants serve best in various regions.

Gardeners already blessed with resident populations can justify laying down their tools for a few moments in order to carefully observe which plants seem most appealing to their butterflies at a particular time. And just for the pure sensuous thrill of watching the creature, suspended like a gorgeous ornament on the lip of a flower, probe with its long proboscis, sipping nectar as the gods and goddesses do. Then watch it flit away again on its brief but brilliant career, leaving us to ponder our earthbound rounds, our choices or lack of choices, our absurd preoccupations. Butterflies make me wish that I danced; they make me wish I could fly, could float free and easy in a sunny sheltered place sweet with aromatic flowers. It's why we garden in the first place, I suppose, dreaming and imagining the possibilities of beauty, its power to set us free.

$\mathcal{J}$UNE

WEEK 22: GOOSEBERRY FOOLS

Berry season is upon us already, so we're keeping a close watch on ripening strawberries and gooseberries, the sweet-and-sour first arrivals, alert for the moment at which they achieve their pinnacle of perfect ripeness. Some people will tell you gooseberries never achieve that point—to non-believers they taste unpleasantly tart, bitter almost, and the wonder is that anyone would bother to grow them at all. As one of our American manuals puts it: "Gooseberries are not particularly popular anywhere except in the British Isles, where a rather unusual dessert called 'gooseberry fool' is highly regarded."

Like many a kid raised in working-class Britain, I was nourished as a youngster on a steady diet of sliced white bread ever-so-lightly buttered, then slathered with gooseberry jam. Our household wasn't big on gooseberry fool, no doubt owing to the cost of cream, as the dish is made of gooseberries stewed or scalded and pounded with cream. But of homemade gooseberry jam we suffered no shortage. A slightly perverse nostalgia keeps me growing them now, abetted by the fact that they're easy to cultivate, requiring far less attention than the higher-profile strawberries with which they share the season.

Another of our manuals advises that "for the average family, six to nine bushes should provide enough fruit." This suggests an unqualified commitment to gooseberries that certainly characterized my own family but can hardly be thought of as "average." These days the two of us get along handsomely on a single bush that bears enough berries to make a dozen or so small pots of jam. I find a pot a month more than sufficient, with a few left over to press upon occasional Brits wandering far from the green and pleasant gooseberries of home. I keep a second young bush, cloned from the first by tip layering, primarily as a back-up lest disaster strike the mother plant. Normally a bush will live about twenty-five years. Ours flourish over in a corner of the vegetable garden where they enjoy full sun, although they will tolerate partial shade. They're said to do best in neutral soil that is moist but well drained; occasionally I'll deep soak them with a trickling hose during summer drought. Feeding's not complicated: heaps of compost or rotted manure applied around the roots in spring. I pile on wood ashes as well, to supply potash which the plants demand. A potash deficiency shows through a browning of the leaf margins, best remedied with a foliar seaweed spray and a dressing of rock potash.

Last spring I was horrified to find scores of little caterpillars chewing my big bush to tatters—larvae of the pestilential gooseberry sawfly. Methodically, one by one, I squeezed the life out of them between thumb and horny index finger, a control method better suited to a bush or two than to the recommended six to nine. This spring not a single caterpillar has appeared.

Only in the matter of pruning might the amateur grower falter, because fruit is produced on both new wood and fruiting spurs of old wood. Some authorities insist the bush be grown on a "leg"—a short stem supporting main branches with side shoots. Other experts recommend a cane approach with each plant producing fruit on three canes that are a year old, another three that are two years old, and a third set of three that are three years old. I've also seen them grown as cordons—a single stem from which all side shoots are pruned back to two centimetres in order to encourage fruit spur growth. Properly done, a cordon occupies very little space but positively bulges with berries that are easily picked. Since gooseberries are by nature eccentric, I've allowed myself a different approach to pruning. I let the bush fan out with about twenty canes, each of which I clip hard so that no side shoots develop, thus encouraging fruiting spurs as a cordon does. The resulting crop, if not exactly overwhelming, is more than adequate. In the grand scheme of things, you don't really want to be overwhelmed by gooseberries as you might with strawberries, say, or fresh figs. Just a taste now and then, sufficient for old acquaintance's sake, and you'll be nobody's gooseberry fool.

As foolproof as gooseberries go, strawberries are another matter entirely. During a recent Russian presidential election campaign, one challenger assailed the incumbent as "a tired old man who should retire and grow strawberries." His insinuation—that the raising of strawberries is so unchallenging it can be left to toil-worn oldsters—is an absurdity that even the heat of electoral battle cannot excuse. With a sublime taste that epitomizes the sweet excitements of mid-summer, the homegrown strawberry is brought to the table only after a mighty struggle against birds, bugs, bizarre diseases and inclement weather. Our crop last year, for example, was a sorry disappointment, but nowhere near the disaster suffered by commercial growers in the Fraser Valley whose crops were reduced by as much as 50 per cent through the cool wet spring.

Everything, it sometimes seems, loves to eat strawberries. The strawberry root weevil is a universal nuisance, especially in the West. The adult lays her eggs in the bud of the strawberry; when her grubs emerge, they set to work eating their host plant's roots. An infestation can effectively reduce a crop by half. The strawberry crown borer—a beetle whose grub feeds on the roots and crowns—is so destructive it has discouraged the growing of strawberries in whole regions. Earwigs, caterpillars, mites, aphids, leaf beetles, spittle bugs, whiteflies, slugs and sowbugs, not to mention thieving birds—they all have a go at one or another part of strawberry plants.

Even more devastating are the viruses and fungi that thrive in the moist conditions strawberries like best. In bad years, we get grey mould rot—a fungus that covers the fruit, especially any berries touching the ground, with a grey velvet-like mould, so they resemble a long-forgotten piece of cheese in the far reaches of the refrigerator. Powdery mildew is another fungus that causes the leaves to turn purple and curl upwards. One of the worst of all is a root disease called red stele, identified by a red centre in the root. The stunted plants wilt in warm weather, producing only a few wizened berries. Verticillium wilt, black rot and various other rots and blights can also occur.

For many years now plant breeders have been working to develop varieties that are more resistant to disease, as well as being bigger and better in every way. Ever-bearing varities have nudged their way into some gardens with the promise of producing a spring crop and then another crop again later in the season rather than one grand June crop so beloved by strawberry jam makers. Where late spring frosts may kill the first set of flowers, they offer the advantage of a second set of blossoms. However, the word on the street is they tend to do less well in areas with hot dry summers. There's also a certain amount of excitement these days over the new day neutrals—plants that set flowers regardless of how long the day is, continuing to produce a modest number of berries from spring until autumn. But aficionados maintain that the taste of the best single-crop varieties has yet to be matched by any of the ever-bearing newcomers.

I consider the hankering for a better strawberry a sure sign of the inherent perversity of human nature, and have had a little taste of its folly myself this year. We all know that strawberry plants must be renewed every two or three years, and that crop rotation is recommended. I confess to having fallen down a bit in this department—I've continued developing new plants every year from runners, and periodically rooting out older plants once they began resembling bristlecone pines, but I hadn't taken the time to begin fresh beds. A springtime top dressing of compost on the old beds and a few invocations to the deities seemed to suffice. But after last year's dismal show, a new regime seemed in order.

First step was to acquire new plants which we obtained last fall from friends who swore by this particular variety for fruit size, taste and general excellence. I selected a new bed, carefully avoiding any spot where tomatoes, eggplants, peppers or potatoes had recently grown, as I had a vague notion that these are all vectors for verticillium wilt. I spaded in huge barrowloads of compost. I painstakingly spread the roots at planting, with the crowns at the perfect surface level, to avoid having them rot from being too low or dry out from being too high. I gave them a thick mulch of grass clippings to ameliorate the worst of the winter rains and prevent damage from frost heaving and cold drying winds. I spent the better part of autumn chasing after a neighbour's rooster which repeatedly came over to scratch under the mulch for worms, in the process uprooting our precious new plants.

The first berries began ripening just a few days ago, so I spread floating row covers over the bed to keep the robins from swiping them all. When I pulled the covers back to pick the first bowl of the season: Voila! Enormous red berries on every plant, far larger than our old varieties ever produced. I plucked one and was just about to pop it into my mouth for a taste test when I saw a couple of repulsive little sow bugs huddled in a cave they'd tunneled into the underside of the berry. A second berry had the same problem. I pondered a moment then realized with dismay that the fruiting habit of the plants and the weight of the great berries combined to have each berry lying on the ground. The plants simply weren't strong enough to hold the big brutes up. Wherever berries rested on the grass mulch, sow bugs were busy on the berries. Fouled sow bug holes are not what one has in mind when one thinks of strawberries and cream at Wimbledon.

Another bitter disappointment lay in store: the berries, although enormous and entirely succulent in appearance, don't have quite the same stunning, ecstasy-inducing flavour our older varieties do. These new and blander big shots have a white pith in the centre that never ripens and needs careful cutting out. Compared with our smaller but sweeter and largely sow bug-free old varieties, these showy newcomers are a dreadful comedown, little better than the tasteless imports in supermarkets. Their improvements remind me of Hollywood starlets vainly pressing towards success through lip and breast enhancement surgery. It serves me right, I conclude, for trying to improve upon the sublime. I do note, however, that among their strawberries from seed, Thompson and Morgan offer a variety called "Mignonette" which is used in France for decorating pastries and dropping into a glass of champagne. Now there's an image I could live with. Voila!

WEEK 23: TOUR DE FORCE

This weekend we again hosted what has become, in a perverse sort of way, the apogee of our gardening year: the annual house and garden tour. On this grand occasion, our garden gates—along with those of about a dozen other island households—are thrown entirely open in order that the general public may, for a modest fee, wander at leisure through the grounds and make of them what they will.

This is the seventh consecutive year our place has been on the island tour, a track record of sufficient length to allow certain generalizations to be safely made. My first observation concerns persons who sit on committees across the nation organizing garden tours, for there are now scores of tours scattered over the landscape. Their organizers are a peculiar breed—people who combine a love of plants and plantings with a knack for social convening and the raising of funds for worthy causes. Sandy is one of them, for she it was who had the bright idea to organize the tour in the first place in order to raise money for our local land conservancy.

She modelled the scheme after two popular tours—one of gardens, the other of homes—in Victoria. But credit for the original garden-tour concept goes to a certain Miss Elsie Wagg who served on a committee to support England's district-nursing service. For sixty years, all sorts of fundraising concepts had been floated to assist the nurses in caring for the sick at home, as well as to support the nurses themselves in their retirement years. Then, in 1926, Miss Wagg had her moment of genius. "We've got all these beautiful gardens in the country and hardly anyone sees them except the owners and their friends," she explained to her committee colleagues. "Why don't we ask some of them to open next year for the Appeal?"

The offbeat idea was an instant hit. In 1927, more than six hundred gardens were opened—many of them on grand estates such as the private garden of King George V at Sandringham, or of renowned gardeners like William Robinson and Ellen Willmott. The gardens were listed in a pamphlet. An admission fee of "a shilling a head" had, by the end of the year, raised more than eight thousand pounds. Once launched, the thing took on a life of its own: Britain's Gardens Scheme is today a hugely successful fundraiser. The several thousand participating properties—the emphasis is now on smaller gardens—are catalogued in an annually updated book and are identified by a yellow poster reading "Garden Open Today."

And of course there are now these fabulous garden-touring package holidays where one can, for example, in the course of ten days, view the gardens of the Cotswolds,

Wales and the Lake District. Here the tour-goer glides from Hever Castle in Kent up to Sissinghurst, over to Barnsley House, through the Cotswolds to Hidcote Garden, then on to Burford House and Biddulph Grange, the Lake District, Chatsworth House, Bressingham Gardens, Beth Chatto Gardens, the Garden of Roses in Saint Albans, Wisley Gardens and Lord knows what other gardens before collapsing from systemic envy and nervous fatigue.

Here's how our own little island tour functions, on its far more modest scale. Tour-goers purchase tickets in advance at twelve dollars apiece. Each ticket contains a map and a brief description of the dozen-or-so properties on the tour. Vistors can then proceed in their own vehicles—bicycles are becoming blessedly more popular—and at their own pace. We average about thirteen hundred visitors spread over a Saturday and Sunday, which is about the maximum our little ferry and its redoubtable crew can be expected to handle.

Simulators ourselves, we soon found our tour being cloned by other cash-strapped benevolent groups in the vicinity. Tours began popping up like thistles all over the region. A certain amount of convivial jostling for position ensued as to who is going on what weekend and who has come up with the cleverest new wrinkle to lure in record crowds.

To those who haven't experienced it, having thirteen hundred strangers tramping through one's house and gardens might seem a daunting prospect. Not so, for the tour is actually a marvellous event—spiritually uplifting and

forcible in shoring up one's faith in the fundamental good-
ness of humanity, at least that portion of it that gardens.
The event generates a huge outpouring of volunteer energy
across the island, everyone from the guinea-pig gardeners
to ticket-takers and lunch providers and cleaner-uppers.
Young and old, halt and lame, hundreds of islanders are
inveigled into lending a hand, and their combined energies
create a terrific buzzing excitement.

Meanwhile, multiple sensations may assail those of us
whose properties are on the tour. Firstly, there is something inherently gratifying about seeing gardens employed
for the common good. Throwing the gates open, even
for just a day or two, can help temper any proclivities
the gardener may have towards abandoning society altogether and giving oneself over entirely to the life of plants,
however appealing a prospect. Plus having your property
showcased on a tour is a magnificent motivator for getting on with certain projects. Psychologically the tour
functions much like an editor's deadline, an arbitrary but
unarguable set point at which one must be finished. There
is, of course, a fundamental fallacy at play here, in that gardens, like novels, are never really finished—one could go
on fussing forever, and probably would if someone didn't
take a firm hand and say: That's that. Certainly lawns can
be mowed, edges trimmed, weeds pulled, shrubs sheared,
windows and floors washed and a general sprucing-up
conducted, which otherwise might not be, were the tour
not bearing down upon us like an iceberg. I sometimes
wonder whether, if we didn't have the goad of the tour, cer-

146

tain bothersome jobs would ever get done. This year, for example, we'd had some trouble with the cascade. Frost heave over winter had budged rocks and cracked some concrete, requiring a major retrofit. Nothing all spring compelled me to tackle the job; in fact I remained entirely uncompelled, almost blasé, about it until this week when the awful prospect of thirteen hundred witnesses to my failed cascade spurred me to action.

You discover, or rediscover, certain propensities within yourself, some of which you'd just as soon not. For example, every year I'm beset by a nagging apprehension that visitors will be sniffing around, like pigs after truffles, in search of things to criticize. That they're coming not to enjoy themselves but rather to expose some awful failure on my part. Like thirteen hundred mothers coming upstairs to see if you've cleaned your room properly. We begin an anxious pacing through the gardens, convinced that the roses won't open on time (yes, one year we had a guy out in his garden with a hair dryer, trying to coax buds open), that the peonies will all be finished, that there'll be nothing in bloom at all, and I'll be definitively exposed as a charlatan and a fool.

Oh, but then the beauty of the day itself! So many sweet-tempered souls wandering around the estate and heaping one with flattery of a most beguiling sort. "Gosh, you've put a lot of work into this place!" they'll gush—music to the workaholic ear. Tour etiquette generally suggests that critical reviews be kept to oneself or be shared with intimates out of earshot of the owners. We did have one free

147

spirit a few years ago who marched to a different drumbeat. "What's so terribly interesting about your garden," she exclaimed unabashedly, "is that everything's growing so beautifully even though it's all in the wrong place!" This year Sandy by chance overheard one dear soul suggesting to her friend that our delphinium stakes, towering above admittedly, but uncharacteristically, modest-sized plants, betokened serious delusions of grandeur on our part.

But critiques are the exception. Indeed, seen afresh through the eyes of so many enthusiastic visitors, the old place begins looking not quite so shabby after all. The sun breaks through. Hummingbirds buzz and butterflies flutter. Laughter and rapt exclamations ring across the grounds. One begins to feel actually rather accomplished, something of a success in life really. Fluffed up with complimentary comments, one's faith in the intrinsic decency of humankind refreshed, one strides out purposefully to greet the next wave of visitors, giving quiet thanks for the perspicacity of a certain Miss Elsie Wagg.

WEEK 24: SUMMER SOLSTICE

We are wafting about the grounds these days, giddy from ambrosial perfumes lingering on the air. Mornings and evenings especially, the crush of scent is almost too much, too heartrending, to be borne. I feel at times a need to weep for no good reason, to sing an aria (if only I could), or simply stand enraptured in this delicious swirl of fragrance.

Just as springtime nights disclose that spring is a season of sound, midsummer evenings do the same for scent. We lie awake in the summerhouse, brushed by floating veils of fragrance. Honeyed, spicy, fruity exhalations drift in and away, ethereal as dreams, elusive, trailing threads of memories behind them, evocative of... what?

There's no gainful employment to be found in trying to describe either the fragrances or the emotional states they stimulate. Words fail us; for the fragrant garden flourishes just beyond where words leave off, where concepts clank to a halt, useless as old farm equipment rusting in a meadow. Farther on from there lies the scented garden, what Milton called a "wilderness of sweets." I suppose the purest moments of spiritual meditation draw close, on occasion, to where the fragrant garden grows. There one simply is, lost to oneself and the world, entirely swept away.

Thereafter, back in the world of spades and stones, we do well to take the advice of Francis Bacon: "And because the breath of flowers is far sweeter in the air (where it comes and goes like the warbling of music) than in the hand, therefore nothing is more fit for that delight than to know what be the flowers and plants that do best perfume the air." I very much like that "breath of flowers"—as though we are inhaling what the flowers are exhaling, and so in some way are joined to them, as to one another and other breathing creatures, through the shared exchange of air.

Successive fragrant pinnacles peak as the gardening year unfolds, none of them higher than this. The old roses, held back by coolish, moist weather, aren't really out yet—

and they're an olfactory Everest all by themselves—but a combination of fragrant vines, shrubs and perennials is more than enough to carry us to dizzying heights. I've already described the old familiar dame's rocket as a powerful attractant to butterflies, and like so many of the plants favoured by butterflies and hummingbirds, it casts a lovely scent, often likened to the fragrance of wallflowers. British author Rosemary Verey writes: "The single-flowered variety makes a splendid plant for the wild garden, where you may walk on a warm summer evening, or at the back of the border—for it is more scented than handsome." Well, handsome is as handsome does, as my old mum used to say, and dame's rocket does handsomely all 'round. How did Wordsworth put it?—"The flower of sweetest smell is shy and lowly."

There's nothing the least bit shy or lowly about the honeysuckles we've got scattered all over the yard. Most of them are an old variety called "Gold Flame"—rampant vines smothered in starry golden tubular flowers suffused with pink, their sex parts thrust out brazenly. At evening time especially, the vines pour out a splendid honey-scented perfume that wafts across the yard and lingers voluptuously. Celia Thaxter described the honeysuckle's scent as "like the spirit of romance, sweet as youth's tender dreams. It is summer's very soul."

One hesitates to mention these sublime fragrances in connection with bedpans and cesspools, but we do know that the ancient craft of aromatic gardening was in part developed to help cloak foul household odours prevalent before the modern blessings of refrigeration and indoor plumbing. The principle is no less sound today, so we've swathed our outdoor composting privy in fragrant honeysuckle. The privy, though seldom offensive to any but the most fastidious of nostrils, is thus rendered splendidly aromatized. The trick with rampant honeysuckles, I've learned, is not to become so beguiled by their siren scents as to abandon discipline. They need to be whacked back regularly, else they degenerate into an unattractive and rather slovenly woodiness.

Something of the same can be said of the sweet mock oranges, old fragrance favourites of which we have several varieties blooming. The headiest of the bunch is a hybrid developed in 1925 in the nurseries of the great French hybridist Victor Lemoine and baptized, rather grandly, *Philadelphus x lemoinei,* "Belle Etoile." And a beautiful star she is indeed, casting a sweet and vaguely lemon-orange fragrance that wafts like gossamer through the garden. Some plants will cast their scents only at certain times of the day—often early morning or evening—while others require moist, warm air for top performance, but "Belle Etoile" is ravishing at all hours, on cool days as well as warm ones. Also herded into the "more scented than handsome" category, it's a loose-limbed shrub that requires no-nonsense pruning back after flowering, lest it give way to gangliness. But just now, covered in clusters of smallish white flowers, she's a specimen of undisputed beauty.

As are the dianthus that have just started blooming with multitudes of flowers in white and every shade of pink running all the way to blazing crimson. Here is a plant where the hybridizers, for all their alleged excesses elsewhere, have worked wonders with single and bicoloured varieties. Powerful but elusive, their scents hint at cinnamon and cloves, as though they bordered an ancient spice road along which they entice us to travel. British author William Robinson wrote of them: "I pray the reader to explore the world of dianthus; they have riches to offer to those who love scent upon the air, scent in the hand or scent in the house. Grow them from seed and if you find a plant with a fragrance new to you, never pass it by without asking for a cutting." I find these little beauties often come spilling over pathways and edgings, making it a simple matter to snip away small rosettes that readily root as cuttings. Just now we've got several trays of new varieties from seed crying out for transplanting, though where they'll ultimately go is anybody's guess, as we haven't room for half of them. That's how it is with pinks— often called clove gillyflowers in old texts—you can never have enough, any more than you can have enough of their enticing fragrances.

152   We find that they grow handsomely alongside another old fragrant standby, nepeta or catmint. Its blue-grey leaves and tiny lavender-blue flowers cast a pungent scent, especially after a midsummer shower. Both long in bloom, gillyflowers and catmint together swarm with feeding bees and butterflies. So does that other old cottage-garden favourite, the herb valerian. Also in full flower now, its tall stems are topped with clusters of tiny flowers in pink,

white and soft lavender-blue. Its scent hangs in the air, rich and musky, like an excess of cheap cologne encountered in close quarters.

But that's how it is just now in the garden awash with this exuberant profusion of perfumes. Creeping thymes, bodice-bursting peonies, trumpeting daylilies, the first opening roses, pungent geranium leaves and dozens of other aromatic plants cast their fragrances into the swirl of scents through which we move. It is intemperate in the extreme, this fulsomeness of fragrance, almost preposterous. We ourselves waft about too, breathless and impetuous, languorous at times, maudlin at others, close to tears, then rapturous with passion. Anything but rational and judicious—but sensible in the truest sense. Impeccably well grounded most of the time, the fragrance gardener enters another level of consciousness at moments like these. So there's no sense discussing mortgage rates or mutual funds or any other rubbish. The gates of paradise have swung for a few moments open and the gardener has gone in.

WEEK 25: BY ANY OTHER NAME

I tend to get depressed whenever I start reading about roses. Not for lack of interest or enthusiasm, but rather from the daunting immensity and complexity of the topic. You're scarcely three paragraphs in, before the author—generally an esteemed past-president of the Royal National Rose Society or something—warms to the topic of rose classification. Then we're off and away on a bewildering ramble

through the thickets of Floribundas and Polyantha Pom-
pons, Wichuraiana Climbers as opposed to Wichuraiana
Ramblers, Climbing Sports of Hybrid Teas compared with
Climbing Sports of Floribundas, Kordesii Climbers and
Repeat-flowering Climbers.

You're well into mental gridlock before being informed
that so much hybridizing has occurred among what used
to be distinct groups that the lines of demarcation have
become hopelessly blurred. Hybrid Tea-type Floribundas,
for example, have stretched like spandex between the twin
buttocks of Hybrid Teas and Floribundas, creating a singular rump out of what had previously been two firmly
distinct entities. Various categories of climbers, ramblers
and pillar roses have been intermingling indiscriminately.
Anarchy seems the order of the day, with wild-eyed hybridizers running riot in the streets while tactical squads of
classifiers bang their shields to try to maintain some sem-
blance of order.

Despite the high drama involved, I feel myself nodding
off, as I used to do when studying physics. Refinements of
argument as to whether Fantin-Latour should continue to
be classified as a Centifolia or be reclassified as a Bourbon
have much the same soporific effect as deep pondering
of Heisenberg's Principle of Uncertainty. I fully recognize this as defeatism on my part, brought on by an acute
awareness of how much there is to know about roses and
what dismal progress I'm making in mastering very much
of it. Even on a good day I have trouble remembering that

Rosa gallica crossed with *Rosa canina* to produce the Alba, and with *Rosa phoenicia* to produce the Damask, or that the Damask crossed with Alba to produce the Centifolia. No matter how many times I've had it explained, I can't keep a *Rosa spinosissima* straight.

There are people out there with an intimate knowledge of these matters and I admire them immensely. I suppose if life were far longer and intellectual discipline more effortlessly acquired, I might make a stab at being one of them, just as I might come to some primitive understanding of all the RAMS and megahertzes whirring inside my PC. But somehow I think not. I seem constitutionally inclined towards denial, to remaining stupendously underinformed about roses, even at the cost of a debilitating drop in self-esteem.

All of this, of course, is sub rosa—one does not disclose such things to the outer world, and particularly not to acquaintances who are dedicated members of the local rose society. I've learned that to deal with such people successfully one needs to possess a few small but reliable snippets—what media types call "sound bites"—that can be trotted out whenever the talk turns, as it always does, to roses. I recall, for example, making a rather impressive splash in a conversation among a group of distinguished rosarians in Vancouver. These were no triflers, these were authorities who could distinguish a Hybrid Perpetual from a Shrub-Grandiflora at thirty paces. Being among them was like having lunch with a tableful of astrophysicists.

They had a number of cut roses with them (they would), all but one of which they could identify. I in turn sniffed at the unknown rose. "Hmmm," I pondered discerningly, "the bouquet is intriguingly evocative of Mme Isaac Pereire." The most knowledgeable of the group sniffed again. "I think you may be right," he said approvingly. "It could very well be a sport of Mme Isaac Pereire."

This was charlatanism of the most reprehensible sort on my part. Although I do know and love Mme Isaac dearly— I even recognize her as a Bourbon—but only because she grows prominently at our front gate. She's in bloom just now, and every morning when I arise and descend from the summerhouse, I take one of her large flowers in my hand and draw it close. Oh, what an outrageous fragrance! Sweet and deeply subtle. The great British rosarian Graham Stuart Thomas (a character with whom the greatest dexterity would be required in effectively employing one's sound bites) describes her as being "possibly the most powerfully fragrant of all roses. The flowers are large, of intense rose-madder, shaded magenta, bulging with rolled petals, quartered and opening to a great saucer-face."

That sort of near-purple prose is more my idea of right writing about roses. I can understand rosa virtuosos poring over thick and learned tomes during the depths of winter, but not now, not when the roses are at their peak of bloom. Now one wants to cast aside musty texts, discard reading glasses, let down one's hair, and romp about the rosery in gossamer underwear.

Here is Fantin-Latour, named for the great painter, but which by any other name would smell as sweet. The handsome bush is covered in blooms, each crammed with scores of blush pink petals folded together like religious mysteries with deeper shadings of pink at the centre. The fragrance is sublime.

Just alongside is Félicité Parmentier, another full bush with green-grey leaves and massed clusters of pale pink blooms. Her new flower buds are pure and perfect, disclosing a tantalizing hint of pink, then opening to a mesmerizing swirl of small petals. Her perfume is unimaginably fine. Sandy's favourite rose, she is perhaps as close to perfection as any plant may come.

But how can one say it when just over here by the weathered fence is Sarah Van Fleet, her glossy apple-green leaves showcasing single soft pink flowers. Her perfume is delicate too, sweetly intoxicating, more than enough to make one forget her murderously thorny arms. She's a dangerous charmer, this one, but we are easily seduced.

Just as we are by Maiden's Blush alongside. Her foliage is a pleasing blue-green, her new canes have a hint of pink, while her flower buds break the palest blush pink then open to a pure and delicate pink that deepens at their centre. Her fragrance too is enough to make you lose your composure and behave in ways that might scandalize the neighbourhood.

Can you even bear to carry on over to Ispahan, a spreading mass of bloom on the hillside, just as she was on her ancestral hills of Ispahan in ancient Persia. Her sprawling branches sag under the weight of hundreds of double blossoms, all a soft uniform pink, casting a halo of heady perfume around the plant.

Then on to Königin von Dänemark, the elegant Danish queen with blue-green leaves creating a marvellous foil for her flowers. Her large soft-pink blooms are cupped at first and then open fully, with their central petals densely quartered. Ethereally perfumed, she is everything a queen would be in a loyal royalist's imagination.

And so it goes around the rosery, one celestial stopping point after another. Rambling Albertine and long-limbed New Dawn reclining against the old woodshed like two beautiful sisters, arms outstretched to touch one another's fingers. Ebullient Kiftsgate climbing into a big cedar tree and cascading down multiple trusses of small white blooms. Rosa mundi throwing a party with her gaudy petals striped red against creamy pink around a coronet of yellow stamens. Maigold glowing against the western sun in a mass of blowsy custard-gold blooms. Beauties every one of them, beyond superlatives. Wandering among them, a niggling small voice in the back alleys of the brain might continue nattering about the importance of being Ernest Calvat and the distinguishing characteristics of Polyantha Pompons. But from far away, across ancient aromatic hills, comes wafting a more compelling voice whispering: be still. We are in the gardens of the gods. We have touched the heart of the rose.

WEEK 26: EVER SO BLUE

The season of inquisitive visitors is upon us, and one of its more endearing rituals is having a guest peer, like Alice into her looking glass, past the pastel beauties of antique roses and sumptuous peonies, towards a distant splash of blue. Of all the colours illuminating the gardens of June, no other quite catches the eye or excites the imagination the way blue does. Shining with vivid intensity and clarity, the blues are a fascinating group, endowed with special powers to attract and to entice. Some are as unsullied as the blue of the Blessed Virgin's veil, the colour of constancy, the one we call true blue. But some of the blues aren't quite so virtuous. They're more apt to be singing the blues in a smoky after-hours club. Something powerful, perhaps even dangerous runs through the inky-blue depths of some clematis and delphiniums, more like the blues born of blue devils, the baleful demons seen in apparitions during delirium tremens.

They're all at play in the garden just now, numerous blooms that fall somewhere along the long blue spectrum between green and violet. Most are mixed with tints and show as qualified blues: baby blue, lavender blue, metallic blue and all the rest. Pure blue—"the colour of the cloudless sky"—is rare enough to make otherwise-steady gardeners lose their balance. Describing blue Himalayan poppies, Penelope Hobhouse gushes: "Such a mass of pure blue flowers is almost as rare and precious as the much-prized lapis lazuli of the ancient world." Rare enough, at least, that gardeners will tolerate aberrant behaviour in certain plants as the price of their pure blue flowers. Blue anchusa's one of these. A loose-limbed perennial closely related to borage, anchusa is a gangly and coarse-looking customer with fleshy stems and hairy leaves, as though it drank beer on the front porch in its underwear. It grows over a metre tall but is prone to sprawling clumsily over its neighbours. You wonder why you bother with it at all—until its small but captivatingly blue flowers first open early in June. Theirs is a cerulean blue of vivid clarity, luminous like blue Mexican tiles from a long way off. While less than ideal for small spaces or precise planting schemes, blue anchusa serves brilliantly near the back of a large border, where its loose limbs can be staked and its coarse foliage disguised.

Colourists tell us that blue flowers create a sense of depth and distance in a garden because they reflect the hues of the sky and the deep blue sea. They seem to expand and deepen space in even small gardens. Perennial blue flax (several dozen finicky little seedlings of which I've just finished potting up) is a reliable performer in smaller spaces, producing clusters of sky-blue flowers over fine greyish foliage. Massed together, their blue can reconcile the bolder colours of nearby flowers, as the brilliant hues of alpine meadows are harmonized by vast blue skies beyond. With a bloom period of many weeks, drought-tolerant and freely self-seeding, perennial flax is a carefree contributor to the blues of June. Opening before dawn and already faded by noon, these small blue beauties are best admired on early morning strolls through the garden; any plant that compels us to view the garden at dawn in summertime is worth having for that reason alone.

Scabiosa is another small trouble-free blue perennial. A member of the eccentric teasel family, this one's more associated with staying home sewing than rambling across wild mountain meadows or singing the blues in smoky nightclubs. It's called pincushion flower from its tufted round centre which resembles a pincushion, its pistils and stamens sticking out like pins. We've got it growing as contentedly as any seamstress alongside clumps of pink and white astrantia. Rounding out that particular little kaffeeklatsch is love-in-a-mist, another romantically eccentric charmer with powder-blue flowers caught coyly in its green mist of threadlike bracts.

The deep blue flowers of spiderwort bloom for only a few hours, usually in the morning, then dissolve into a drop of thin jelly, a melodramatic habit that gives *Tradescantia x andersoniana* one of its common names, widow's tear. But we need shed no tears for this tough customer, a native of the rich woodlands of the mideastern and central states, because it's all but indestructible. Good in any soil, sun or shade, best with lots of water, it produces long, deep green, arching foliage like thick grass. It continues putting out its three-petalled flowers throughout the summer and expanding its clump at a rate that demands regular division. Named garden varieties come in a range of colours, the vivid blues being especially fine. Like anchusa, it's inelegant at times but indispensable.

Any talk about indestructible plants pretty soon sees hardy geraniums pushing their way into the conversation. These are the old cranesbills—nicknamed for their long seed pods which resemble the beaks of cranes—that have made such a dazzling comeback in popularity. Some are vigorous, drought-tolerant workhorses capable of suppressing even very aggressive weeds. Their flowers come in lovely hues of blue, pale violet, mauve. I once made the grotesque miscalculation of giving a slide-show lecture in Victoria that contained not a word about hardy geraniums. After my presentation, I was approached by a remarkably energetic woman who gently scolded me for the omission. She turned out to be none other than Phoebe Noble, Victoria's eminent hardy geranium expert. She writes of Johnson's Blue: "When this geranium is in full flower in June I think it is the best plant in the garden," which is how we feel too about its lucent blue flowers. She does concede: "By August, if I have been negligent, the flowers are faded and the leaves are brown and tatty and I wonder why I give it such a prominent position at the front of a long border." Then she adds that this untidy stage can be avoided by shearing the plant right to the ground to force a fresh crop of leaves and possibly a few late flowers.

Most splendid of all are the stunning blue spires of giant delphiniums. I have over time come to the conclusion that the better part of gardening involves assiduously cultivating those plants that enjoy one's particular premises and

162

banishing those that do not. Delphiniums have taken to our place like the proverbial duck to water, despite getting very little of the regular watering and deep rich feeding they're supposed to require. They simply like it here, in a way that rhubarb, for example, doesn't. I'll take the trade-off any day. We mostly grow Pacific Giant hybrids in whites and dreamy lavenders but most of all in blues—pale blue, pink or lilac-flushed blues, and especially rich true blues.

Gardeners for whom delphiniums don't come easily can be excused for labouring to grow them anyway, so great are the rewards. Hungry slugs love few foods more than the springtime shoots of delphiniums. I pick the slimy fellows off by hand, place them in a bucket, carry them a vast distance (by slug reckoning) and deposit them in the woods. Later on, wind and rain batter delphiniums merci-lessly, and the confidence of the stakeholders too. But when the spires do eventually stand in stately groups as they are just now, elegantly massed with blooms of the truest blue— oh, this is a vision of such exquisite purity and beauty, it would lift the spirits of the most world-weary among us and restore our jaded faith in the sublime.

The glorious effects of summer blues can be enhanced by careful placement of adjacent colours. As the legendary English gardener Gertrude Jekyll put it: "Any experienced colourist knows that the blues will be more telling—more purely blue—by the juxtaposition of rightly placed com-plementary colour." In designing a blue garden, Ms. Jekyll advocated using almost exclusively pure blues. The purple blues of campanulas and lupines, for instance, "would not be admissible." Whites and pale yellows she considered best for keeping blue flowers "ever so blue." Lime-green, silver and grey foliage all work well at intensifying blue. While not "blue garden" people ourselves, we do boast a few small examples of our own just now: the vivid flowers of blue anchusa lolling against a Jerusalem sage and an Arabian thistle. The silver-grey foliage of the sage and thistle, and the sage's luminescent sulphur-yellow blooms together do indeed make the anchusa flowers look "ever so blue." Following a looser discipline, we have wild opium poppies blooming alongside many of the delphiniums. The brilliant red of the poppies flaming against the sublimely blue spires of delphiniums appeals to me as perhaps a bit reckless but entirely correct.

$\mathcal{J}$ULY

WEEK 27: FOOLS FOR FAWNING

I was sitting at my desk early this morning, pondering mightily, when a blur of movement out the window caught my eye. Thirty yards away, across where the little creek trickles between lawn and woodlands, stood a deer, a doe, slender and lovely in her cinnamon pelage. Her large ears were cocked, alert, her glistening black muzzle sensed the air. Then I saw the reason for her caution: behind her, stepping daintily out from the sword ferns and horsetails came two tiny fawns. They couldn't be more than a few weeks old, with vivid white spots running in lines along their reddish-brown coats. Once on the grass they began to frisk like goat kids, kicking up their skinny rear legs and making ridiculous fake sorties around one another. The dam, satisfied that no danger lurked, took to cropping grass while her little ones cavorted nearby. But suddenly her head was up again, her fluid body rigid with attention, all senses alert. The twin fawns froze as well. I could hear nothing through the open window but the twittering of birds and the gurgle of the creek. But the dam sensed danger some-where and, as quietly as she'd come, slipped back into the woods with the fawns at her heels.

These are our first fawns of the year, later than usual, and it did my heart good to see them. Nothing quite epito-mizes sweet innocence and vulnerability the way a small fawn does. "Bambi lovers" I hear defensive hunters call-ing anyone opposed to their blood sport, but what hope is there for any rough customer unable to get mawkish over a fawn? Of course, a gardener fawning over fawns is either a fool or an affable masochist, for with each new fawn, as Yeats put it, "a terrible beauty is born." Those locations at which deer and gardeners interface are the grounds of epic battles in which the devious cunning of the deer is pitted against the desperate ferocity of the gardener under siege. For all their sweetness, new fawns ultimately add to the besieging hordes. This is no petting zoo: it is Leningrad at its bloodiest, Masada at its most heroic.

166   It's easy to pick out gardeners in deer country for they have a slightly manic look about them, as though they'd inhaled too often before becoming besotted by the more sensible addiction of gardening. It takes no effort to strike up an animated conversation with these characters; you simply ask them if they've had much trouble with deer lately. It's like asking the parents of especially reckless teenagers how their kids are doing. Their pupils dilate;

their lips quiver; strange facial tics kick in. They try not to get themselves wound up, but they can't help themselves, poor dears, and within minutes they're off and running on a mad monologue concerning what the deer have eaten, what havoc wreaked, and what new stratagems they are themselves devising in defence.

This is where you get all the demented talk about dangling bars of soap from apple trees or sprinkling lion and tiger dung among the brassicas. It's a bit embarrassing, really, to hear mature people carrying on in this way, speaking with such heartfelt earnestness about the repulsive powers of blood meal suspended in nylon stockings. Their talk brings on that same prickly sensation one experiences when being compelled to listen to overdisclosive associates at the coffee machine detailing the collapse of their latest relationship. What can you possibly say to a deer-bedeviled gardener who insists upon speaking enthusiastically about deer-proof plants? Does one have the right, indeed the obligation, to rain on their parade by warning that clematis and tulips—notwithstanding whatever weighty tome may list them as "close to" deer-proof—won't last five minutes out there in the real world of deer-eat-all? "I don't think there's anything they won't eat if they're hungry enough," one battle-scarred veteran of the deer wars told me.

Not long ago I heard some enterprising Americans on CBC Radio extolling their new water fence. This setup has an electronic beam that, when broken by intruding bodies, triggers an eruption of water from sprinklers which will,

167

to hear the Yankee traders tell it, so startle and terrify encroaching deer, they'll flee in confusion never to return. Sure. Or there's always the electric fence: A gardener told me recently of a young buck that stuck its head under his electric wire, got zapped, causing it to bolt straight forward in panic, thereby entangling the wire in its antlers, then crashed around the garden in a maelstrom of tangled debris, wreaking more devastation than a midsummer cyclone.

Grizzled veterans know that there's nothing like a good stout fence for keeping the rascals out, but even here wisdom whispers to beware of false security. A fence may be as impregnable as the walls of Troy, but it still requires a gate to be serviceable, and there's the breaching-point. At our place, whatever breakdowns of security occur are due solely to particular persons leaving a gate open, about which words are invariably exchanged (and flagrant lies told) once the dust of battle has settled. In the meantime, there's a deer in the garden to be dealt with.

Trying to guide an intruder out of the compound usually reinforces my belief that the craftiness deer show in gaining access to your plants masks a more general dull-wittedness. To wit: I throw wide open all available gates. I move slowly and gently towards the intruder, cooing soft encouragements for it to be on its way. Sensing a threat, the deer crashes off to the far side of the garden, knocking down and trampling whatever it can en route. I repeat my slow approach from a fresh angle calculated to best nudge the creature towards a gaping open gate. No such luck: the deer goes bounding off on another destructive dash to the far side. Repeated several times, this ritual succeeds in reducing large portions of the garden to rubble and vexing me badly. I begin to address my nemesis in harsher terms. I abandon slow and steady coaxing in favour of a hostile charge. I've been known to hurl stones, never with any measurable success, and one time nearly put a rock through the greenhouse. By the time the obtuse creature finally escapes through a gateway, I've worked myself up into a dandy lather and am well prepared for a civilized discussion of who left the goddamn gate open in the first place.

But deer are no more created equal in the matter of intelligence than humans are. Last year we had a yearling buck hanging around, usually by himself, not in a small group as most of our regulars are. Smart as a whip, this little guy would show up whenever we set to work in the garden. He seemed to realize that we'd be leaving the gate open as we passed in and out, providing him ample opportunity to slip inside unnoticed when our backs were turned. Grubbing away at some chore or other, I'd look up and there he'd be, munching contentedly on a rose bush. Yelling at him to get out would do no good, though he plainly took my meaning. I'd have to walk towards him menacingly. But there'd be no idiotic dashing all over the place for him. He'd just calmly trot back out through the gateway by which he'd entered, with a look on his face like "Geez, what are you being so grumpy about today?" This little chap was like an Albert Einstein cast up, through who knows what genetic or environmental twist, from the dimwitted herds.

169

Mind you, who is any gardener to talk about dim-wittedness? As the summer wears on, the deer take to reclining in shady spots on the lawn, laconically chewing their cuds and appearing to watch with bemusement as we go tottering back and forth with wheelbarrow loads of compost or firewood or flats of seedlings. "Ho hum, what fools these mortals be," the deer appear to be musing. And we in turn cast a benign eye at them, forgiving their infuriating incursions, their persistent tearing at the apple trees, their debarking unprotected saplings by antler rubbing. Troublesome pests on the one hand, these terrible beauties are also lovely creatures to have around—"moving parts of the garden" Sandy called them once—and never more so than on shining mornings when tiny fawns first appear and frolic on the grass.

WEEK 28: HERE BE GIANTS

We've had a giant cow parsnip blooming in a back corner of the garden for the last few weeks. You might say looming as much as blooming, for it really is a monster, twelve feet tall, at least. Its central stalk stands thicker than a fore-arm, fleshy and juicy looking, a swampy green mottled with rusty red, and thin ridges running down its length. The huge dissected leaves spread a metre or more wide. Massed at the top of the plant, the flower heads look like enormous floating disks, a squadron of galactic spacecraft, smaller ones circling the central mother ship. The umbels of tiny white flowers resemble Queen Anne's lace on a colossal scale. This is what marketing people might call an impact plant—startlingly large, with a tropical and vaguely sinister aura. Although the garden's rife with other wonders at the moment, your attention is drawn repeatedly back to this imposing specimen.

We were first attracted to cow parsnips while hiking in lush mountainside meadows on the Queen Charlotte Islands. They held their graceful flowering heads on six-foot stalks, tallest of the wildflowers and grasses on those verdant slopes. The effect in that wild mountain setting was stunning. Those were the native perennial, *Heracleum lanatum*, which are not universally admired because they're poisonous to livestock and capable of causing severe dermatitis if touched by humans.

Some time later, we spotted giant cow parsnips blooming en masse along a stretch of highway on Vancouver Island. While driving, gardeners habitually pay more attention to what's growing along the roadside than to oncoming traffic, and although hazardous, this tendency has its rewards. Naturally we stopped the van to investigate further. These were not the troublesome native, but a naturalized exotic, the giant *H. villosum*, a biennial from the Caucasus. We realized, as gardeners do upon encountering certain plants, that we simply must have some at our place. A mental note was taken as to the precise location and a plan devised for returning in the fall to dig out a few for transplanting.

Now I realize a scheme like this gives rise to complex ethical questions concerning the morality of pilfering wild

171

plants. The last thing beleaguered wild places need is hordes of spade-wielding enthusiasts excavating "free" fawn lilies and trilliums. But when it comes to wildling exotics—especially exotics robust to the point of aggression—situation ethics surely must come into play. Having weighed all factors judiciously, we concluded that a raid upon the giant cow parsnip patch was indeed a permitted use.

Our collecting expedition was not an outing in which a serious botanist would take great pride. To begin with, the only parking possibility was across the highway from the target zone, requiring us to sprint with our spades across the busy road and back again bearing plants. The miscalculation here was in not anticipating the true size and weight of a giant cow parsnip root ball. By the time we'd lugged three back to the van, each time narrowly avoiding death or mutilation from thundering trucks and throbbing muscle cars, we declared the expedition an unqualified success and fled homeward.

The following spring the plants came out of the ground like growly bears after hibernation and soon shot up to eight or nine feet high. They seemed an altogether splendid addition, dramatically statuesque alongside Pacific Giant delphiniums and Arabian thistles tall enough to play in the NBA. Carried away, as gardeners are prone to become over new acquisitions, I rhapsodized about cow parsnips while delivering a particularly brilliant slide-show lecture. But afterwards I was approached by a man with a cautionary tale to tell. "I lived in an old neighbourhood in east Vancouver," he told me. "We had those giant cow parsnips in the

172

back yard, but they escaped down the alley and pretty soon the whole neighbourhood was overrun with them. They were everywhere!" I assured the fellow that we were far too diligent to ever allow our plants to set seed and sent him on his way. It's an amazing thing, isn't it, how gardeners won't take fair warnings seriously until they've been menaced by the same danger themselves. Despite fair warning, we somehow managed to let one of our plants seed freely, and the following year there were literally hundreds of offspring that had to be painstakingly plucked from impossible places. Never again, I say to myself, casting a wary glance at today's flowering monsters. For all of that, they're irresistible, and if you've got the space for one, with rich, moist soil, and can trust yourself to lop the enormous flower heads off before they set seed, the giant cow parsnip is a guaranteed show-stopper.

On a more reasonable and less threatening scale, garden angelica is another oversized biennial with a dramatic presence. It resembles cow parsnip in growth habit—a strong upright central stalk, large and deeply divided bright green leaves, and multiple umbels of tiny flowers massed in rounded umbrella-like clusters. Although a native of northern Europe, it too has a distinctive tropical ambience. The flower heads are already past their prime now; in June they have a lovely lime-green cast, much like lady's mantle flowers, that plays beautifully against soft pink roses or thalictrum. Closely related to the carrot, angelica shares with other umbelliferous plants the virtue of producing small flowers that are highly attractive to butterflies and many of the tiny beneficial insects we wish to attract into our gardens. Now its globular seed heads have taken on a lovely wheat colour while its smooth, pale green stems have developed a pinkish-mauve cast. We let ours self-seed, then easily pluck out unwanted offspring without any of the impending sense of menace a seeding cow parsnip poses.

We use angelica as an ornamental, although it has a long and venerable tradition as a culinary herb. Its young leaves are used in cooking fish, the roots and stems for flavouring liquors, and the crystallized stalks for confectionary decoration. The stems can also be blanched and eaten like celery. I don't know why I mention all this—such revelations only serve to provoke anxiety that one isn't traipsing about like Martha Stewart baking cakes from scratch and decorating them with icing you've produced from your home-grown crystallized angelica stems.

Better to move quickly along to another impact plant—the Japanese butterbur, *Petasites japonicus*. This one's not what you'd call a garden star exactly: as one of our manuals puts it, this lusty perennial is "not often planted for ornament except in rocky, poor soils where better plants will not grow." And it's invasive to boot. You'd only really bother with it if you had a lot of space and a bit of an attitude problem. But it does have its moments. Early in spring, huge and slightly surreal purplish-white flower heads emerge from the earth, each on the tip of a short stalk. Later on, enormous leaves unfurl, rounded and spreading more than a metre across, held singly on a stalk like a rhubarb stalk, only purplish with deep white ribbing.

The shiny green leaves have a soft kid-leather texture; by now they've become mottled with rusty red. These plants are especially dramatic by water, and we have them growing alongside our woodland creek where it widens into a sunny pool. Over the course of the summer, big banana slugs rasp expanding holes in the leaves, leaving some as only skeletal outlines. For a time last winter, the huge leaf skeletons lay spread across the pool bank, like doilies discarded by green giants, making an eerily lovely picture.

But for real rock 'em sock 'em drama, nothing quite matches gunnera, the giant South American perennials which produce the largest leaves grown anywhere in temperate zones. These awesome beauties can reach three metres tall with leaves over two metres across held on stiff stalks. The leaves are puckered and deeply veined, scratchy as sandpaper, the reddish stems bristling with small spines. Clusters of little flowers are borne on peculiar spikes nestled at the base of the plant. Gunneras can singlehandedly create the feel of an ancient tropical jungle. We have one in a large pot in the vegetable garden, awaiting transport to a permanent home. The trick is finding a big enough space to accommodate it. They need heaps of organic material and plenty of water to support their stupendous growth each year, and winter mulching even in our balmy conditions. In short, they are not a plant reasonable people would cultivate. But, as one of our manuals puts it: "Given space (they need plenty) and necessary care, these plants can be the ultimate summertime conversation pieces."

I'm not sure a conversational coup is the primary reason some of us are drawn to these big bruisers. Undoubtedly there are subconscious motivations at work here, perhaps not all that dissimilar from the urge to drive the big trucks and muscle cars that almost ran us and our cow parsnips down. One's therapist might gently suggest that making bold statements through oversized plants serves to block performance anxieties in other realms. Who knows? What I do like about all of these big impact plants is the tremendous vitality with which they surge from the earth and the stupendous size they achieve in a single growing season. These speak to the awesome powers latent in fertile soils and seeds.

WEEK 29: OF EMPIRES AND VAMPIRES

Our garlic crop's just about ready for harvesting, a summer ritual that wouldn't be complete without pondering again one of the great mysteries of our period in gardening history, namely: Why don't more gardeners grow their own garlic? There are growers out there risking extreme hypertension from trying to raise all sorts of impracticable cultivars, but do they have even a tiny sliver of soil for one of the greatest plants of human civilization? Baffling. The raising of garlic is so delightful in the doing and so enormously rewarding that you'd expect to see bulbs of it curing in elaborate braids at every turn. But no. Most of the garlic eaten by Canadians is produced in California or Mexico and comes with all the charming chemical inputs associated with big agribusiness. Its taste is mediocre and its shelf life short, despite being sprayed to prevent sprouting. Perhaps most galling of all, this ersatz garlic is an imposter, an insipid imitation, debasing an otherwise magnificent lineage.

Still, it's what many gardeners eat, if they eat garlic at all. I fully realize there's no point arguing when it comes to matters of taste. In my own family—as Irish working class as the potatoes we grew and ate with daunting singlemindedness—garlic was never featured in the family cuisine. Like sex, it was not discussed, but was understood to be a foreign substance most generally associated with the exhalations of Italian immigrant labourers riding at close quarters on the bus.

Such are the malicious twists of history, for garlic—a member of the royal lily family—is one of humankind's most ancient cultivated crops, prized over millennia for its culinary, medicinal and magical properties. Chinese herbalists were prescribing it for various ailments more than six thousand years ago. Look to ancient India and Babylonia, to classical Greece and Rome, and you find proof that the rise of civilization and the cultivation of garlic go hand in hand. The great pyramids were built on garlic power. In ancient Rome, the seat of empire, it was renowned as the "herb of Mars," bestowing strength and courage upon the conquering legions. Aristophanes himself—not somebody we normally think of as an aging playboy—credits garlic juice with restoring masculine vigour. Pliny believed its "very powerful properties" could drive off snakes and scorpions.

Transylvanian werewolves and vampires would cringe before its cloves. The Black Death and similar plagues could gain no toehold, we're told, wherever garlic was eaten in abundance. While consecutive civilizations rose, flourished and fell away, a belief in the healing and protective potency of garlic endured. Crackpot modern theorists may proclaim "the end of history" all they want, but I've not heard any proclaim the end of garlic. In short, garlic goes on.

Impeccable in its pedigree, garlic is exceptionally easy to cultivate, harvest and store. The most commonly grown varieties are of *Allium sativum*, although the precise identities of different strains are often obscure, as befits a plant of magical properties. The clumsily named elephant garlic, *Allium ampeloprasum*, is actually a leek that produces a mild-tasting bulb and is not to be taken seriously. The strain that has stood our household in good stead for many years has a central stalk around which about a dozen large, wedged-shaped cloves are clustered. This is typical of rocambole varieties, including Chinese, Ukrainian and Yugoslavian strains. Other varieties, sometimes called "soft necks," have no stem running through the bulb. Whatever the names, one looks for a variety that will produce large cloves that have easily removable skin and superior taste, texture and pungency. Don't underestimate skin removability; we used to grow a variety that was admirable in every way except that you couldn't, short of violence, ever get the skin off the cloves.

The largest cloves of the largest bulbs are retained as seed stock, no matter who might have other ideas. The seed stock is sacred. I like to plant in late October, monsoons permitting, as fall planting is ideal for maximum bulb production. They require a period of cold weather to sprout and then a good three months at least to grow to maturity. In colder areas a thick winter mulch will protect the new plants while still allowing that critical burst of early spring growth, but spring planting may be required in areas of extremely cold winters. Garlic likes well-drained, sandy loam where no other onion family member has grown for three years, although remembering what has grown where for three years is easier said than done.

Not entirely sanguine that my crop rotation is everything it might be, I compensate by vigorously spading several wheelbarrow loads of compost into the raised bed before planting, in the primitive but steadfast belief that abundant compost covers all other shortfalls. I carefully separate each clove so as to retain its skin and not plunge it stark naked into cold ground. I plant them, blunt end down, so that the pointed tip is just below the soil surface. After a month or two of cold weather, our cloves often show new tips by Christmas, which stimulates a tremendous sense of good omens for the year to follow. However, if they fail to show, I begin fretting that all is lost. They continue their herky-jerky growth through winter warm spells. I mulch the bed with the first grass clippings of spring, and pretty much leave them alone after that, except perhaps for a splash of water in a dry spell. Some enthusiasts—the sort who'll coax their elephant garlic bulbs into weighing a kilogram apiece—will bung in high potassium and phosphorous fertilizer to boost spring bulb development, but I don't myself follow this buns-of-steel approach to the ancient herb.

By June the stalks begin producing seed heads, often on an artsy twirl of the upper stem, reminiscent of Oscar Wilde. These I systematically snap off in order to concentrate all the growing energy into bulb formation. I love the smell of garlic juice on my fingertips during this chore, like the essence-of-tomato scent you get pinching out side shoots on tomato vines. Once the tops have yellowed or fallen over, I lift the bulbs and let them cure by hanging on the dry and semi-sunny back porch for a week or two. Persons with creative impulses and time on their hands can braid the stalks together for wonderful retro-peasantry effect. With neither time nor creativity on my side, I just cut the stalks a few inches above the bulb and tie clusters of them together with twine. After curing, we store them in a cool and dry place with the onions.

And there it is: simplicity itself. Thereafter, you've got a ready supply both for gourmet extravaganzas in the kitchen and for clever turns in the garden. Garlic sprays—sometimes with onions and chili peppers added—are a venerable standby for deterring leaf-chewing insects. As companion plants to roses, garlic helps deter pests and is believed to enhance the fragrance of the blooms. Even compost made from garlic and onion scraps is said to help. True believers maintain that garlic tea makes a spray potent enough to control epidemic diseases like late blight on tomatoes and potatoes, which seems to me like believing that televangelists can heal people crippled with arthritis, but there's no denying that the power of faith is indeed a marvellous thing.

There's simply no end to the course of miracles attributed to garlic. I recently saw a report about a German clinical trial which concluded that older people who take garlic daily have more flexibility in their major blood vessels and lower incidence of heart disease than those who do not. Gardeners know more than enough about stiffening backs, but perhaps not as much as they should about the stiffening of blood vessels that occurs naturally with aging. Garlic, according to researchers, can lower cholesterol levels and blood pressure and reduce blood clotting which is a factor in arteriosclerosis. Grand news indeed, but hardly a surprise to devoted garlic growers. Then, just as they were beginning to make some sense, the scientists had to botch the business: for full effect, you have to take your garlic in a daily tablet. Not raw. Not cooked. A pill. The cynic within immediately began wondering who had funded this particular study. I mean, can you imagine the brawny builders of pyramids popping a 600 mg tablet a day? Count Dracula recoiling in terror at a necklace of strung pills? Does anyone really believe it was "garlic supplements" that helped old Aristophanes keep his pecker up? No, no, I say, a thousand times no! Our civilization will undoubtedly fall as all others have before it (some days it seems well on its way). Garlic pills may go the way of leeches and bloodletting.

But garlic shall endure, I'm sure of it: the herb of Mars, bestowing healthfulness and courage and, where appropriate, restored masculine vigour.

WEEK 30: POPPYCOCK

Our gardens are ablaze with poppies at present, and there's no more perilous interlude in the gardening year. Undeniably exquisite, unquestionably evocative of ineffable sentiments, poppies are also notorious for provoking more outlandish behaviour and florid oratory than a senator gone to the bottle. The papavers put people over the top in a way that few other flowers—indeed few other life forms—can. We may linger overlong over our daylilies, we may on occasion be a tad too effusive about our fuchsias, but neither produces the fantastic excesses that poppies do.

Just listen to the language that gets flounced about as soon as a poppy or two pops open. "The acme of grace," Louise Beebe Wilder calls them, while you're chatting together at an intimate gathering, "the best of laughter, the rarest embodiment of all that is delightsome, careless, touchingly fugitive." All true enough in its own way, of course, you couldn't agree more. Just as you're going to add a clever observation about the frothy charms of filipendula, Celia Thaxter bustles over and begins waxing about how poppies produce "splendour so dazzling as to baffle all powers of description." Quite so, but this doesn't deter some people from trying to describe them anyway. Among the worst is old John Ruskin, who can sniff out a

182

poppy conversation the way turkey vultures can scent carrion. Here he comes now, sauntering across the room, as though by chance. Seldom stuck for words, Ruskin shakes his wattles, strikes a meaningful pose and solemnly intones: "[T]he poppy is painted glass; it never glows so brightly as when the sun shines through it. Whenever it is seen against the light or with the light, it is a flame, and warms the mind like a blown ruby."

The old blowhard really is overstating it a bit, having a mind warmed "like a blown ruby," but these ostentations are commonplace in poppy talk. By this point you begin getting an uncomfortable feeling, as when you're cornered at a party by someone who specializes in psychobabble. You take to scanning the room for escape routes. But old Ruskin, once he's got the wind in his sails, is not one to shut up. "It is an intensely simple, intensely floral flower," he tells you knowingly. You presume that an "intensely floral flower" is much like an intensely choral choir, but refrain from saying so, in the hope that the conversation will peter out. No such luck. "All silk and flame," he carries on, staring raptly at a point well above your head, so that you wonder if he's talk-ing to you, or to God, or simply to posterity. "A scarlet cup, perfect edged all round, seen among the wild grass far away like a burning coal fallen from heaven's altars."

Blown rubies and now burning coals to boot, this has gone just about far enough. You begin subtly scuttling sideways, like a crab, towards the nearest exit. But the old codger, more nimble than you'd expect, cuts you off with a small but effective countermove and carries on. "You cannot have a more complete, a more stainless type of flower absolute," he tells you. Or a more tedious conversation, you're thinking to yourself, now pinned against the draperies. "Inside and outside, all flower. No sparing of colour anywhere, no outside coarseness, no interior secrecies, open as the sunshine that creates it..." Swept up in his own prose, the old duffer closes his eyes to ponder the magical effect he's conjured, giving you just enough time to slip sideways and away.

But there's no sure sanctuary from bizarre encounters at poppy time. Ducking through the kitchen, you bump once again into the always-charming Celia Thaxter. "The orange of the Iceland poppy," she exclaims out of nowhere, "is the most ineffable colour." You would have thought that ineffable was not subject to gradation: that to be "most ineffable" is rather like being most pregnant, but never mind. "It is orange dashed with carmine," Celia blushes, "most like the reddest coals of an intensely burning fire." Poppy talk is full of fires and flames. You agree with her wholeheartedly, discreetly lift a glass of punch from her silver tray and keep moving.

Over in another corner, Robert Browning's holding court. You overhear him proclaim "the poppy's red effrontery," at which his clutch of gathered admirers all sigh. You do a quick 180 degree turn, only to run right into Louise Beebe Wilder again. Such a character, Louise. The talk quickly turns from Shirley poppies to California poppies which she describes as "foregathered in blithe haphazardry." Rather than routing everyone within earshot, this peculiar figure of speech attracts Celia Thaxter back over. As dear as she is to all of us, poor Celia can't help herself when it comes to California poppies. She launches immediately into a soliloquy, having first handed you the serving tray so as to leave her hands free for illustrative gesturing. "It is held upright on a straight and polished stem," she tells us, not for the first time, "its petals curving upward and outward into the cup of light, pure gold with a lustrous satin sheen; a rich orange is painted on the gold,"—here she makes delicate painterly gestures—"drawn in infinitely fine lines to a point in the centre of the edge of each petal, so that the effect is that of a diamond of flame in a cup of gold." We've already had Ruskin's warmed rubies, we may as well have Celia's flaming diamonds as well. "It is not enough that the powdery anthers are orange bordered with gold; they are whirled about the very heart of the flower like a revolving Catherine-wheel of fire." She whirls her right hand histrionically, almost spilling the drinks. "In the center of the anthers is a shining point of warm sea-green, a last, consummate touch which makes the beauty of the blossom supreme." She finishes speaking, her uplifted face flushed with rapture. Even Louise is uncharacteristically at a loss for words. You have the disconcerting sense of being out of your depth, floundering in a sea of flaming jewels.

In the cold and sober light of dawn you might be inclined to dismiss all this purple poppy prose as of no consequence. Surely, you say to yourself, horse people or Harley-Davidson people are every bit as fanatical in their enthusiasms, and who's the worse for it? But not so. Like the tormented souls who end up stalking movie stars, poppy admirers soon stumble from devotion into delusion. Opium and field poppies are often their undoing, for these thrive as brilliant itinerants, nomads that wander wherever they will, self-seeding abundantly, hybridizing recklessly and popping up in stunning new colours all over the map. They are a wild bunch, far beyond anyone's control, free spirits that will not tolerate the fusty rituals of horticulture. The less you do for these vagabonds the better.

Fair enough. The only trouble being that admiring gardeners can begin believing that they themselves are kindred free spirits. They tumble headlong into the delusion that they too are colourful gypsies at heart, unfettered by mortgages, careers or compost heaps, free to wander the wild hills and fields, perhaps lingering for a while beneath a shady oak to play the pan pipes and take what beauty they may. There's no need to belabour the point: this is daydreaming of an entirely frivolous and potentially catastrophic sort. Who's looking after the summer pruning while all this merry pipe-playing's going on? Who exactly is picking, shelling and freezing the peas while everyone's off cavorting as free spirits? With a list of chores longer than the road to Mandalay, the gardener risks everything by idle fantasizing about life as a carefree gypsy rover.

A bad end awaits. Flaming silken petals fall in due course from the opium poppies, revealing statuesque seed heads, each balanced like a tiny urn on a tall stalk. Now a seductive danger slithers in as the gardener, long since accepting that the open road of whimsy inevitably curves back around to the potting shed, begins musing on Dryden's "sleepy poppies." Their flowers have carried us to heights of ecstasy scarcely otherwise imaginable. Intoxicated, we now decide, with poor pathetic Coleridge and all the rest, to enter the ancient pleasure dome through a tiny slit in their seed heads. Even Celia Thaxter, of all people, the very embodiment of gardening respectability, found herself under their spell: "I muse over their seed pods," she confided in me as the party was winding down, "those supremely graceful urns that are wrought with such matchless elegance of shape, and think what strange power they hold within. Sleep is there, and Death his brother, imprisoned in those mystic sealed cups."

Best to leave them sealed, Celia darling. Set these precarious yearnings aside. We have glimpsed the splendours of Xanadu in the brief and glowing brilliance of the flower. It is enough. Now go to sleep and dream.

WEEK 31: ARMED AND DANGEROUS

The days have turned searing hot. After the wettest six months ever recorded in these parts, we're now dry as old bones in Death Valley. We are forced to savour the garden after the heat of the day has abated, walking out in the cool of an evening made divine by the perfumes of lilies. As daylight fades, bats slip out from their roosting places and flit about, hunting moths and mosquitoes. Grey ghosts seem to move through the gloaming, ghostly plants that come alive as twilight fades. Thistles and their allies.

187

An old Scottish tale is told of how, one gloomy night in the tenth century, a band of marauding Norsemen sought to capture mighty Staines Castle by stealth. Perhaps more bold than bright, the furtive Norsemen removed their foot-gear to wade through the castle moat. But the moat was dry and rank with prickly thistles. Pricked and pierced beyond enduring, the hapless attackers cried out in agony, rousing the castle, whose defenders swarmed forth and roundly defeated the disadvantaged Norsemen. Thus, in commemoration of this great event, was the lowly thistle exalted to floral emblem of Scotland, inspiration for The Most Noble and Most Ancient Order of the Thistle of Scotland.

Landowners beleaguered by weedy thistles know full well how the routed Norsemen must have felt. Thistles are pugnacious plants, symbolic of defiance and surliness, and the bane of many a mild-mannered gardener. I've just gotten through scything down several threatening patches of them in the arboretum—we leave them as long as possible for the sake of butterflies, but scythe them clean to the ground before they set seed. And as the Staines Castle stalwarts appreciated, not every thistle's a bad thistle. A number of them perform beautifully in the summer garden, and we reluctantly accept that we have turned the corner into high summer when we begin to sing their praises.

For sheer drama and excitement, none quite matches the giant Arabian thistle, *Onopordon arabicum*. They're a near relative of the Scotch thistle—indeed, one burly Scots visitor insisted to me they were Scotch thistles, the very ones planted in a colonnade so that the vacationing Queen

188

may enjoy a view of them from her bedroom windows at Balmoral Castle. Unlike the plodding Norsemen, I know better than to argue with a Scot. At our place, these grey-leafed giants sometimes grow up to ten feet tall. Their glory is in their height and foliage, with enormous silver-grey leaves as sharp as scimitars and etched with white skeletal lines. The stemless leaves grow directly from an upright central stalk. When you touch them the leaves feel crinkly, like old parchment. Their serrated edges bristle with needle-sharp points, and if you back into one while busy in the vicinity, you can get a smart stab in the buttocks for your trouble. The stout centre stem has spiny leaflike growths down its length, like the spikelets along a dinosaur's spine.

By late June or early July these statuesque beauties achieve a pinnacle of splendour. Their inconspicuous flowers begin to open, the flower heads perched on multiple small branchlets at the top of the plant. They're a bit of a joke for a plant so large—even stumpy bull thistles put out bigger blooms. We cut the flowers off to extend the foliar show through July, otherwise the plants fall apart badly after seeding. If you don't cut the heads off, they'll freely self-seed around the garden, but unwanted offspring are easily plucked out, with none of the wrenching agony associated with Canada thistles. Arabian thistles grow as biennials, so that you can transplant juvenile volunteers during their first year. This week I made it my business to pot up a dozen young volunteers which we'll set out in the fall in spots where they'll show to fullest advantage next summer—they're terrific with blue delphiniums and soft pink roses, or skirted with big ornamental alliums. They do all the good things that other silver-grey foliage does, only on an enormous scale. Fully grown, these exotic characters loom in the garden like enormous ghosts in Arabian nights.

Smaller, but every bit as beautiful in twilight, Miss Willmott's Ghost, one of the eryngiums, is not a true thistle at all, but completely thistle-like in manner and appearance. We have one flowering just now alongside a grey granite sculpture of a cloaked woman, Miss Willmott's Ghost trailing behind the woman of stone like a dark silver shadow. The plant has a central stalk of arresting metallic blue-grey, and multiple-flowering shoots. Each flower head, balanced on the top of a shoot, looks like a teacup formed of stiff and finely pointed bracts that arch outwards, their fine edges etched in silvery white. At the centre of the cup, covered in tiny flowers, sits a cone about three inches tall, like a giantess's thimble. At first the cones gleam silvery green, gradually turning blue-grey. This plant too will die after flowering, but for now Miss Willmott's Ghost—named for the renowned British plantswoman—shimmers in the twilight garden with an unearthly beauty.

There are a number of other worthy eryngiums, none quite so dramatic, but some a little easier to keep around. We also have the familiar sea holly, a stiff-branched, thistly perennial that grows almost a metre tall. Hardy, tough and drought-tolerant, it produces spiny, dark green leaves and gorgeous small flower heads like steely blue acorns surrounded by a corona of spiny blue bracts. Up to now, we haven't had the smaller but showier alpine sea holly, but we have about thirty babies in pots, from seed, and great hopes of their joining the show next year. All the eryngiums prefer full sun and will do better in poor dry soil than in rich moist conditions.

The globe thistle, *Echinops,* is another admirable summertime performer just now coming into its own. A hardy perennial, it grows in thick clumps of erect and rigid stalks, about a metre tall, with coarse, prickly, deeply cut, greyish-green leaves. Each stalk is topped by a small, perfectly round steel-blue flower head packed with tiny flowers. Loose clusters of these small metallic blue globes float together in intriguing constellations. We enjoy the play of their blue spheres against the flattened yellow flower heads of nearby yarrows, or in association with echinaceas. Their globes will last long into fall, making a handsome complement to late summer phlox, Michaelmas daisies and rusty Autumn Joy sedums. Bees and butterflies adore their tiny flowers. Globe thistles also prefer a sunny, well-drained spot with sufficient moisture for their summertime surge of growth, after which they're drought-tolerant. If the globes are cut when they first form, they will hold their shape and colour as outstanding dried flowers. A number of forms are available, with the improved "Taplow Blue" favoured for its intensely blue flowers.

And we couldn't have the pipes skirling an anthem to thistly plants without bringing in spiny bear's breech, *Acanthus spinosus.* This is neither a true thistle nor even a

pretend thistle like the eryngiums, but still it has a thistly something or other about it. Its large and arching dark
green leaves are polished and glossy, deeply cut and spiny-
pointed like a thistle's. But its flowers are not—they're
borne on tall and stately spires massed with funnel-shaped
flowers in soft mauve and white. Mauve can be difficult in
flowers, associated in the mind, as Penelope Hobhouse puts
it, with "mourning and middle-aged widows... It becomes
more attractive and positive when its sheen recalls that of
faded satins and velvets, themselves redolent of past riches."
Bear's breech is far from mournful, I think, because the
strong whites in the flower give a contrasting brightness
to its mauve. In any case, the effect is lovely. We have one
grouping at the base of a clematis "Etoile Violette" that
climbs about eight feet up a rough obelisk, then bursts into
a cascade of deep violet blooms just as the acanthus spires
blossom under it. Terribly clever. Another acanthus grows
alongside a villosa hydrangea whose lacecap flowers and
flannel-soft reddish-green leaves provide a lovely contrast
to the polished foliage and stiff spires of the bear's breech.

All very fine indeed. Strolling the gardens of summer,
especially in evening and most especially by moonlight, I
find these various thistly plants create an exotic and mysterious ambience, a thrilling ghostliness, along with a
reassuring sense that, should mischievous Norsemen come
creeping barefoot through the night, they'll get more than
they bargained for.

192

$\mathcal{A}$UGUST

WEEK 32: THE DEVIL FINDS WORK

By the time August waddles onto the stage like a wheezing, sweaty Falstaff, most gardeners have begun to entertain anew the delusion that any day now they will enter, as though by wizardry, into a blissful state of refined and languid leisure. They imagine themselves, correctly fine in dress and person, reclining in their pleasure grounds, unencumbered by all duty save the sweet savouring of the beauty they have wrought. Water trickles and gurgles through ferns in a cooling little trill, while songbirds twitter from the shrubbery. Marvellously, nothing requires soaking or weeding or tending in any way. There is no imperative whatsoever but to relax in dappled shade and have the garden at last repay you in full for your industriousness earlier in the season. "The end of labour is to gain leisure," Aristotle observed, and, although not a strict

Aristotelian, you rejoice in the leisurely end to which your labours have brought you.

Needless to say, such moments of anticipated tranquility require an apt setting. One can hardly contemplate the paradise garden from a plastic chair on the driveway. You really need a loggia or open portico, perhaps a leafy arbour or grotto, a summerhouse or pergola. Which runs you smack up against one of the fundamental drawbacks of August, namely the harsh light it casts upon the inadequacies of your leisure-time infrastructure. Where there ought to be a cupola with Georgian-style benches, sitting upon which one might sip spritzers while discussing matters of high art and world affairs, there is instead a dull-witted deck crammed with derelict barbeque parts and offering only transitory shade under a tatty market umbrella that constantly threatens to topple in the wind.

Until it can be adequately savoured, quality leisure time of the imagined sort must be put on hold temporarily while necessary upgrades to the venue are undertaken. Much thoughtful planning and subsequent heavy labouring are required to construct a summer sanctuary of fitting elegance. Garden design books and magazines are enormously helpful at this stage. You'll see a stunning photograph of a brick wall draped in flowering *Clematis montana,* beneath which a curved marble bench invites one to sit and contemplate the divine. Another photograph shows a cunningly contrived stone outcropping that bids one recline and relax beside a waterfall among the cool green leaves of massed hostas. Or an oaken bench, tucked in an alcove of clipped yew, affords a marvellous view down a central path framed in architectural topiary and leading towards a tantalizingly distant vista.

This sort of inspiration works wonders at our place in overcoming any lax tendencies towards lying about and scratching oneself from boredom. Last year it got us moving on the new deck and summerhouse project at the south end of the garden. We already had a rough-hewn and admittedly eccentric, but perfectly serviceable, all-season house at the north end. It has a deck of sorts attached, draped in fragrant honeysuckle and mock orange. Our handmade deck furniture, while not of polished teak, is sufficiently comfortable for simply sitting down, relaxing and enjoying.

But there's a dreadful ineluctability about the compulsion to continue building new fixtures for leisure, even though the compulsion's folly has been amply demonstrated many times before. Close by the house we have a stone alcove, fashioned by my own blood-stained hands out of the hillside in order to provide a cool grotto into which to retreat during hot summer days. It is carpeted in Scotch and Irish moss, with a small cascade and pool alongside. The idea was to recline on the soft mosses, listening to the gentle plashing of water while sipping a glass of chilled wine and reading Margaret Atwood's latest. Unhappily, our old dog Fen decided in her dotage that this was just the spot wherein she could execute her toiletries

195

and, in the way of old dogs, she'd accept no amount of dissuasion. Even with vigilant pooper-scooping, the thrill of the place as a reclining spot was lost.

Never mind, there were other options. On the eastern side of the garden, a rustic cedar bench, its clunky design softened and silvered through years of elegant weathering, sits beneath a rose arbour looking westward. From here we can view the garden ascending the hillside to the west, its massed blooms backlit beautifully by the afternoon sun. Alternatively, on the crest of the western hillside, another wooden deck looks down across the entire expanse.

At first glance, this might appear to be a sufficient number of resting places for two people. But no, a seasoned gardener scanning the scene would realize straightaway that something is amiss. None of these vantage points affords a view from the southern end of the garden. Many flowers, as we know, like satellite dishes, face due south. From all existing viewpoints, we were seeing them from behind, on their north side, so we'd end up peering over the back of flower heads, as though occupying cheap seats in a crowded opera house.

It simply wouldn't do, so half the yard got disarranged as we busily set about pouring cement footings, heaving great piles of timber about and generally transforming a perfectly settled spot into a tumultuous construction zone. After a few years of this behaviour, you begin to feel like one of those people who live in a state of permanently renovating their home, tormented souls who cannot find contentment without a pile of drywall in the kitchen.

I've already described the gratifying results of the summerhouse project, pleasures that are unquestionably worth the short-term sacrifice. Not that we're spending excessive amounts of time lolling around in the summerhouse on languorous summer afternoons, even though the flowers can now be viewed from their proper south-facing perspective. Because it soon became apparent to us that, looking northwards as it does, this new edifice affords no good views of the moon. Nor do our other leisure spots. And no garden, as everyone realizes, can be considered complete without a properly located moon bench. Plans are already being hatched for a new arbour at the extreme north end of the garden, beneath a big cedar tree. A Kiftsgate rose growing there needs some support anyway, and the arbour will allow it to cascade gracefully, while we'll have a perfect view of the whole garden bathed in moonlight from the rising moon.

Perhaps when that little project's done there'll be some quality leisure time around here, and that could lead into serious discussion of patio accessories. A sling lounge chair might be a bit easier on the old backside than the sturdy mock–Cape Cod lawn chairs I made. A little bistro table with matching chairs would be cute for coffee breaks. Maybe a deacon's bench or a gliding love seat. We've always wanted a hammock—in fact, there's one hanging around here in storage some place, but we've had no opportunity to set it up. How about one of those gas-fired patio heaters with a push-button ignition system, for sitting around outside on a cool evening?

197

I tell you, there's no end of opportunities for leisure just lying around out there waiting to be tapped. You know in your bones that when you finally get around to joining the leisure classes you'll agree wholeheartedly with Cicero: "Leisure consists in all those virtuous activities by which a man grows morally, intellectually and spiritually. It is that which makes life worth living." Yes, I couldn't agree more. It is the end towards which we labour, as Aristotle told us. Meantime the deck looks as though it could really use a fresh coat of stain, and that's a job best done while the weather's still hot and dry. Better put down Margaret Atwood and get on with it.

WEEK 33: OTHERS DON'T LIKE IT HOT

Now the heat's really beginning to build, as we've sweltered through several weeks of cloudless skies with daytime temperatures roaring up into the thirties. These blast-furnace conditions, where one's skin seems to scorch within minutes of exposure, are not my idea of the good old summertime. They ignite in me what I think of as an uncharacteristic grumpiness that can degenerate by mid-afternoon into smouldering misanthropy. I begin ruminating pessimistically about global warming and ozone depletion. I develop murderous resentments towards boneheaded politicians squandering our hard-earned tax dollars on stupidities while the Earth burns. Perversely, I seek out gardening acquaintances who are more than ready to trade in their complaints over the cold, wet spring for updated lamentations about drought and desiccation.

Long after mad dogs and Englishmen have retreated to cooling shade, gardeners can be caught out in the midday sun, moving soaker hoses around, fretting over leaf burn and predicting the end of civilization as we know it. I remember my father, home from his night-shift work, gardening shirtless in the full heat of Toronto summers with his entire back blistered from sunburn.

After repeated warnings about the harmful effects of ultraviolet rays, made worse by thinning of the ozone layer, most of us now know better. Increasingly, gardeners can find themselves trapped between the demands of garden maintenance on the one hand and the prudence of avoiding exposure to ultraviolet sunlight on the other. Living the privileged, if underpaid, life of the self-employed, I normally reserve the quiet early hours of the day for writing; but when the heat wave's on, I rise at dawn and get most of my outdoor chores done before the solar furnace gets fired up. I cherish these lovely early hours in the garden, the plants moistened with silvered dew, the cool air charged with refreshing expectancy. Then, as the heat builds, I retreat to shady sanctuary, in the spirit of Stephen Leacock's "While we welter / In the swelter / Of the Pestilential Heat / Drinking Sodas / In Pagodas / At the Corner of the Street."

Pale of skin and red of thinning hair, I have, when younger and not nearly so wise, suffered enough brutal sunburns to last, or end, a lifetime. I was one of those kids who, when compelled to go to the lake or some wretched outdoor pool, would huddle in the shade swaddled in protective clothing while swarthy boys dove and swam and frolicked in the sunshine with pretty girls. A wallflower longing to become a sunflower, I tried the frolicking thing a few times myself, only to be ignored by the girls and burnt like a potato chip for my trouble.

In recent years, if I had to be out in the sun for any amount of time, I'd wear the gardener's traditional wide-brimmed straw hat, cotton T-shirt and loose cotton pants. But now we're told even that arrangement is insufficient. A typical cotton T-shirt, for example, will prevent sunburn, but will allow 50 per cent of harmful ultraviolet B rays through to the skin, and up to 70 per cent if the shirt is wet (not that most gardeners are into the "wet and wild" T-shirt scene favoured, I'm told, in certain alehouses.) Open-mesh baseball caps and open-weave straw hats—standard issue for many summer gardeners—are equally ineffective. I suppose one can slather oneself in sunscreen and carry on for a bit, but between dirt sticking to oily arms and the sweat of honest labour washing the screen away, it's not exactly a long-term solution. For the right price, you can get a designer outfit fashioned from certified sun-protective fabrics, but even absolute personal protection doesn't answer the really big question facing us, namely: What are these confounded ozone holes doing to my precious plants? Most gardeners, I think, would uncomplainingly endure the risk of malignant melanomas if they were certain that their irises weren't languishing as well.

This year I think our plantings are staggering from a double whammy: long periods of unseasonably cool and moist conditions suddenly interspersed with clear days of mercilessly scorching sun. The plants are caught, like unfortunate youngsters cursed with a parent who swings between affection and rage for no discernible reason. The only good news in all of this is that any leaf-burn, die-back, yellowing, bark-cracking or other mishap may now be conveniently blamed on global climate change rather than on one's own ineptitude.

Having created the ozone-depleting agents of our undoing, science is now plodding along to catalogue their consequences. Most of the underfunded research being done in the field is directed towards the impact increased UV-B is having on food crops. That's the type of ultraviolet radiation reaching ground level with greater intensity as the ozone shield perforates. (Here I do want to acknowledge being conscious of coming across as a bit of a zealot on the topic, perhaps embodying Winston Churchill's definition of a fanatic as "one who can't change his mind and won't change the subject." So I won't.) Several trends of interest to plant people are already evident. Some plants, it seems, are much more sensitive than others to ultraviolet radiation, and there's a remarkable range of sensitivity among different species and among cultivars of the same species. The "most sensitive" category includes members of the pea and bean families, the squash and melon families, especially cucumbers, and the mustard and cabbage families.

Researchers tell us that effects can include impaired photosynthesis and leaf chemistry, plant stunting, increased branching, leaf discoloration, reduced biomass and diminished seed yield. One study of cucumbers exposed to 12 per cent ozone loss—a frequent occurrence already across Canada—showed a reduction of leaf size of about 20 per cent, with the plants being far more sensitive to drought stress. At ozone depletion of 20 per cent, soybeans showed chlorosis on their leaves, indicating destruction of chlorophyll. Flower production and viability of pollen were also impaired. Fungal infections—of which we're enduring more than our fair share this foul, wet year—appear to increase with greater UV-B exposure. Water-stressed plants seem to have lower UV-B sensitivity than well-watered ones, as do phosphorous-deficient plants, so it may be wise to hold on the soaker hoses and the epsom salts.

Certain plants appear to be better than others at protecting themselves or repairing damage from radiation. One defence mechanism involves producing compounds, called flavonids, in the upper epidermis of the leaf tissue, that prevent harmful rays from penetrating deeper. Plant breeders and biotechnicians, indefatigable improvers by nature, are now seeking to manipulate plants for higher UV-B tolerance, just as they've done for disease resistance and higher yields. One expert in the field, Dr. Alan Teramura of the University of Hawaii, writes that "either by using conventional breeding practices or by using some molecular techniques and biotechnology, we might be able to mitigate some of the damaging effects of ultraviolet radiation on crop plants. However, this type of breeding around the problem is not an option for native plants. It is not an option, probably, for forest tree species. It is possible only for crops." Another band-aid is to grow uv-sensitive plants under glass because it blocks ultraviolet radiation.

"In the full furnace of this hour," wrote poet Archibald Lampman, marking a Canadian heat wave a century ago, "my thoughts grow keen and clear." In mid–heat wave, gardeners can become remarkably keen and clear about new projects aimed at cooling down the landscape. With science advising us to expect increasing levels of ultraviolet radiation through the foreseeable future, it's a good idea to study the sun-soaked garden carefully to determine where shade from trellises, bowers or other structures might help make the midday garden a little more livable for people, plants and creatures. The planting of shade trees in particular takes on a greater urgency than in other seasons. For several consecutive summers we've been planning to introduce some high shade over our gardens, only to abandon the scheme each winter as unnecessary. But things came to a rolling boil one scorching mid-afternoon this week when I was touring the gardens with a distinguished visitor. "Don't you think you should get some dappled shade onto this garden?" my broiling guest suggested with a singular lack of tact. And of course we should, and will this coming autumn, blast me if we don't. We've decided that a half-dozen Skyline honey locusts, strategically placed to create pools of filtered shade along pathways, should shelter us from taking any more heat from sizzling visitors. Meanwhile, torrid letters to the editor about myopic politicians and the environmental costs of rampant consumerism are a time-honoured way of venting during the blistering and grumpy days of summer.

WEEK 34: NIGHT-CLUB LADIES

It's still too darn hot, but by supper hour a lovely quality of light and air shimmers across the clearing, enticing us to get outdoors. When we emerge as creatures of the evening the garden is divine. As often as not, I'll find myself at dusk doing a spot of hand watering, in part because some plants are parched as mad prophets in the desert, but also for the sheer pleasure of being in the garden. A hushed, rich fullness descends, intoxicating fragrances perfume the air, and the plants exhale a cooling freshness after the heat of the day. Nighthawks skim across the evening sky and bats skitter in and out of sight like fragments of dark dreams.

204

For the past few weeks the trumpet lilies have reigned over this twilight time, their intense perfumes lingering on currents of warm air. These are the flowers of Hera, goddess of the moon and childbirth, and the sacred symbol of Britomartis, whom the Minoans five thousand years ago revered as Great Mother. Lilies sprang from the milk of Juno, spilled from her engorged breasts as she nursed the infant Hercules. And grew as well from the tears of Eve when, expelled from the Garden of Eden, she realized she was with child. They stood in a vase (if medieval artists are to be believed) near the Virgin Mary when the angel Gabriel appeared unto her announcing her immaculate conception. Lilies are the sacred flowers of motherhood and fecundity; an evening garden fragrant with their scent is a place mysterious with female secrets, where ancestral memories waft about whispering of virgins, goddesses and the wonders of fertility rites.

Understandably intoxicated, and a bit mad at the best of times, lily fanciers have taken this venerable fertility symbolism as carte blanche to engage in a hybridizing binge of mind-boggling dimensions. Everyone, it sometimes seems, is out in the potting shed busily propagating and hybridizing lilies: there are now more than seven thousand registered lilies and God knows how many more living beyond the registry. "Within the last few years," wrote Bebe Miles some years ago, "the number of strains and clones offered has increased to the point where a lily catalogue is a bewildering array, even to the experienced lily grower. For the gardener who just wants a few lilies, the situation is rapidly reaching a point of no return." Like an innocent bystander caught in the crossfire of a gangland turf war, a bemuddled gardener is almost required, as Miles puts it, "to take a course in genetics before choosing a dozen lilies." Unchaperoned by any competent classification system, this hybridizing binge predictably provoked fierce disputes over names and categories, reminding us that lilies also adorned the lion frieze in the Nineveh palace of the mighty Assyrian warlord Assurbanipal.

But like the Assyrian Empire, our trumpet lilies have faded now, leaving their unsightly sticks to feed the bulbs for next year. Several other plants, each an evening star in its own right, have stepped into the breach. None is as lovely as the lily in daytime—in fact, the three replacement plants I have in mind hang about all afternoon looking non-descript and vapid, like bored teens outside a 7-Eleven. But by evening they come into their own, none of them with more élan than the common evening primrose. A metre or more tall, with coarse, hairy leaves and stems, this wild-ling has little to commend it by day, but come early evening, it puts on a spectacular show. One by one its new flower heads, scrolled like cheap cigars, begin to tremble and unfurl. Hints of yellow appear, as when a sulphur butter-fly emerges from its puparium. The flower seems to pause for a moment and then in a sudden swirl of movement unfurl fully to a beautiful pale yellow trumpet. Here's how American plantswoman Helen Field Fisher described this exceptional moment: "[S]urely no flower is more dramatic in its opening. Like glamorous night-club ladies its blos-soms wait for exactly the right light effects in sunset colors, then suddenly throw back their green cloaks and swirl wide the skirts of their golden evening gowns." Fisher goes on to say that the genus name, *Oenothera*, means "wine scented" and that "when the heady fragrance of these flowers floats across the garden, the night moths quickly gather."

Evening primroses are a native biennial that was long dismissed as "common." Some gardening encyclopedias still don't bother to mention it, and one discounts it as "a weedy plant growing over much of the U.S." and of passing interest only because "the root was eaten as a vegetable by Indians." It's yet another of the North American wildflowers that needed to go to Europe to get a pedigree. There it found a place of prominence in discriminating gardens, so that Penelope Hobhouse praises its "pale yellow flowers glowing at dusk" and recommends a "haphazard natural seeding" alongside blue ceanothus or purple-leaved *Cotinus*.

I doubt that our second star, evening scented stocks, have ever stuck their noses into a nightclub, and certainly they've never made sensational entrances in a swirl of golden skirts. Scrawny little annuals from the mustard family, native to southeastern Europe and Asia, these are not what you'd call charismatic plants. Working hastily along the front of a border, I've sometimes almost torn them out as weeds, what with their scraggly little lance-shaped leaves and inconspicuous purple flowers. They're fussy little customers, too. If allowed to become root-bound in pots in spring, they may refuse to bloom later on. Planted out, they require frequent watering, full sun and rich soil. Even when pampered, during the heat of day they seem to have an air of truculent defeat which, cowering in the shade myself, I feel is not entirely inappropriate. But what a transformation when you step out of an evening and experience their heady scents floating through

207

the garden. It's hard to believe that the puny flowers can produce such abundant perfume and cast it so widely. Evening-scented stocks are spindly, little, one-trick ponies, but their single trick is sensational.

A third star in the twilight garden, nicotiana is not as drab by day as the other two, but still at its finest in the gloaming. Sometimes called "flowering tobacco," it's a member of the often-disreputable nightshade family. Most commonly planted are strains of *Nicotiana alata,* which in the wild grows about a metre tall with large, fragrant white blooms that open at dusk. It's been hybridized extensively—though not with the same devil-take-the-hindmost frenzy as lilies. Varieties now bear flowers that remain open by day as well as night in a spectrum of colours including pure white, an appealing lime green, cream, salmon, rose and red, all the way out to crimsons and purples. However these "improvements" come at a cost— reduction or loss of fragrance. For evening scent especially, growers recommend Grandiflora, which has large white flowers shaded yellow that show well at twilight.

With lots of space available, we prefer big *Nicotiana sylvestris,* a native of Argentina that sometimes stands two metres tall, muscular with large tobacco-like leaves. Its slender tubular white flowers hang in tiered clusters and are tailor-made for hummingbirds. A bit downcast-looking on hot summer days, it perks up in the late afternoon, emitting a fine fragrance and assuming a stately grandeur that in Hobhouse's opinion makes it "almost as beautiful as a lily." The nicotianas continue flowering until frost.

We've had sylvestris survive the occasional mild winter to bloom again—nicotianas are perennial in warmer climes but treated as annuals in our northern gardens.

With lilies to pick up the slack after the antique roses and honeysuckles have finished their big flush, and these three scented stars to carry on after many of the regal lilies have lost their crowns, and with summer phlox, snakeroot and others still to come, the evening garden blessedly remains a haunt of intriguing scents right through the blistering weeks of high summer.

WEEK 35: MID-LIFE CRISIS

These are the dog days of summer when people living normal lives generally have the good sense to take things slow and easy; they'll head to the cottage or beach, or simply flop down on the back porch to guzzle cold beer. This is as it should be, but unfortunately not how it usually is for gardeners, because along with the regular chores there comes as well, inescapable as yellow jackets at a picnic, an imperative to make some hard-nosed decisions. For, by August, the garden's shortfalls have become unarguable. In May, one can beguile oneself with assurances that the best is yet is to come, that problems will correct themselves once the annuals fill in or some other miracle occurs. By August, we know, the age of miracles is over.

There may be disappointments aplenty: ridiculously misplaced plants, leering gaps and black spots, shrieking colour clashes, unaccountable die-back or a general wiltedness that betokens serious lack of spunk on the part of certain plants. On the worst of the dog days, the garden may seem an incontrovertible disaster. The days may simply be too bloody hot for reasonable thinking and one would be better off reading a Danielle Steele and admitting that life has its limitations. Or it could be that one is entering a mid-life crisis in the garden. I didn't even know there was such a thing until I picked up a book titled *Growing Pains: Time and Change in the Garden* by Patricia Thorpe. But there it was in plain black and white: I and several million other gardeners, it seems, have entered a phase of entirely predictable crisis.

A garden, like life, in Ms. Thorpe's intriguing analysis, passes through a series of stages. Starting a garden, she writes, is a little like starting a love affair. You can coast for a while on all the early excitement and enthusiasm. How true that is. Remember those intoxicating days of wine and roses, before you'd ever heard of crown canker. The carefree bliss of life before botrytis blight. The unalloyed joy of believing that perennials are plants that live forever. Like lovers in springtime, we planted with carefree abandon, heedless of future consequences.

210 Thereafter, according to Thorpe, we entered a second stage—what she calls the years of encouragement—when our plantings hit full stride, and the successes of several seasons inspired a phase of bullish expansionism. We stretched ourselves boldly to the very borders of our properties, some of us even spilling over onto sidewalks and public boulevards, where we had no legal right to be. Artificial boundaries could not constrain a vision as grand

as ours, no hedge was so high that we could not bound over it acrobatically to sow our wild seeds wherever we wanted.

All across North America over the last twenty years, Thorpe writes, more people embarked on more ambitious garden making with less information and less help than at any time in the last two centuries. A similar wave of enthusiasm for gardening swept across the continent in the first three decades of this century. The difference being that back then there were still plenty of skilled growers around to dispense advice, and, as well, there was a ready supply of experienced labour. Today, by bleak comparison, we have only the labour of our own love. Gazing out now through the heat haze at your vast expanse of gardening experimentation, you find yourself seeing only mistakes and terrible miscalculations. Monstrous plants running rampant. Obscene-colour cat fights. Everything a jingle-jangle. No coherence. No unity of theme. No proper proportions. Disasters in every direction.

You have entered the third stage—what Thorpe calls the "years of crisis." Having known so much once, you now recognize how very little you know of all there is to know about gardening. "You are," writes Thorpe, "poised between the garden of your fantasies and your slowly accumulating knowledge of what you may actually achieve some day." Add to this an awareness that aging muscles and bones cannot quite do what they did so vigorously twenty years ago, and you have the preconditions of despair.

What's to be done?

Rather than retiring to a hammock with a good novel and a cool drink, as would any reasonable person under the circumstances, gardeners insist upon trying to set things right. They begin making plans for next year's garden so as to avoid the deficiencies of this one. If trees, shrubs and perennials are in the wrong places and needing to be transplanted in the fall, the reasoning goes, then we'd better decide now where they're going to be relocated. All apparently prudent, of course, except that the heat of summer is not a prime time for decision making, as tempers are apt to fray more quickly than usual. Raised voices in the August garden usually indicate a decision-making session gone sour.

Or indecision seizes certain gardeners. They hesitate, they vacillate, they shilly-shally. They reread their Vita Sackville-West and Gertrude Jekyll, those larger-than-life gardeners who could thrill to a summer border splendid with a foreground planting of pale mauve verbena, clouds of white gypsophila, violet-blue *Salvia pratensis* and pink-white spires of *Acanthus spinosus*. Oh, why can't I too do something clever like that? the vacillators ask, eventually concluding that life is unfair and they themselves are abject failures.

Other gardeners exhibit a formidable decisiveness. They are resolute and determined, free of hesitation. "We'll dig that beauty bush out in October and put it over there," they'll announce to whoever will listen. This bravado is great if you actually know what you're doing. Or don't care. Some gardeners don't give two hoots about the highblown principles of garden design and never will. "I just squeeze plants in wherever there's a bit of room—I'm a shove it in and love it kind of gardener," one woman told me recently. And, most important, she was entirely happy with her haphazard results.

Sandy and I fall into a third category which might be called the Gut Reaction Approach to garden design. It involves plopping plants in at random during the dormant season, then waiting to see what summertime serendipity happens by way of composition. Our experience with a Dortmund rose exemplifies the method. The first year our Dortmund flowered, it produced luminous trusses of a brilliant red that seemed somehow evocative of a Nevada brothel. "That rose will have to go," we said, "it's just too too." That fall poor Dortmund got unceremoniously booted to a distant corner. The following summer her generous blooms seemed altogether more appealing than they had, provoking a decision to move her back into the inner sanctum again. Another year or two we decided to banish her once more for causing such a commotion among the soft pinks and yellows. Poor Dortmund became our version of a migrant worker, forever on the move and never properly appreciated.

213

The fundamental problem here, of course, is that these critical determinations about plant placement often must include the opinions of other parties. If one were free to decide on one's own, things undoubtedly would be easier. But no, some decision making requires a protracted period of discussion, with the sun belting down and tempers running short, then sudden squalls erupting over who is or isn't listening to whom.

Post-decision trauma can also be a factor. Decisions made but not written down can blur over time and eventually lack any sense of decisiveness. "I'm really delighted we decided to put the *Tilia cordata* over by the garage, aren't you, dear?" The rhetorical question, framed a few weeks after the fact, may be met by a stony silence indicating that that's what *you* wanted, but it wasn't what was decided at all. Changes of heart are another matter. Some gardeners begin reconsidering their decisions mere moments after making them. "I don't know about that gunnera after all," they'll murmur—this subsequent to a harrowingly protracted decision-making ordeal, which only recently concluded with a firm commitment to place the gunnera just there.

Personally I'm inclined to not discuss any of these matters in the heat of summer. Far preferable, it seems to me, to await transplanting time in the fall, then make harum-scarum last-minute decisions as you're dashing about trying to get everything settled in before winter. Meanwhile a cold beer on the porch strikes me as a mighty fine idea. From that mellow vantage point, one can philosophize at length about how a garden's mid-life crisis is really an opportunity, a transition period, a time of reassessment and replanting that will eventually result in a more mature garden of enhanced loveliness. A knowledgeable plantsperson like oneself readily accepts that all gardens require a systematic remaking every decade or so, and none of it is a cause for panic.

After the breakdown and tears of mid-life crisis, after the summoning up of new courage and the development of new visions, the gardener reconnects with the essential truth of the craft—that it is the actual doing of it that's important, the mucking about with soil and seeds, pushing boulders uphill, bending plants to our will and bending ourselves to the willful ways of plants. Fitting ourselves into the lay of the land and the blowing of the wind. It is the long-term process of making a garden that we must love if we are to persist. And persist we must, those of us with real sap running in our veins, because, really, what else is there to do?

WEEK 36: SUMMER WHITES

Friends were regaling us not long ago with tales of their adventures last year in some of the great English gardens including, naturally, the white garden at Sissinghurst. There they considered themselves fortunate not to have been trampled underfoot by the crush of sightseers jostling for the perfect camera angle. Our friends' photos of the event show throngs of unlikely looking gawkers milling around a few bewildered white plants. Nevertheless, white gardens remain quite fashionable, and generous use of white in planting schemes is usually rewarding, never more so than in the late summer garden.

It's easy to understand why seasoned gardeners may lose their heads over whites. For one thing, they're splendidly versatile: they can light up a gloomy corner; in repetition they can bring a sense of unity, even of formality, to what otherwise might be a hopeless hodgepodge of hues; they can mediate between and reconcile fiercely clashing colours, and through the subtle tricks of contrast give strength to nearby pallid colours. At twilight and by moonlight the whites shine with a thrilling luminescence. Especially in late summer, white foliage and flowers can create an atmosphere of cool and refreshing spaciousness, a soothing interlude between the blazing reds and yellows of high summer and the flaming tones of autumn.

At our place just now, a Huldine clematis draped over the rose arbour spills a lovely mantle of cupped white flowers, each with a faint mauve blush and soft green centre. In the dappled shade of a small crabapple tree, oak-leaved hydrangeas are blooming with large panicles of ivory-white flowers. Out in full sun, a drift of summer phlox creates a brilliant shining snowbank of white bloom, while the Matilija poppy still displays a few of its enormous flowers of pure white crinkled petals around a centre of golden yellow stamens. These big beauties are main-stage performers, feature attractions that wouldn't be out of place at Sissinghurst itself if only there were sufficient room.

But there's another, far more subtle, group of whites at work in the garden now—plants whose beauty lies in masses of much smaller flowers that create frothy inflorescences against which other plants show to greater advantage. Alongside the main pathway we have a charming small composition featuring the little pink rose The

Fairy reclining against fluffy white pillows of The Pearl and of baby's breath. These frothy fillers' work is to frame the rose, to give it a setting that will enhance the beauty of its blooms, like bridesmaids gathered around a blushing bride. The Pearl is a sturdy old favourite with an extended summer blooming that can light up any garden. Although it's a yarrow, it doesn't have the flat-headed boot-camp brush cut of most yarrows, but rather a galaxy composed of multiple miniature white globes that create an airy effect. Notwithstanding its dainty appearance, this perennial is a workhorse, hardy in all zones, tolerant of drought and an exuberant spreader in moist ground. Even in our dryland conditions, it spread to the point of a few pearls too many, giving the appearance of all foils and few features. We began to rogue it out a year or two ago, but left enough to still shine brightly, like Herrick's "A girle, Rubie-lipt and toothed with pearl."

The other, even frothier foil is the familiar baby's breath. This hardy member of the pink family is beloved by florists for good reason: its many-branched panicles bear thousands of tiny white flowers, creating a silvery mist that seems to wrap itself with airy grace around larger plants and coarser leaves. "See-through flowers," Vita Sackville-West called them, while Gertrude Jekyll praised the "grey-white clouds" of their inflorescences. Patrick Lima describes the single-flowered types as "ethereal to the vanishing point" and recommends the grafted double cultivars Bristol Fairy and Snowflake. Hardy to zone three, gypsophila loves sun, sweet earth and good drainage. Its deep taproot sustains it through extended drought, but makes transplanting next to impossible. Soggy ground is its nemesis, and we often lose a few plants during particularly wet winters.

Just behind this composition, a drift of gooseneck lysimachia appears to have gathered like a gaggle of inquisitive geese. A native of western Asia, sometimes called Japanese loosestrife, this hardy perennial has sturdy stems with dusty green leaves, each stem culminating in an elegant taper of small starry white flowers that resembles the neck and head of a goose. A solid performer in the mixed border or wild garden, it enjoys moist and fertile ground and will droop disheartedly if it gets too dry. In damp conditions its foliage remains strong after flowering. Anyone who has kept geese knows that they are creatures of great merit and an independence that borders on insubordination. Gooseneck lysimachia's the same: given free reign, it'll wander into places where it's not wanted and cause mischief. It's at its best in large drifts, where the illusion of a gaggle is created, and kept from wandering.

White mugwort is not a name to conjure images of slender elegance, but it's the common name for *Artemisia lactiflora,* another Asian beauty closely related to The Pearl. Most garden artemisias are aromatic herbs with finely cut silver leaves and undistinguished flowers. But lactiflora (literally "milk-white" and also called "ghost plant") is altogether different, having dark green leaves and attractive flowers. Attractive to some, I should say. "Once I purchased

218

nine *Artemisia lactiflora*," sniffed American plantswoman Helen Van Pelt Wilson, "and found myself in possession of something very near a weed." In August it produces flowering stalks about two metres tall that bear creamy plumes of tiny ivory-tinged flowers. Again, these are not spectacular in themselves but make pleasing companions to other plants. Penelope Hobhouse recommends placing them alongside gleaming yellows which can subtly connect to green leaves in a way that pure white flowers couldn't, or including the artemisias in a blue-and-grey colour scheme where they can enhance pure bright blues. We've got several growing alongside a thalictrum of matching height whose airy clusters of powdery blue flowers go wonderfully with the ivory artemisia flowers.

Behind them in this composition of big perennials with small flowers towers the great black snakeroot. A stately late summer bloomer native to woodlands from New England to Tennessee, it is sometimes called Cohosh bugbane. Its slender flowering stems reach two metres or more, producing multiple slim towers composed of many pearl-white buds and tiny flowers, conjuring miniature steeples massed in a mountain village. Like all these airy summer whites, snakeroot combines a graceful appearance with a vigourous constitution. It prefers rich, moist acidic soil and partial shade, though ours is thriving in full sun.

There is something intrinsically appealing about all these small-flowered beauties, especially their lending of themselves for the benefit of other nearby plants.

Living as we do on Planet Hollywood, where vulgar self-promotion pushes itself forward past humility and benefi-cence, these tiny-flowered summer whites provide a refreshing reminder of the considerable charms of sim-plicity and selflessness.

SEPTEMBER

WEEK 37: BLIGHTED LIVES

Terrible developments in the vegetable patch: an attack of late blight has come down upon us like the wrath of Jehovah. Almost overnight, dozens of tomato vines, heavy with large green fruits, were laid waste. Common in other locations as well, these blights have become a bane of West Coast vegetable growers. They spring like the scions of Lucifer from fungi that thrive in cool and humid conditions. Their target plants are of the nightshade family—tomatoes and potatoes. We know that tomato growers generally face adversity of some sort or other— blossom-end rot, freak frosts before harvest, or giant tomato hornworms defoliating whole vines overnight. But none seems more malignant, nor more dispiriting, than these vile blights. Growers suffering from an attack give every indication of serious mental disorder. Some have a wild-eyed and dishevelled look about them, as though they'd run away from home and been drinking cheap whisky far into the night.

Two different blights, twin virulences, assail us. The first, sensibly called early blight, strikes around mid-July, blackening everything in its path, like Sherman marching towards Atlanta. If this one gets a toehold in the garden, there's little opportunity for hope. You salvage what new potatoes you can and dust off grandma's recipes for green-tomato-everything. Soon after, the second shoe drops as late blight descends to finish the evil work its sinister twin began. Plants yellow and die overnight. In potatoes, the fungus spreads inwards through the tubers, sometimes in collocation with bacteria, causing an evil-smelling soft rot.

In calm moments, one realizes that there's no end of pests and diseases that assail gardeners everywhere—powdery scab, root-knot nematodes, fusarium yellows and all the rest. But a strong case could be made that none is so disheartening, none so repugnant and hateful as this poxy pair of blights. What agony to stand helplessly by while your potato and tomato vines develop dark blotches on their leaves, which almost overnight wither to a twisted black and rot, to behold your half-ripened tomatoes turn to a disgusting mush before you've had even one succulent juicy mouthful—oh, what a vile, filthy and dreadful disease this is! This fungal curse come to blight our lives like some gruesome fate inflicted by malignant spirits.

222

Small wonder that we veggie growers have a desperate look about us nowadays.

Our potatoes went down first, in mid-July. Despite my old dad's repeated admonition that a substantial potato patch is the cornerstone of economic security, the advancing blights of recent years have forced us to trim our patch drastically. Grudgingly, we content ourselves with two trenches, perhaps thirty plants in all, for summer and fall eating. I planted Pontiacs for the early crop and Yukon Golds for later, in a bed where neither potatoes nor tomatoes had grown before. Though the cool, moist spring was ideal potato-growing weather, the Yukon Golds succumbed in July. Their leaves developed small dark brown areas which rapidly multiplied to cover the whole plant. Within days the tops lay withered and twisted on the ground. Right alongside, the Pontiacs were not near so badly infected, nor were the tomatoes, off in separate beds. I'd planted mostly early-fruiting tomato varieties—Oregon and Oregon Spring, which were developed for our coastal climate, and Sweet Million cherry tomatoes, which had in the past shown themselves somewhat resistant to blight.

"Cover your tomatoes," the radio garden show experts warned us all summer. As in any wartime situation, dark rumours spread like wildfire through that portion of the gardening community assailed by blight. It's in the soil, some whisper. No, it's floating in the air, others tell you. The rain carries the spores, or whatever they are, some insist. Not quite right, another expert adds, it's raindrops hitting infected ground that splashes the disease up onto the plants. On and on they debate the matter, long into the early hours, like insomniacs on all-night talk radio.

Approaching blights sound a call to arms, and one wants to believe that no gardener—least of all a vegetable grower—will lay down her tools and refuse to fight. But, as in any other group, we have our share of defeatists and idealistic idlers. "Perhaps we won't get it this year," some tell themselves, surrendering to gross denial unconvincingly dressed up as optimism. "Well, what can you do about it anyway?" others snivel. "Whatever happens, happens." This is the Neville Chamberlain approach to blight—all very well meaning and gentlemanly, but in the end disastrous—and most gardeners will have none of it. Green and gentle creatures by and large, when threatened from without, stout-hearted gardeners harden into Winston Churchill, ready to fight them on the beaches, fight them in the potato trenches, and fight them on the raised beds of history.

Thus it is that even in this dark hour, when early blight has already done its deadly work and late blight descends to polish us off, gardeners are counterattacking with an ingenuity that excites both astonishment and awe. Some have confined their tomato vines indoors, like children too tender to be sent out into a rough-and-tumble world. Others have thrown up greenhouses of questionable sturdiness to deflect the black rain of blight. Some have more modest little plastic tents beneath which their tomatoes huddle like campers waiting out a deluge. Clever characters have encased each tomato plant in a perforated designer plastic bag, as though they'd taken their vines to the dry cleaners.

In extreme cases, even more desperate measures have been resorted to. Although we generally keep it to ourselves, we've known all along that certain gardeners are easy prey for peddlers of quack cures. They are naifs, ever ready to put their faith in mail-order miracles or the healing touch of charlatans. Thus it was that last year a shocking number of growers fell victim to the false hopes of copper. I imagine this coppery hoax must have started from the traditional use of copper spray against blight. Word of copper's magical properties was whispered everywhere, like an urban legend, until it assumed a mystique of near-mythic proportions. Otherwise quite reasonable people took to piercing the stems of their tomato vines with lengths of copper wire in the forlorn hope that the plant would absorb healing copper into its system and thereby repulse fungal spores. I was fervently urged to do the same myself, then rudely mocked as a cynic when I declined. Zealotry inflamed by desperation seldom remembers its manners. Shamelessly, certain growers heaped copper amulets around the base of their plants, like devotees of some bizarre horticultural cargo cult. It seemed appropriate at the time not to comment on these peculiar rituals, lest offence be taken, but some were being conducted with such fervent intensity it really was hard to keep a straight face at times.

This year I've heard no talk of copper at all—it must have moved on, as these things do in the course of miracles.

But the blight is still with us. Some friends began reporting serious crop losses during the summer. By mid-August we began bringing in ripening tomatoes. Then several days of wind and rain in late August and all was lost. Scattered in three separate beds, virtually every vine developed dark mottling on their leaves and stems. The still-green tomatoes showed grey-green splotches under their skin; these quickly turned darker, like bruises from a brutal beating. Desperately we clipped away infected leaves and fruit and carried them off to be burnt. A few plants continued producing sound fruit, and those in the greenhouse were fine, but within a few days most of the outdoor vines had withered completely, their fruits hanging forlornly like Christmas ornaments on a long-dead tree. We've had to tear the whole works out and burn them. No great pots of homemade tomato sauce to get us through this winter; no organic dried tomatoes to spice up winter salads, no homemade salsa. Oh, woe!

"With blight," Sandy said in a dispirited moment, "there's either fight or flight, and I'm for flight." That's heresy to us Churchillians, of course, but perhaps she's right—there is, after all, a limit to how much time and effort one wants to devote even to tomatoes. These are dark reflections, I know, at what should be a time of celebrating the bountiful harvest. But not so dark as the gloomy hours of blight, standing out on a corpse-littered battlefield, the stench of rotting tubers and fruit in our nostrils, the foul black rain still falling.

WEEK 38: AMUSING OBERON

A flock of garrulous chickadees splashing in the little pools of our cascade this morning drew my attention to the maidendhair ferns growing down the bank alongside the cascade. I was startled at how the pale green fern fronds appeared to be scorched along their lips from the sun. But on closer inspection I realized that the brown tips were actually spore cases along the rim of each frond. The frond edges, rather than burnt, were curled over to protect the little cases, like cabbage leaves rolled in Lilliputian perogies.

I think the northern maidenhair fern is one of our loveliest natives. You can find it growing wild from Alaska clear across to Newfoundland, more often than not alongside mountain brooks and wild streams. Their shiny purplish-black stems and delicate fronds fanned out like miniature palm trees are especially beautiful when misted by the splash of falling waters. Its sister species, the sublime "hair of Venus" was among the great magic plants of Roman mythology. Its elegant fronds, which shimmer with a silvery sheen when placed under water, evoke the goddess of beauty and love, she who arose glittering and splendid from the foam of the sea.

Magic symbolism comes naturally to ferns, which alone is reason enough to include them in our gardens. Before scientific inquiry finally unlocked the mysteries of fern reproduction, it was believed that the plants produced

227

seeds on only one night of the year, Midsummer Eve. The seeds were highly prized for the magical property of making their bearer invisible. Oberon himself, king of the fairies, derived his invisibility from the seeds and was fiercesome in defence of his secret, driving off other would-be seed-gatherers.

The scientific explanation is almost as arcane. The tiny spore cases that attracted my attention this morning are called sporangia. They form along the tips or undersides of fronds, each containing many hundreds of spores. A single fern may bear thousands of sporangia clustered in distinctive patterns called sori. This is a plant poised for massive reproductive possibilities. When the sporangia burst, multitudes of spores explode as a fine dust into the air. When I brush past the big western sword ferns that are a native groundcover in our woodlands, they throw up clouds of rusty dust at spore-bearing time. Wafted along, fortunate spores alight on moist ground. There they develop into a heart-shaped, fascinating little plant called a prothallium. This peculiar growth looks nothing at all like a fern. The prothalium is a true hermaphrodite, producing both sperm and eggs. The sperm are fantastic swimmers, thrashing strenuously through the depths of drops of dew or rain water. A successful sperm fertilizes an egg and thus is conceived yet another growth, this one called a sporophyte, which eventually grows into the plant we recognize as a fern. Given this arcane double play of a reproduction process, it's little wonder our sturdy fore-

228

bears put the whole business down to the concealments of darkling fairies.

Nevertheless, the process is astonishingly efficient. Ferns are one of Earth's most ancient plant forms, thriving on our planet for more than 350 million years. They were at their most spectacular in the Carboniferous period when huge ferns towered as tall as modern trees, a time remembered as the Age of Ferns. Although the great fern forests are no more, their descendants still grow all over the globe in spectacular diversity. Occupying a fertile middle ground between the simplicity of ancient mosses and liverworts and the complexity of more recent seed plants, ferns have adapted themselves to an astonishing range of conditions: growing under rocks in scorching deserts, underwater, high on mountain sides and well north of the Arctic Circle. Over half the known species are tropicals, including big tree ferns, some of them familiar to us from fern bars or the homes of compulsive misters. About 360 species are native to North America, particularly concentrated on the damp West Coast and in the humid northeast.

At our place, having a splendid show of ferns is a complete no-brainer, as we're surrounded by them on all sides. Along with the delicate maidenhairs and the big evergreen sword ferns, we have the lovely deciduous lady fern, whose vase of lacy and graceful bright green fronds stands more than a metre tall. The little evergreen deer fern huddles on the floor of dark woods and the adventuresome licorice fern roosts in mossy niches high up in craggy bigleaf maples. Bracken fern—gorgeous after the first frosts have polished it rusty gold in woodland glades—is a nuisance otherwise, with deep-running roots, forever popping up where it's not wanted.

It seems to me ferns belong in almost any garden, in part for their magic, of course, but also for their adaptability. Many do best in shady, moist and acidic conditions, so they're naturals in any respectable shade garden. Others are perfectly suited to stony, sunny and dry places. The shade-loving species, by far the majority, are invaluable in woodland plantings, either in massed groupings of ferns alone or as foils for other foliage plants and flowers. I love how the delicate fronds of the maidenhair fern play against the large glossy leaves of hostas or bergenias; or the whopping big gunnera, stout as a sumo champion, foiled beautifully by the lacy fronds of lady ferns.

Once established, ferns need little attention other than watering during periods of drought and perhaps a bit of cleaning up at season's end. Their roots tend to be quite near the soil surface, so some care must be taken in cultivating around plants. A mulch of peat moss, leaf mould or compost in spring and fall helps protect roots and conserve moisture. Many are easy to transplant and divide. We move them around like furniture, especially the big sword ferns which initially covered our garden site. When we were clearing the area, we dug them out with a grub hoe and spade, then grabbed a handful of leathery fronds and dragged the huge root balls into the woods for replanting.

After getting themselves straightened out, the transplants settled right in and soon looked as though they'd been growing in that very spot since before dinosaurs passed this way. They are one of the few plants that will thrive handsomely in the inhospitable conditions underneath western red cedars and bigleaf maple trees—a zone where many a gardener has come to grief trying to coax exotics to grow.

Increasingly nurseries stock a wide variety of ferns for outdoor gardening, although the names of many can be daunting. "The only thing against ferns," groused Helen Van Pelt Wilson, "is their jaw-breaking names which botanists make worse by changing them all the time." In any case, purchasing plants is certainly preferable to digging up wildlings. In Victorian England, growing ferns in vivariums became such a rage that street urchins earned their meagre living by pillaging the countryside of ferns and selling them in London to supply the demands of fern mania. The diligence of these fern robbers soon decimated native fern populations. Oberon, I'm sure, was not amused.

I saw a similar pillaging at work down at the Seattle flower and garden show a few years back. One prize-winning demonstration garden that year consisted of a chunk of ancient temperate rain forest—an old cedar stump, huckleberry bushes, rotting mossy logs, sword ferns and all—that had been torn from Lord knows where and trucked to the convention centre for display. Perhaps these were fragments rescued before the onslaught of industrial clearcutting, as our own little maidenhair ferns were. But ferns, like the ancient forests in which they thrive, are plants of

231

magic, and if we wish to attract into our gardens the fairies, sylphs and other magic elements that live in ferny woods, a thoughtful and respectful approach is of the essence.

WEEK 39: AUTUMNAL EQUINOX

It's been quite some time now since we buried our dear old border collie, Fen, who'd been with us for all but the first of her seventeen years. She was a sweet old thing, and a faithful companion, especially whenever there was a bit of gardening to be done. A worker by instinct, she liked to fall in alongside the wheelbarrow as we'd trundle great chunks of Mother Earth from one place to another. If one of us was working over a particular bed, old Fen would settle down close by, to observe the work and mostly to listen. In her canine wisdom she appeared to understand what Hazlitt meant when he noted "Silence is the one great art of conversation." She seemed to appreciate instinctively that gardeners are more content if they're able to chat away while busy in the garden, preferably to a companion who can be relied upon not to chat back. An occasional yawn or muffled grunt would be the extent of Fen's contribution.

I did all the talking. The stream of observations I'd direct her way comprised a very specific and particular form of communication that could be called—and quite possibly has been called by some manic garden magazine editor—hortichat. It is an elaborate language, highly ritualized and indicative of a brain finely attuned to performing a given task—say, pruning the clematis vines—

while simultaneously discoursing to the dog, but utterly incapable of fine pruning while listening to the latest neighbourhood gossip or trying to plan next Saturday's dinner party. Hortichat is a one-way street: all outputs, no inputs. Undoubtedly, left and right brains are involved in some way.

Hortichat suffers none of the drawbacks inherent with two-way garden dialogues. These invariably involve your stopping whatever task you're performing in order to conduct a conversation in amiable fashion. Where we live there are no neighbours close enough for spontaneous conversation to erupt across the backyard fence, but I'm fully familiar with the immense complexities of discourse across lot lines, the refinements of diplomacy required for establishing and maintaining a genial coexistence with whatever personalities destiny, for good or ill, selects to plop down alongside you. Except in extraordinary cases, these over-the-fence interchanges are tightly circumscribed by neighbourly etiquette, which is not the case at all when dealing with members of your own household, who are apt to drag you off to confer on some perceived attraction or calamity just discovered. Don't misunderstand me: there are times when garden conversation is entirely correct and highly desirable, but this is not, and never will be, hortichat in the true sense, nor should the two disciplines ever be confused. Verbal intercourse, agreeable as it may be, exposes one to the likelihood of getting drawn into protracted discussion about whether one is performing the task at hand adequately. It offers the distinct possibility of your

233

being enjoined to abandon the job at hand in order to assist with some other chore you aren't especially interested in undertaking. Unchecked, conversations can degenerate into full-blown planning sessions at which impossibly complicated garden design problems need to be sorted out while the clematis are left hanging.

A chat with the dog, on the other hand, albeit a one-sided affair, offers none of these hazards, and I sorely miss old Fen for her discreet companionship. I suppose—in fact, I know—that some people talk to their cats while gardening, though I can't understand how they delude themselves into believing that any cat is the least bit interested in what they have to say. I tried it myself, back when we used to have a great lazy feline loafing about the place, but I couldn't avoid feeling rather a fool for making disclosures to a creature whose indifference so plainly bordered on contempt.

Since Fen's passing—we still glimpse her ghost now and then in her old familiar corners—I've had to focus on developing relationships with other creatures in the garden. It's not the same thing at all, of course, but I've found that, in a pinch, wild animals can make passable substitutes. In fact, I'm not entirely convinced that the recent renaissance of wildlife gardening isn't a thinly veiled attempt by gardeners to lure in unwitting wildlife for conversing purposes.

Birds are variable. Some, such as rufous-sided towhees, are in my experience very attentive listeners, head cocked thoughtfully, brilliant beady eyes, and only occasionally given to a cry that sounds like shrill self-pity. A row of plump robins on a fence can be addressed with scintillat-

234

ing wit, so long as one represses the suspicion that they're dismissing you as a tiresome windbag whom they'll tolerate only for the opportunity you afford them to swoop in and gobble a juicy earthworm. Winter wrens I find altogether too bossy, as are hummingbirds, and the ravens in our neighbourhood are outright rude.

Reptiles and amphibians aren't always entirely satisfactory either. I've enjoyed the occasional good session with a tree frog, but they're inclined to be secretive and given to camouflage, traits more appropriate to cocktail party badinage than to wholesome hortichat. Plus they have an unfortunate compulsion to croak at inappropriate moments, the way certain people respond to something you've said by babbling on as though you'd said nothing at all. We have no toads in our vicinity and more's the pity because I have a notion they'd be quite convivial in a quietly contented way. For companionable silence it's hard to beat snakes, whose exquisitely active tongues make no sound at all. There is, however, something disconcerting about their having no visible ears. Although they appear to be gazing in rapt attention with unblinking eyes wide open, one has the sense sometimes that they're a long way off, perhaps still back in Eden, hissing sibilantly to themselves about the business with forbidden fruit.

Like politicians, insects bring out the worst in most of us. I've concluded that a certain minimum brain size on the part of the listener is required for successful hortichat. Some beetles qualify, and you should have at least a few words for disturbed earthworms. But horse flies, deer flies,

235

mosquitoes, wasps, no-see-ums, face flies and other tor-
mentors—once provoked, I have no hesitation in snarling
incredibly vulgar and vicious threats at their sort.

None of these wild creatures, in short, is altogether satisfactory the way a loyal dog is, and it may be that repeated
disappointments with fauna is what eventually leads
many hortichatterers to step over a certain fine but crucial
line and begin directing their remarks to plants. No less
an authority on peculiar behaviour than Prince Charles
himself has bid us talk to our plants, on the grounds that
they will be happier and healthier for our dropping the
occasional bon mot in their direction. This I believe and
practise faithfully. However, I'm not sure I'd call it hortichat. It lacks the savoir faire, the philosophical cut and
thrust of that art form which should be, as Shakespeare put
it, "pleasant without scurrility, witty without affectation,
free without indecency, learned without conceitedness,
novel without falsehood." Instead, this fashionable talking
to plants has an ambience that is too blatantly supportive,
as though one were a member of the helping professions
and the plants were disadvantaged clients.

236   In addition, it would be unwise and unrealistic to
expect uniformity of response from all genera and species.
Plants, like people, have their own predilections. A row of
stout rutabagas trudging off to work with lunch buckets
under their arms might respond well enough to a hearty
"Good morning!" But try the same blue-collar cheeriness
with certain hybrid peonies and they'll snub you with-

eringly. Rugosa roses don't at all mind being shouted at if they've clawed you badly during pruning, but you shouldn't expect the David Austens to tolerate the same rough language. In the past I've managed to coax a crop of broccoli through a very bad spell of clubroot, but no amount of exhortations and heartfelt appreciations will do any good when late blight assails the tomatoes. Try as you might, they will not be counselled out of their victimization.

Still, notwithstanding these several provisos and caveats, generally speaking, hortichat is good for plants, pets and plantspeople. There's only one fundamental difficulty with it: namely, that society at large fails to appreciate the palliative role played by hortichat in helping soften the blows of dirty weather, crop failure and vile infestations. Sometimes I fear for the fate of gardeners caught in mid-conversation with a cauliflower. I can visualize perfectly competent plantspeople being dragged off to nursing homes or therapeutic residential settings because they were observed repeatedly conversing with song sparrows. Which is why it's highly advisable to have an attentive hound around the place and always speak softly.

237

WEEK 40: HIGH AND DRY

There's a plaintive sound in the air these days as crickets and grasshoppers play the final lines of their plangent songs. These are not laments for summer's end nor songs of regret that they idled away precious hours when they might have been working against the onset of winter. No, they play for love and procreation. Meanwhile, having not idled away precious work opportunities, we're now entirely trapped in a predicament common to dedicated vegetable growers everywhere—being inundated beneath an avalanche of garden fresh produce. Excessive zeal for seeding earlier in the season eventually results in a cornucopia of fruits, roots and leafy greens that grotesquely exceeds any reasonable demand. All the earlier fussing and fretting—about how conditions were too cold for adequate germination, too dry for robust growth, too infested with pests and diseases for any measure of success—now lie exposed as weak-kneed defeatism. Truckloads of beans and beets, cabbages and corn come thundering into the kitchen. We have a good-sized pantry and a twenty-two-cubic-foot freezer that's been so jammed to capacity for weeks it's all but impossible to fetch anything out of it.

During the seven years we lived here without electricity, Sandy used to can untold jars of produce, but we eventually concluded that life is too short to spend most of it sweating over a steaming canner. Mercifully, our root crops can stay in the ground over winter, which helps, but not enough. There's also a bumper crop of winter squash coming on, so we'll once again be reduced to hiding them under beds and couches all over the house. Of course a certain amount of surplus can be pressed upon politely smiling acquaintances, though we refrain from the zealotry of bartering sacks of mixed vegetables in exchange for automotive repairs or dental work. Personally I find it discouraging to acknowledge how many tonnes of vegetables are required in trade for a root canal. A roadside stand—as indicative as any finance minister's blustering, of serious miscalculations in the ratio of supply to demand—is out of the question.

One alternative to adventures in the underground economy is the food dehydrator. It excels on the simple principle that dehydrated food takes up far less space and is far easier to store than its fresh, frozen or canned equivalent. Plus there's a certain frisson in drying food, participating as one is in an ancient art, indeed the oldest known method of food preservation; perfectly preserved samples have been found in the excavated tombs of ancient Egyptians.

While our enterprising forebears relied upon the sun or fire to dry their foodstuffs, we postmodernist gardeners can choose from a variety of compact and efficient electric dehydrators. Our first experiments, however, involved a contraption that occupied a murky middle ground between ancient fire pits and high technology. A friendly neighbour—a person notorious for dumping excess produce into an already-glutted marketplace—dropped off several large boxes of ripe pears and along with them an antique dehydrator fired by kerosene. In those days we read by the light of kerosene lamps and kept perishables in a kerosene refrigerator, so there was nothing suspicious about a kerosene dehydrator. Youthfully enthusiastic, we cored and quartered the pears and spread them on mesh trays inside the dryer, lit the kerosene wick, and stood back to await results. All went as planned and the pears dried beautifully in a couple of days. The moment of triumph arrived. We would taste our first dried pears. How interesting, how unmistakable: the fruit had absorbed some weird fumes from the impurely burning kerosene and tasted more of petrochemicals than pearishness. They weren't just distasteful, they were utterly inedible and we cast them out and the Dickensian dehydrator with them.

Undeterred, we entered phase two, which involved a prototype dehydrator of my own design and construction. By this time we had evolved from the age of kerosene to the age of propane. When not using the woodstove, we cooked on a classic fifties propane range that boasted four top burners, each of which had its own pilot light that burned day and night, consuming propane at a prodigious rate. I calculated that, if trapped, the heat generated by the four pilots would suffice to nicely dry our surplus produce. Our history here for the better part of three decades has been pockmarked with similar calculations on my part, leading me to conceive of myself as something of a Buckminster Fuller without brains. I roughed together a large wooden chamber that sat rather cunningly on top of the stove. By this point the neighbour—for reasons that don't concern us here—was no longer dropping off pears, but we were producing abundant apples of our own. Lacking any mesh trays inside the handmade dryer, we decided upon dried apple rings suspended on strings running through their centres. We carefully sliced and strung the rings while I considered whether to apply for a patent. The failing here was not in my apparatus, but rather in the apple rings which persisted in breaking apart and tumbling headlong, like fallen Lucifer, onto the pilot lights where they hissed and scorched. My idiotic chamber eventually went the way of its kerosene predecessor.

Soon after that, my parents shipped out to us their own electric dryer, an upscale unit with ten mesh trays, heating coils and a fan. The whole box can be maintained at a uniform temperature, with settings between 38 and 63 degrees Fahrenheit, considered ideal for thorough drying while preserving nutrient values. The dryer operates on about 1,000 watts and maintains efficiency by recycling its warmed air. Some foods, such as mushrooms, will dry in as little as an hour, while very moist stuff, like tomatoes, may take a whole day or more. A spinoff benefit of having the unit running in the kitchen this time of year is that the heat it gives off is just enough to take the morning and evening chill out of the air, so firing up the wood stove can be delayed a little longer.

Plums, apples, tomatoes and zucchinis are among the worst offenders when it comes to running an autumn surplus. When all's said and done, there's only so much tomato sauce, plum butter and applesauce any household can decently accommodate. As for zucchinis, the less said the better. A single sugar plum tree in our yard rains down sweet small plums like manna from heaven. We simply split these open, pop out the stone, spread them on the drying racks and within a few hours they're reduced to wonderfully sweet and chewy treats. In the depths of winter they can be rehydrated for baking. Excess apples, rhubarb or berry fruits all make excellent fruit leathers. We render them down as though making thick apple-sauce, puree the fruit in the food processor and then spread it thinly on plastic wrap stretched over the drying trays. After perhaps six or eight hours of drying, when the leather is no longer spongy in the middle, we flip it over, peel off the plastic wrap and continue drying for a few more hours. Wholesome and nutritious, fruit leathers are invaluable on camping trips or day-long hikes, and many's the time they've saved me from the unspecified perils of airline and ferry food.

For extended backpacking trips (as though gardeners haven't brutalized their backs more than enough already) a lightweight soup mix can be concocted by drying herbs and vegetables such as peppers, onions, garlic, mushrooms, tomatoes and celery. After drying, simply powder them in a food processor or blender, lace up your hiking boots and be off! When I'm not scrambling over glaciers myself, one of my winter mainstays are the zucchini chips that Sandy makes by the bagful. She slices young zucchini into thin rounds, partially dries them, dips them in a mixture of balsamic vinegar and soy sauce, then a coating of Parmesan cheese and spices and a final session in the dryer. Vastly more addictive than potato or corn chips, these zucchini treats are just the thing when sprawled on the couch watching *Hockey Night in Canada* and wondering if there's meaning in the universe.

242

But the ultimate triumph of the kitchen dehydrator has to be dried tomatoes. These are so easily done in vast quantities that one can only marvel at the princely sums commanded by "California sun-dried" tomatoes at the deli. Not this year, of course, but usually we bring in scores of ripe tomatoes lined up like army recruits awaiting processing. We slice them into thinnish rounds and pop them into the dryer. They can be completely rehydrated by a long soak in water, but for that gourmet sun-dried taste, we pour boiling water over the dried slices, drain them after about thirty seconds, then place them in a small jar of olive oil. They are the essence of tomato, the very soul and spirit of tomato, excellent in all respects and provocative of much swaggering self-satisfaction. Tossed into a salad of midwinter greens, they offer a piquant reminder of the sweet delights of midsummer eating and of the fundamental worthiness, known to our ancestors, of dehydrating the harvest excess while crickets and grasshoppers play their plaintive songs of love.

*O*CTOBER

WEEK 41: SWELLED HEADS

A few years back, writing my first gardening book, I waxed enthusiastic about hydrangeas. "What's most appealing about hydrangeas," I pronounced, "is that many of them sustain their full glory late in the season when so much else is shrivelled and wizened." I went on to say that at our place "we've put our faith in hydrangeas in the way some people believe the facile promises of electioneering politicians." In hindsight I now marvel at how insightful one can be, albeit unconsciously, because now, far wiser in the ways of hydrangeas, I find the analogy to promise-'em-anything politicians especially prescient.

Don't mistake me: I haven't abandoned youthful enthusiasm. I still consider the hydrangea to be an altogether admirable plant, easy to propagate, undemanding in its culture, magnificent with long-lasting blooms, and the dried-flower arranger's delight. A combination of types, once established, can provide a scintillating presence in the garden from early summer through to first frost. We've got a glorious Annabelle, for example, that's just recently finished flowering. A selection of the smooth hydrangea native to the eastern U.S., she seemed a languid and melancholy character during her first few years with us, but no longer. Now she shines brilliantly through the late summer, recalling Edgar Allan Poe's "For the moon never beams without bringing me dreams / Of the beautiful Annabel Lee." Her sumptuous ivory-white trusses couple an appealing freshness with antique charm, as Annabel Lee herself must have done for poor Edgar in their kingdom by the sea.

Our Annabelle sits in a crowd of blue-flowering macrophylla, that omnipresent shrub in West Coast gardens which helped inspire our initial enthusiasm for the clan. A stroll through some of Vancouver's older neighbourhoods this time of year is made glorious by enormous blooming hydrangeas planted many years ago. Glorious in some eyes, that is, but not all. Their fulsome mop-head flowers are the object of both inordinate pride and derisive scorn, depending upon one's circle. In colder parts of the country, the same dichotomy of enthusiasm greets the peegee hydrangea which is also at its finest this time of year as its long panicles of creamy white flowers age into a stunning pinkish bronze. Vigorous, dependable and ravishing to enthusiasts, the peegee is dismissed in one of our encyclopedias as "far too common a plant in American gardens."

Perhaps so. But three times we've attempted to get a peegee established at our place, all without luck. Although hardy and vigorous, growing to seven metres or more, this is one commoner that seems a bit too particular for our methods.

I like most hydrangeas immensely, even those pint-sized little French hybrids with the huge encephalic heads. But I've come to understand over time that hydrangeas have a way of provoking peculiar behaviour in people. I remember not long ago visiting a very chichi gardening shop in Vancouver—one of those places with a clever name and assorted garden fixtures to die for—and being scandalized to see several staff members slinking into the shop, giggling like schoolkids, carrying trusses of hydrangeas that, it quickly became apparent, they'd stolen for dried-flower arrangements from nearby gardens.

Or consider the far-flung fixation with altering the flower colour of certain varieties through manipulating the acidity of the soil in which they grow. Some pink-flowering types, we know, will bloom pink in alkaline conditions, blue-pink when the soil is neutral , and blue when it's acidic. A blue macrophylla, on the other hand, will flower pink in acidic soil. This has to do with the plant needing to absorb aluminum from the soil in order to produce blue blooms, and aluminum being soluble only in acid conditions. Fair enough. But why is it the case, you have to wonder, that so many people whose acidic soil produces blue flowers are determined to have pink, while so many whose alkaline soil naturally produces pink blooms are equally mad to have blue? Does it reveal something best not revealed about human nature that those lusting for blue are out pouring aluminum sulphate or potassium alum onto their alkaline ground, while those craving pink are dumping dolomite or superphosphate all over their acidic earth? Wouldn't house exchanges be easier? As often as not, the consequences of this acidic cross-dressing are mottled blossoms of pink-blushing blue that are every bit as charming as the pure colours. The whole business seems to me uncomfortably like the behaviour of those restless spirits who are forever dying their hair and tanning their hides within a millimetre of melanoma, all for the sake of looking like something nature would prefer they didn't.

Riding high above the common clamour for colour change at any cost, we ourselves leave our mop-tops free to be what they will—in our acidic soil generally an electric blue that flashes at you from fifty paces off with an insistence that leaves you wondering whether a dash of pink might not be such a bad idea.

White-flowering types like the beautiful Annabelle make virtuous companions for both the neon blues and baby-doll pinks. Among my favourites is the oak-leafed hydrangea whose worthiness increases the further we fall into autumn. This ruggedly handsome shrub is native to the southeastern U.S. and prized as much for its foliage as its flowers. Resembling large oak leaves, in summer the leathery leaves are dark green with felted undersides, then colour beautifully as fall progresses. By November, the foliage is stunning wine red. Its flowers appear in midsummer as large trusses of creamy white gradually mellowing to antique pink. Our shrubs are only a few years old and have thus far shown a certain weakness of character when it comes to holding up their flowers for all to see; the big trusses tend to end up flat-faced on the ground, where they don't show to great advantage, but give the shrub a slightly pathetic air, like a dog that's fouled the carpet. Annabelle behaved that way too for a while, and I suspect that certain hydrangeas, like teenagers, test your mettle before really coming into their own.

I wouldn't say the same for our villosa hydrangeas. Native to China and Nepal, they're robust customers that can grow up to four metres high with large pointed leaves and juicy stems, both flushed red and felted with soft hairs. Best in dry soil and shade, the villosa spreads large clusters of lace-cap flowers in white, pale pink or purple. The ones at our place—raised, I should confess, from purloined cuttings—have an appealing cast to their flowers, ivory washed with antique pink. When you prune the bushes properly, that is. Somehow I managed to prune ours at the wrong time last year, cutting away the flower buds in the process, and we've had scarcely a bloom this year. Their headlessness naturally got me wondering about potential connections between hydrangeas and Hydra, the fabulous many-headed snake that infested the marshes of Lerna and whose many heads—unlike hydrangea heads—regrew as fast as they were cut off, until the mythic beast was slain by Hercules. But no: hydrangeas are named for the cuplike form of their seed capsules.

Back to pruning. It's easy enough to grasp the principle that the pruning regime differs for shrubs that flower on last year's wood, like macrophylla, and those that flower on new shoots, like the peegee. God knows how many times one has reread a pruning handbook to refresh the fading memory about how hydrangeas that flower on old wood are pruned immediately after flowering, while ones that flower on new shoots are pruned in late winter or early spring, before buds break. No, what one really needs is either an effective course in time management—freeing one up to get out there and do the pruning when it should be done—or, perhaps preferably, a master gardener willing to labour for minimum wage who'll do the job properly at the appropriate time.

The one type I've had absolutely no problem with pruning is the climbing hydrangea. Native to Japan and Korea, in maturity this hardy climber makes a breathtaking display. Clinging with rootlike holdfasts, it can climb twenty metres up a tree, then in June break out in abundant clusters of lace-cap flowers that swathe the whole tree in white lace. Requiring a cool, moist root run, and not a plant for small spaces, it's an excellent choice for a north-facing wall or to cover an old stump or waste ground. Thus it was that I conceived a grand scheme back when we were roughing in the garden a decade ago. One patch of ground on the hillside was so appallingly riddled with fractured sandstone, we grew weary of unearthing and wheelbarrowing the rubble away. In one of those flashes of intuition that not even years of troublesome experience

249

will dissuade me from indulging, I alighted upon a solution both practical and aesthetically pleasing. We would simply mound up the unearthed stone on the stoniest patch of all and build an elevated deck above the heap. This would both rid us of the wretched stone and provide a lovely vantage point—and, most cunningly of all, the heaped stone hidden beneath the skirted deck would provide a perfect hibernaculum for the garter snakes we were anxious to encourage as slug predators.

Climbing hydrangeas were grafted onto this scheme some weeks later when the deck, cobbled together from recycled materials whose inelegance predated the current vogue for the distressed look, loomed like a naked bunker on the hillside. We bunged in a climbing hydrangea at the base of the east-facing wall, confident that within a year or two this fast-growing climber would smother the deck's ugly infrastructure with flowery lace.

Today, some years later, we're still waiting. Several miscalculations undermined the scheme. The first, and perhaps keystone flaw concerned the relative attractiveness of the covered stone heap as a hibernaculum. For reasons best known to themselves, and perhaps to a handful of renegade herpetologists, the snakes shunned it absolutely, preferring winter quarters of any description over the intended hibernaculum. Always busy filling vacuums, Mother Nature chose instead to populate the cool, damp rock heap with abundant slugs. While the snakes were preoccupied elsewhere, the slugs would slide out from under the deck and set about rasping the new growth tips off the climbing hydrangea. No other hydrangea in the garden do slugs so much as deign to slime across, but climbing hydrangeas they crave. The upshot being that the hydrangea remains a stunted little customer, slugs abound, snakes snooze elsewhere and the ungainly deck still looms.

Some might lose heart at reversals of this sort, but not gardeners, and certainly not hydrangea growers, who've long ago accepted that these fulsome beauties have a way of bringing out the peculiar sides of people, confusing steadfast pruners and confounding even the best-laid plans for slugs and snakes.

WEEK 42: THANKSGIVING

A disgusting disease has beset our Korean dogwoods. We have half a dozen of them planted in prime garden spots, as they are trees of surpassing beauty through much of the year. The youngest of them withered and died over the summer. The oldest—now perhaps ten years old and four metres tall and until this year altogether wholesome looking—has suffered terrible splitting of its bark on the south side. The bark cracks open and lifts away from the bole; wood bugs slip in under the loosened bark and set up filthy little squats. The tree, now in a lacklustre mimicry of its normal autumn glory, steadfastly declined through the growing season to produce new shoots in its canopy, instead sprouting vigorously below the damaged parts of its trunk. I've cleaned its wounds and given the tormented trunk shade from direct sunlight, and pulled away all but two of the new basal shoots, calculating that one may be required to reinvent the tree if the whole top dies away. Perhaps the tree is doomed entirely, I don't know, but next year should tell the tale.

I strike this melancholy note today, when we should be celebrating our blessings, not bemoaning our misfortunes, because, absurdly, I feel a sense of responsibility for what has befallen the dogwoods, as though I were to blame for one's distress and even for the other's dying. That somehow I'm at fault here, guilty of criminal negligence causing death. I could put my anxiety down to the dregs of residual Catholic guilt still swilling around in my system, but I think not. In my experience, Catholics and Jews, Presbyterians and other hardline Protestants each have their own exquisitely refined traditions of guilt, but so too do gardeners. Simmering guilt is one of the great hazards of horticulture.

Virulent and common as the cold, garden guilt has any number of symptoms. Guilt over having a lawn, perhaps, or over cutting it with a polluting power mower. Guilt over not having torn out your frivolous exotics and replaced them with a native plant garden. Residual guilt from prolonged and deliberate cheating on water restrictions. Continuing guilt arising from dereliction of duty. On a scorching hot day you neglect to open the vents in the greenhouse, only to discover, later in the afternoon, all your cucumbers roasted beyond redemption. Or you'll absentmindedly leave a hose soaking a certain plant for a few hours, which somehow elongate into a few days, and by the time you think to turn off the tap, the poor plant has drowned as woefully as an ancient mariner lost at sea. Bedding plants left too long in their flats, shrivelled into the throes of a gruesome and premature death, have a great way of crying "Murder!" and setting loose the dogs of guilt.

But while we may feel guilty for the good we might have done but failed to do, a deeper turpitude attends the wilful committing of a moral offence. This may involve distracted mindlessness rather than malice to begin with, like the time last spring when I went to prune some dead wood out of a Kiftsgate rose we'd painstakingly trained to climb into a big cedar tree, and I somehow succeeded in accidentally cutting most of its perfectly healthy main stems. This is an honest mistake and understandable given the crush of duties to be done. The offender might easily be absolved were he to confess to a stupid error and be done with it. But like Richard Nixon, the gardener instead seeks to escape blame by resorting to premeditated false-hoods. "It was just lying there on the ground!" he exclaims after accidentally uprooting or trampling upon a favourite plant of his companion. "I can't imagine what happened to it." This is an outright lie, as transparent as the fibbing of a delinquent schoolboy. An occasional cowardly lie, of course, would do no long-term damage, but having got the hang of it, the gardener becomes a repeat offender. He lets on to admiring visitors that he grew from seed some fabulous specimen just acquired at great expense from a nursery. "Completely organic, of course," he boasts of his vegetable patch, although he's been surreptitiously side dressing his monster vegetables with potent chemical fertilizers. Repeated over time, these transgressions open a crack through which the maggot of guilt wriggles into one's soul.

Guilt's filthy offspring, shame, soon slithers into the garden too. We define shame as the painful emotion arising from a consciousness of something dishonouring, ridiculous or indecorous in one's conduct or circumstances. Or, if not most painfully, often most publicly, in one's garden. Consider, for example, the innermost feelings of the persons responsible for the riotous colour combinations produced in certain rhododendron and azalea gardens. Speaking of inelegant combinations, just this year we had a malingering clematis for the first time burst into bloom with oversize flowers of a rather heinous vermillion. These blooms hanging alongside the golden goblets of a Maigold rose created an effect atrocious enough to offend the sensibilities of an oyster. Shame may be induced by a thing which is shockingly ugly or indecent, or of disgracefully bad quality, and that certainly covers a number of my grand gardening schemes over time. A couple of such disasters scattered around the garden, and you begin to suspect—no, to be certain—that visitors and passersby are sniggering behind your back. Yes, the garden's a disgrace just now, but what can be done? Humiliated, the poor gardener is dragged into a debilitating shame brought on by loss of esteem and reputation. Shame, like guilt, is a slow and melancholy poison.

Given that guilt and shame are such mighty forces at play in the garden, it's axiomatic that learning to handle them skilfully is as integral to the education of a gardener as learning to transplant adeptly. Thus many gardeners become masters of transference, smoothly offloading guilt and shame by blaming someone else. If you inadvertently order cos lettuce seeds when you intended to get buttercrunch, you don't acknowledge your error—you blame the seedhouse for mislabelling their seeds. House guests, neighbours, kids and dogs are all excellent to blame for breakage in the garden caused by your own clumsiness or haste. If a plant dies thanks to your ministrations, you can blame global warming, unscrupulous nurserypeople, or mysterious diseases hitherto unknown to science.

While gardening with a companion exponentially raises the odds for experiencing guilt and shame, it also presents fantastic opportunities for employing their whips and stings for one's own purposes. A few years back, some smart advice giver made a bucket of money with a book titled *When I Say No I feel Guilty*. Only an out-and-out rogue wouldn't feel guilty when one's dear companion is toiling in the garden, smeared with dirt and tormented by biting bugs, sun blazing down, while you're reclining on the chaise lounge contemplating questions of ontology. Gardeners are nobody's fool, and they soon learn to exploit this potential for inflicting guilt on inactive companions. Wails of distress emanating from the herb garden, pathetic

255

cries of woe from the shrubbery—there's all sorts of chi-
canery that can be employed to inspire guilt and shame in
companions who aren't pulling their wagon.

Excessively robust partners, on the other hand, can be
brought to heel by holding them accountable for any mis-
haps that might occur, whether from their bullishness or
not. You know the sort of person I mean—out there on a
Sunday afternoon, making a grand production over, say,
pruning the "Kiftsgate" rose while you're trying to indulge
in an hour's peace and quiet curled up on the couch with
Timothy Findley. Let them have their self-important pos-
turings. All you need to do is saunter out in due course,
find an inept pruning cut or two, drop a sarcastic or dis-
appointed word, inducing just a shimmer of shame in the
do-gooder, and you've seized the moral high ground, notwithstanding their sweaty labours while you reclined in
leisured languor. I tell you, these are the moves of emotional maestros, subtle as spider's silk spun among the
garden's complex web of sin and redemption.

WEEK 43: LATE GRACES

As we tumble down the darkening tunnel of October, two
splendid gifts from the great gardens of Japan illuminate
the grounds—Japanese maples and Japanese anemones.
Both have been lovely for months, strengthening their
claim as eastern stars of the autumn garden.

Many gorgeous small maples have come to us from
Japan including the vase-shaped Nikko maple, the

Fullmoon maples, the Trident, Amur and Hornbeam maples and the diabolically named Red Devil maple. Given the time, space and capital, one would have them all. The name Japanese maple, however, properly refers to a single species, *Acer palmatum*. Native to Japan and Korea, this little tree has been developed into fantastic variations in size and shape, leaf form and colour. There are scores of named cultivars, ranging from dwarf weeping shrubs to elegant trees ten metres or taller.

Like many another gardener, we started our affair with Japanese maples with the familiar small red Atropurpureum. With an impeccable reputation for vivid and consistent autumn colour, this little spreading tree plays lovely tricks with sunlight. Its deeply lobed leaves have a shiny upper surface that reflects light cleanly, while dark shadows seem to dance among the spaces beneath the leaves. Backlit by the evening sun, the foliage glows with a brilliant fiery translucence. Steadfastness of leaf colour throughout the growing season and prolonged retention of autumn foliage recommend this tree, but it's easy to acquire a Japanese maple that disappoints on both counts. Unprincipled nurseries stand accused in some quarters of growing trees from seed, rather than grafting, with the result that an unwary purchaser may buy a tree that produces gorgeous spring foliage that quickly becomes muddy and nondescript, or that falls off at the first breath of cold weather.

Among the loveliest members of the *palmatum* group— they're all lovely in my books—are the little cutleaf, threadleaf and laceleaf types. With graceful weeping habits and delicate leaves as finely divided as the elfin fingers of the little people, these are trees, or shrubs really, for special spots. Our first of these small charmers was a red laceleaf that we placed in the rock garden where it weeps over the little cascade, underplanted with ferns and mosses. Its lacy foliage is now a brilliant crimson. To complement its brilliance, we've added several green laceleafs, which have lovely green bark on the new wood and pale green leaves.

After their autumn glory, all these trees retain a twiggy elegance in winter. The spreading vase shapes of many types make especially pleasing winter outlines. None is a better winter performer than the coral bark maple, a green-leafed tree whose young stems are a gorgeous coral colour that glows especially warmly in winter sunlight. Three times we've tried to introduce this wintertime stunner into our gardens; three times it has grown for several years, then abruptly died from a fungal infection. When I see one growing elsewhere I want to weep. But, as comely as it is, we will not try again. I'm a devout believer that certain plants, much like certain people, for reasons of their own, are unhappy in some locations and should not be compelled to endure a life they do not wish to live. And so, with regret, we've severed our tenuous ties to the coral bark, the way one is sometimes compelled to break with an attractive but ruinous companion. Never mind, we've half a dozen other types, and so count ourselves blessed.

Many of the Japanese maples have a satisfying horizontality in their growth habits. Their branch and leaf patterns are layered in subtle tiers that somehow hint of restfulness and tranquility of spirit. The textured layers of leaves and the uncluttered planes of space between the leaf layers suggest light and darkness—perhaps, in a metaphysical mood, even being and not-being—played against one another. If one is destined to find enlightenment sitting calmly in one's garden beneath a tree—and surely we are, or else what's the point?—it might as well, if we can fit, be beneath a splendid little Japanese maple.

And what a marvellous season our Japanese anemones have had! The first of them began blooming in August, then exulted through a dampish September, and held their heads high until the first monsoons just recently swamped them. As author Allen Lacy writes: "No plant of autumn brings more joy than Japanese anemones." Long-lived as well as long-blooming, these slender beauties bring a carefree gracefulness to the fall garden, a distinctive delicacy that plays well against the stouter plants that mostly take centre stage at this blustery time of year. The soft pinks, roses and whites of anemone flowers have a freshness and clarity we more associate with spring and early summer. They seem almost to dance through the garden, like clusters of schoolgirls passing a retirement community.

But they're tough customers in their own right, able to withstand foul weather and the abuses of clumsy gardeners. Native to China, Japan and Nepal, they're hardy members of the buttercup family, along with the springflowering anemones, including the Grecian windflower. All of them derive their name from the Greek for wind, *anemos,* and whether in spring or autumn, all seem to dance beautifully in the breeze.

Japanese anemones emerge as clumps of low foliage in spring, made up of dark green and deeply veined leaves, somewhat like maple leaves, and pleasingly coarse in texture. Late in summer the flower stems rise like thin wires a metre or more high, supporting loose sprays of smallish flowers of delicate pastel tints with a vivid inner circle of yellow stamens at the centre. There are a number of named varieties, all of them splendid. Honorine Jobert is a marvellous old type producing large single white flowers with brilliant yellow centres. "It flowers for months rather than weeks," enthuses Penelope Hobhouse, "and is lovely in a pink and white colour scheme in sun, or at the edge of woodland with dark-leaved shrubs." Equally attractive, Whirlwind bears semi-double white blooms. Queen Charlotte is a semi-double pink, while Prince Henry bears smaller deep rose semi-doubles, and Kriemhilde is a charming soft pink. Slightly shorter than these, and similarly hardy, the Chinese anemone is often lumped in with its Japanese cousins, especially the popular September Charm which has gorgeous silvery pink single flowers. Hardiest of all is *A. tomentosa,* Robustissima, which is sometimes called the grape-leaved anemone. Less than a metre tall, this cultivar is similar to other Japanese anemones, having attractive dark green foliage and brilliant metallic pink flowers. It's hardy down to zone three, but its robust name may also refer to its reputation as a rampant spreader.

Japanese anemones are said to dislike wind, summer drought and soil that gets soggy in winter, but they seem quite content with our winter wet/summer dry regime. They do prefer a cool root run in rich moist soil high in humus, and good drainage is essential. They'll tolerate full sun in cooler climates, otherwise partial shade is best. These are not casual transients in the garden, and won't tolerate being moved about on every new whim. Like herbaceous peonies, they expect a good deal of careful thought about placement beforehand. Once established—and this takes a while, for they won't be rushed or hustled along—they require very little care. In colder locations, they'll benefit from a loose mulch in winter (conifer branches are often used) though it's recommended this not be applied until after the ground has frozen, to avoid trapping too much moisture around the roots. Slow to establish, they eventually spread into the large clumps in which their flowers show to best effect. Plantings don't need dividing other than to contain the spread, as some can be invasive. To increase plants, we divide the clumps in spring just after growth has started. Older plants don't divide well, and often root cuttings are a better bet for propagation.

261

The ethereal clouds of flowers these beauties produce go wonderfully with large-leaved hostas and bergenias. We had a smashing show this year with pink and white varieties played against late-flowering monkshood, and against a little dogwood tree, complementing the pink flush in its autumn leaves. As well, their airy flowering stalks sway splendidly above late asters and goldenrods or over ornamental grasses or large ferns. At their best in large drifts, they're terrific transitional plants along the borders of woodland plantings.

Long after most other flowers have exhausted themselves, the anemones maintain a charming carefree grace, and when at last their delicate beauty collapses, as it finally has this week, we know that the best is behind us and that dark times are at hand.

WEEK 44: ALL FALL DOWN

We are now entirely shrouded in the drifting mists and melancholy of late autumn. The garden seems full of wistful farewells and sombre forebodings. Compared with the rest of the country—basking amid crimson maples, brilliantly golden aspens and all the rest—autumn on the Coast is a comparatively colourless and lacklustre collapse into dreary grey. In an exceptional year, our native bigleaf maples might put on a decent show, but usually their leaves turn a callow yellow, blotched with fungal brown spots, then fall off miserably. Our omnipresent red alders don't even make the effort—they seem to just throw down their tatty leaves in disgust. This is hardly the "Miles and miles of crimson glories . . . Miles of shoreland red and golden," celebrated by poets elsewhere across the land.

But somehow I don't detect any great outpouring of sympathy from other parts of the country towards those of us who must endure this wishy-washy mediocrity of a fall. Sometimes I suspect those east of us are snickering at our

262

insipid autumn show. Not surprising, really. I don't think I'm breaking confidentiality in disclosing that the coastal grower, while envied and perhaps even admired from afar, may not necessarily be loved. I suppose the chummy notes written in February to celebrate the first daffodils, then mailed to blizzard-battered friends on the Prairies or back East, haven't helped. The loose talk of roses still blooming at Christmas. The slightly swaggering tone when describing marvellous semi-tropicals hardy enough for our yards. All of this might easily be misinterpreted as smug self-satisfaction, not likely to endear us to frostbitten colleagues elsewhere. Perhaps pale and pithless autumns on the Coast are nature's way of balancing the scales, of bringing to the coastal gardener just a smidgeon of humility.

A more likely response, as we know, is the redoubling of efforts to overcome our shortfalls. Gardeners are like people who endlessly take self-help courses and seminars to try make things better. We are chronic improvers, not necessarily of ourselves, but certainly of our landscapes, so it stands to reason that we'd gird our loins to try to surmount the mediocrity of a coastal autumn. Let native trees insist on being drab if they want—we'll flaunt the current vogue for native plant gardening by importing trees from elsewhere to create a panorama of gold and crimson glory that would make any Ontarian weep.

This is certainly the route Sandy and I have chosen, a madness that in part involved transforming our old goat pasture into an arboretum of sorts. Enormous holes were dug, huge boulders unearthed, mountains of leaf mould and compost buried, and numerous young trees planted, all bearing impeccable credentials in the matter of autumn colour. Preliminary indications are that the purple maple and copper beech seem up to snuff; and certainly the smoke trees and Japanese maples are giving their best. But I'm not entirely confident about the liquid ambers. Though reputed to produce a stunning autumn display, ours didn't do a whole lot last year. One of them insisted upon clutching its tatty but still-green leaves until well after Christmas, by which time we'd ceased to care very much. It was around then that someone said never acquire a liquid amber without first seeing it in fall colour, as some of them "do it" and some don't. I fear the same may hold true for black gums, which also come with a reputation as autumnal superstars. It takes a considerable act of faith to picture our ratty little specimens that way, but faith we stoically maintain. We went through a similar trial some years ago with a Japanese angelica tree. We tolerated its morbid thorny arms all winter and its pestilential suckering all summer in order to enjoy its celebrated fall colours. Instead, the big leaves turned a dull rusty shade, reminiscent of old autos in a wrecking yard, and fell off in less than a week.

264

Still, we're far from dismayed. We continue resolutely trundling in sumacs and box elders, vine maples and Korean dogwoods—anything we can find to raise the colours. This is because we coastal growers—notwithstanding occasional secessionist blustering from politicians of limited mental reach—want desperately to be Canadians in the fullest sense of the term. Especially in autumn.

Nobody does autumn better than Canadians. We might be tentative and equivocal in our springs, when late snowstorms and floodings confuse the general enthusiasm. We may become overheated and grouchy during summers more suited to mosquitoes than to humans. Our winters make us a laughingstock. But a Canadian in autumn is a creature of magnificent truth and beauty. Here we stand on a crisp October morning, pioneers in spirit, intrepid adventurers amid hills of crimson glory. Caught up in one of nature's most spectacular transitions, we become a visionary people. "Autumn," one of our writers, Charles Sangster, put it long ago, "like an old poet in a haze of golden visions, dreams away his days."

Just so. Dreamers of dreams and seers of visions—that's us when the maples, aspens and all the rest set about their gorgeous dying-down. Especially gardeners—those of us who've nurtured and coddled plants through the frosts and droughts and thunderous calamities that may assail a Canadian garden. Basking in the final weeks of the growing season, we enter a golden time when philosophical musings fall thick and fast as autumn leaves and melancholy reflections drop like rotting fruit along the pathways of our daily rounds.

Certainly a wistful looking-back is part of it. How long ago it seems now (yet only yesterday) when the first winter aconites broke from cold ground to hold aloft their tiny golden globes, brave beacons of hope against the receding dark of winter. Oh, to see again the saffron sheen of crocuses, whites and golds, purples and pale mauves, as all the earth began to sing with springtime! Blood-red roses and delphiniums blue as a clear June sky. The sunburnt beauty of summer—bleached grasses and aromatic herbs, lilies over which a heart might break, exotically perfumed evenings. Sweet bliss long gone. Archibald Lampman called our autumn "Golden, rose-red, full of divine remembrance..."

Though hopeless sentimentalists, gardeners are a people toughened by adversity, familiar with the pain of loss. Throughout the year, we've watched small beauties bloom and fade. The snowdrops dying away gave us intimations of mortality before most of the garden had even awakened. And so it continued, one sad departure after another, made bearable only by brilliant new arrivals. Now we're down to the last of them, and we face the end with a spirit tempered through repeated small bereavements.

Despite our obscene outbursts at the time, we can now glance back with equanimity at crushing reversals suffered earlier—the rose trellis flattened in a snowstorm, those damnable caterpillars ravaging the basil, a lovely young dogwood browning off and dying. What seemed at the time to be adversity of the most appalling sort shrinks now into insignificance. Our histrionics at the scene of the disaster seem in hindsight somewhat overblown, the language unnecessarily rough. For beyond the golden haze of Indian summer we hear the jackboots of winter tramping. Full of foreboding, we glance backwards now, realizing that the most harried of the hectic days of May—when there was always more confounded garden work to be done than possibly could be done—the very worst of these was a blithesome frolic compared with the depths into which we shall soon tumble.

We fall prey to regret and something very close to grief. Perhaps we squandered precious moments in fretfulness and agitated inattention. Maybe we were fool enough to let the oriental poppies open without really pausing long enough to ponder the ravishment of their unfurling. Given the chance, did we gaze with rapt attention into the heart of a tree peony flower, seeing there her mysteries too deep for speaking? Grief runs even deeper than regret, stirred by an awareness that this marvellous expedition through the gardening year is drawing to a close. We cannot escape its symbolisms—I really don't think we want to. The season reminds us, as poignantly as attending the funeral of a loved one does, of the brevity of our short time upon this mortal coil. However full of raptures and delights, miscalculations and regrets, it's quickly gone, and there we stand amid a rain of falling leaves.

The whole affair might have us wallowing in self-pity of the lowest sort were we not such aficionados of autumn. But we are far from morose. Bliss Carman struck just the right note a century ago: "There is something in October sets the gypsy blood astir." Yes. Vagabonds at heart, we leave behind the shining mornings of midsummer when the garden reached its jubilant apotheosis of peonies, roses and delphiniums. We forsake the juicy succulence of a peach plucked ripe from the tree, the jovial explosion of juices from a vine-ripened tomato. We tuck a few essentials into a backpack and set off across the crimson hills, knowing we'll return soon enough, versed in the splendid circularities of the gardening year and the poetry of passages.

November

WEEK 45: ALL SAINTS' DAY

Winding the garden down for winter after the giddy flights of the growing season can be a dispiriting affair, so it's wise to incorporate a few rewarding routines to enliven the process. None succeeds more amiably than an extended outing with the compost grinder or shredder. A machine whose sole purpose is the pulverizing of large organic matter into smaller gobbets might seem at first blush an inessential extravagance, another noisy and polluting contrivance like the nefarious leaf blower, corrupting what should be a haunt of ancient peace and quiet.

Perhaps it is. But for anyone running large gardens—particularly gardens abundant in leggy perennials, vines and canes—a shredder can transform the drudgery of dealing with their debris into an almost transcendent enterprise. Gardeners who've wrestled with volumes of fuzzy verbascum stems or accumulations of Jerusalem artichoke stalks know how difficult such material is to deal with. Putting it out for garbage collection is out of the question. So is burning. Nor does this tough leggy stuff go gently into a compost heap. Thick and woody, it resists decomposition, instead forming intractable mats like the knitted twigs of a beaver dam. Trying to turn a heap of these entanglements is an invitation to hernia. Months later the stems are still there, impervious to the high principles of composting.

After one too many of these episodes, I thought to dice the stalks up with a machete as I laid each layer of them on the compost heap. I started strongly, giving the pile six or seven great bloodthirsty slashes, but soon lost heart. Gardeners with abundant space can, as I used to, simply dump this organic debris in a secluded corner and wait a year or two for it to eventually rot. But I always resented trundling the raspberry canes and fireweed stalks off in this way, and as often as not their piles would be colonized by stinging nettles or quack grass before they'd decomposed, and in the end would contribute nothing to the garden.

270 The ultimate solution, I suspected, lay in acquiring a power shredder to really dice the stuff up. Deep in the bowels of my old toolshed is stored an ancient gas lawnmower, its grass-cutting days long over. For years I dreamed of converting it into a shredder. I allowed this dream to linger, even though I have no aptitude at all for the mechanics of moving metals parts. As our piles of resilient stalks grew, and the resilience of my spinal column

slackened, I took to casting acquisitive glances at commercial shredders for sale in garden centres. Unhappily, many seemed flawed by both daintiness of design and flimsiness of construction. Some seemed little more than food processors with delusions of grandeur. All suffered from aperture inadequacy—modest little openings through which slender stems might be fed one at a time, and which seemed guaranteed to clog up within minutes. Plainly the manufacturers' primary concern is that some bozo doesn't stick an arm inside, have it chopped off, then sue for billions. These safe but pricey gizmos, I realized, are tricycles whereas I needed a Sherman tank.

Then I met Jerry. A gentleman blessed with exceptional skills in both gardening and metallurgy, Jerry lives in busy retirement in Victoria. His vegetable gardens are magnificent—onions as big as basketballs, his house festooned with grape vines and fig trees sagging with fruit. His secret: relentless shredding and ploughing back in of organic debris. He led me out back of his house to where he has a workshop jammed with acetylene torches and tanks and other tools of the metalworker's trade. He had several shredders that he'd made from old rotary lawn-mowers, designed to sit on top of a forty-five-gallon drum. Debris is fed in from the top and is cut to shreds as it falls through the spinning blade into the drum where composting takes place. These units were a bit small-scale for my grand purposes, but then I spotted a deluxe model, the top of Jerry's line: a large shredder fashioned from steel plate with a vertically mounted steel cutting blade inside a large

271

chamber, powered by a five-horse Briggs and Stratten, the entire apparatus welded onto a sturdy four-wheel wagon like the one I used to drag around on my *Toronto Telegram* paper route, so the shredder can be wheeled to wherever debris has been piled. This was what I'd been after. We fired it up and it roared like a ravening carnivore, its great blade whirling with a lust for cutting. I was enthralled.

Genteel haggling ensued. Jerry invited me to make an offer. I demurred. Jerry mentioned a ballpark figure. I countered with another, somewhat lower, figure. An amicable mid-point was achieved. We loaded up the machine and shook hands, then I sped homewards, a man reborn.

Back at the homestead, I stationed the wagon alongside a heap of surly stalks: Arabian thistles, fireweed, foxgloves, and other leggy brutes. I fired it up and shoved in a wrist-thick stalk of an Arabian thistle. Great roaring and gnashing of teeth ensued, and out the other end dropped a tidy heap of shredded fluff. In went the brittle fireweed stalks, in went the floppy foxgloves, in went heaps of bedraggled lamb's ears, and out came green gold. I believe I achieved ecstasy for several minutes.

272   Things only got better. In the three years since I acquired this beauty (I call it Beelzebub because of its fierce roaring), I feel my life has been transformed. It first comes into play in midsummer when Sandy does a cleaning sweep through the ornamental gardens, producing large heaps of delphinium, foxglove and other stalks, along with prunings from the spring-flowering shrubs. These are ideal shredder fodder, packed with fresh green

matter. Shredded, each heap occupies at most one quarter its original volume. About the same time, the broad-bean stalks get processed, along with garlic tops and Russian kale plants, roots and all. I have to be careful not to include dirt or stones that can both blunt the blade and be fired back out like shrapnel. In part, the machine is so efficient because Jerry skipped on the safety features of commercial models. I wear thick leather gloves and my logger's helmet with ear and eye protection and hope for the best.

The autumn vegetable patch produces great piles of corn stalks, blackberry and raspberry canes, comfrey and borage plants and squash vines. Contributions from the ornamental gardens include sunflower stalks, monkshood, Shasta daisies, campanulas, herbaceous hibiscus, summer phlox, lamb's ears and sundry shrub prunings. I don't add peony or rose foliage in the mix, for fear of spreading diseases. (Rose prunings we simply throw outside the fences, where accommodating deer strip them bare.) A late winter swing might include prunings from trees, shrubs and grape vines.

Once Beelzebub has gnashed the stuff to shreds, I heap it inside a standing tube of galvanized wire about a metre in diameter and two metres tall. There's no need to fuss with consecutive layers or rot activators the way compost connoisseurs do—just pile it up and let it go! Fermentation begins within days, the piles quickly becoming too hot to touch and smelling pungently, as billions of bacteria, fungi, algae and actinomycetes set about breaking down the organic matter. After a week or two, as fermentation slows from lack of oxygen, I break open the cage and either restack the near-compost for a second cooking or spread it in the gardens as mulch.

Returned to the earth from which it came, the shredder's output, like all compost, contributes mightily to healthy soil and a more productive garden. I can live with the shredder's brief bursts of noise and modest consumption of gasoline knowing that it is taking what might otherwise be waste and transforming it into life-sustaining humus. At the end of a successful shredding session I feel much as Michelangelo must have felt gazing up at the ceiling of the Sistine Chapel. Nowadays I've taken to loitering about with my shredder wagon, ready to pull it to wherever a random bit of debris might be found, while the rest of gardening takes a decidedly back seat to the sublime science of shredding.

WEEK 46: OUR ROOTS GO DOWN

The rains have begun in earnest now, driven by buffeting winds whose force we forget over the course of summer. We're lashed by wet whips as we dash from house to car. Between storms the air lies heavy with vapours, pungent with the fermentations of decomposing leaves. I rise now in the dark to the sound of dripping water and big trees soughing in the wind. My first chore's to set newspaper and kindling in the woodstove and strike a fire to warm the chilly house. A bit of creative denial is called for now, when cries and whispers remind you that this is only the beginning of the darkness.

In these dispiriting conditions, few prospects are more heartening than the reassurance provided by orderly rows of root crops that will see us through the winter. The blood of our agricultural ancestors pulses a little more warmly in our veins with the knowledge that we are well stocked with edible roots against the harsh months ahead. No amount of waxing skis or planning midwinter getaways to tropical beaches can buoy one's spirits quite the way a row of bulging rutabagas can.

I can't say the same for winter-keeper beets or winter radishes. We've grown them both with variable success. Root maggots so play the deuce with any radishes at our place, we've all but surrendered the field to the conquering maggots. Winter-keeper beets, even when meticulously mulched, seem not to care for life in soggy soil, alternately soaked and frozen. In very short order they ended up crusty and wizened-looking, pulpy at heart, like people addicted to supermarket tabloids. No, you'd hardly want to put your faith in these two underachievers during the bleak descent into darkness.

Jerusalem artichokes or "sunchokes" are far more reliable, but still something short of ideal as a dietary staple, except perhaps for hermits or misanthropes. Neither from Jerusalem nor an artichoke, these are members of the sunflower family and native to eastern North America. Indigenous peoples customarily ate the knobby tubers, and early European arrivals quickly came to appreciate their worth. Sunchokes became a staple winter food for European settlers and even enjoyed a brief whirl of popularity in Europe before being upstaged by the superstar tuber from the Americas, the potato.

No argument about it, Jerusalem artichokes have their fine points: a uniquely sweet and nutty flavour and fresh crisp texture, low starch and calorie counts. They're easy to grow, producing heavy yields for scarcely no care, hardy as all get-out, and impervious to pests, diseases and droughts (except for some subterranean dweller—a mole or vole, I suppose—who gnawed away contentedly at our tubers all one winter). Their taste improves after frost, and they do best left in the ground all winter under a heavy mulch. Many's the time I've scraped back a layer of snow and rooted out a tuber or two for grating into a midwinter salad. They can be boiled or baked like a potato, steamed, sautéed or stir-fried.

Why, we could ask, would gardeners entirely throw over such a noble tuber in favour of potatoes? Would there have been an Irish famine if Jerusalem artichokes had been grown in Erin alongside blight-prone potatoes? History itself turns like a worm on such choices.

But the sunchoke is a wildling, fundamentally unwilling to adapt to the discipline of the vegetable patch or the marketplace. It can, and left unchecked will, become an invasive weed, each new tuber developing into another leggy perennial. I've finally contained ours inside a metal

276

barrier, but we're still pulling out wildlings from places where they're not wanted. Knobby and sometimes small, the tubers are tedious to clean and all but impossible to store anywhere except in the ground. Once exposed to air, even in the refrigerator, they shrivel miserably and quickly lose their crispy appeal. They're tubers to be plucked and eaten, not stored for days on supermarket shelves. Perhaps that's for the best, because they do excite flatulence in many digestive systems and certainly can't be served to company without provoking "You're very brave to serve these" kind of comments.

No, we must dig elsewhere to strike the real bedrock of winter cuisine: the great triad of traditional winter roots made up of carrots, rutabagas and parsnips. Here are worthy roots indeed, taking pride of place in the root cellars of the nation and on the dining tables of those who would walk in the footsteps of our forebears.

These are easy crops to grow, preferring light, well-drained, neutral soil. For each of them, before planting, I dig the bed deep and work in lots of well-rotted organic matter. Stones in the soil will cause carrots and parsnips to fork and go hairy, like boys who take up smoking cannabis too early in life. Growers cursed with intractably stony ground rely on raised beds and on planting stubbier varieties. In extreme conditions, some enthusiasts still manage to raise full-bodied parsnips by forcing a crowbar deep into the soil and working the bar to create a tapered hole. The hole is filled with good soil, into which several seeds are planted, the process being repeated every fifteen centimetres down the stony row. In my books, anyone going to that much trouble is a true-blue rooter.

I plant parsnips and overwintering carrots in the same bed, usually in late June. Certain experts recommend that these two be kept well apart because they are attacked by the same pests, but I keep them together in one raised bed under a floating cover of Reemay cloth which is very effective at keeping off their principal pest, the carrot rust fly. Over the years I put in more than my share of time trying to repel this pestilential fly by repeated side-dressings of coffee grounds, wood ashes and other recommended but questionable deterrents. I plant rutabagas, or Swedes, in July, usually in a bed where early spinach, peas or beans have been cropped off. Like most brassicas, rutabagas germinate in no time at all. Carrots are a bit slower and parsnips are notoriously unhurried about getting underway.

The trick with all three is to keep them consistently watered and weeded. Thinning is a sine qua non, as roots will refuse to develop at all in crowded conditions. I hill some soil up over the bare shoulders of both carrots and parsnips to prevent exposure to sun. Rutabagas prefer their shoulders bare, eventually bulging their great bellies like certain characters who suffer from an unfortunate pride of portliness. I cover the beds with a deep mulch of grass clippings to suppress weeds and keep the soil uniformly moist for good root development. At this point one begins experiencing preliminary warm fuzzy feelings of a winter well prepared for.

Other than the pesky carrot rust fly, our trusty work-horses suffer little from diseases or pests. We do have to add a trace of boron to the soil every few years lest boron deficiency cause the rutabagas to develop hollow hearts. I read that parsnip canker and rutabaga soft rot can be problems in some areas, especially in wet soils. Aphids will sometimes colonize the undersides of rutabaga leaves, but a rude jet of water from the garden hose makes for effective decolonization.

Winter's first frosts sweeten the turnips and parsnips. After that, I heap the beds with heavy mulching materials, to keep the earth from freezing deeply. Seaweed is ideal, if one can beat the opportunists to the beach and get a glistening load after a November gale. Straw's a good second choice.

There's a particular delight attached to trudging into the vegetable garden on a sombre afternoon, pulling back the protective mulch and unearthing a gleaming orange carrot or purplish rutabaga. Plucking parsnips can sometimes be a less-than-poetic experience if their great roots run too deep, forcing an absurd tug-of-war as you try to wrench one out from the fierce embrace of Mother Earth. Roots in hand, I restore the mulch and mark where the row's been harvested with a stick pushed into the soil.

Harvesting and cooking these big, juicy roots is the antithesis of fast-food cuisine, what with all the washing, scraping and dicing. In our early homesteading days here we survived on a winter diet heavily weighted with the traditional "poor person's" dish—potatoes, rutabagas, carrots and apples boiled and mashed together into a hearty but less-than-elegant lump. Nowadays, as often as not, we'll shred carrot, rutabaga and parsnip into a salad and eat 'em raw. One can think of Tess of the D'Urbervilles, near the nadir of her lonesome exile, hoeing rutabagas out of the frozen ground of Hardy's imagination. Or I remember my dad, back when I was a child in England, bringing home big sacks of parsnips from a nearby farm for the making of parsnip wine. There's a traditional weightiness to these roots, a genuineness that suggests good faith, free of deceit or fraud. They are the products of plain dealing, and on their broad shoulders the gardener is carried genially into the depths of winter.

WEEK 47: VANITY FAIR

I've long maintained that gardeners in general are not a vice-ridden group. We're typically far too preoccupied with pruning, planting and all the rest to have much time for malice. We normally confine our anger to weeds, raccoons, neighbourhood dogs and other vagaries of a universe poorly engineered for accommodating our grand planting schemes. We're given to neither greed nor thievery, and our notions of lasciviousness typically involve a fragrant bloom of some sort.

Still, I've no doubt that were we to poke around long enough in any garden, we might unearth some juicy morsels—some shocking perversity or other that would surely give rise to scandal were it widely known. And chances are that any deplorable traits we'd discover in the heart of even the purest gardener would lie more among the tangled webs of vanity. It's been said that virtue wouldn't get very far if vanity didn't keep it company, and the same may well be true of a garden. We gardeners are creators, after all, artists in fact, our work exposed to the praise or disapproval of a critical world. Notwithstanding all the blather about the process being more important than the product, at heart we want people to admire what we have wrought, to appreciate our subtleties of design, how cunningly we've worked our materials into arrangements that both charm by their simplicity and astonish by their deeper resonances. Like any artist, we seek acknowledgement. We're not angling for praise, of course, nothing so coarse as that—most gardeners are the farthest thing from those poor souls of genuinely modest attainment who excel primarily in positioning themselves along the crowded pathways of praise.

With ardent plantspeople it's quite the opposite, at least initially. We are, if anything, unduly modest. Perhaps our gardens were a triumph this past summer, the talk of the town, and we ourselves acclaimed as artists of considerable accomplishment. Strolling the grounds we may have looked upon the glories we had wrought with an altogether healthy sense of satisfaction. But we would not preen for all the world, we would not strut. We'd rather put our tour de force down to the caprices of the weather, to luck and happenstance, to everything, in short, except our own hard work and skill. The trumpet lilies may have been divine in July, the wisteria in its prime sublime enough to make snide cynics sob, but we discount their excellence, and apologize instead for half-heartedness among the cabbages or the pathos of roses sodden with June rain.

Then destiny may have shown its crueler profile. Perhaps you threw a garden party or hosted a wedding in the yard, or were conned into having your place displayed on a local garden tour. The weather was perfect, the gardens splendid, the guests convivial and the event an uncontested smash. You were heaped with kind remarks. Visitors stood in wonder at the harmonies you'd achieved—the aptness of having drifts of alyssum and frothy alchemilla spilling over a sandstone wall, their powdery lime-yellow flowers contrasting brilliantly with the texture of glossy bergenia leaves. "So simple, but so effective!" you'd hear them exclaim. Even the normally taciturn turned effusive under the enchantment of your plantings.

You were, of course, modest in your acceptance of their gushing. Gratified, naturally, you felt no need to preen. "Oh, it's not everything I'd hoped for really," you let on, though in your heart of hearts you knew you'd far surpassed your own expectations. You insisted upon pointing out some small disappointment off in a hidden corner, at most a minor failure, entirely insignificant amid the undisputed triumph.

But basking in the afterglow of your achievement, perhaps you began to question whether your modesty might not be misplaced. Perusing Schopenhauer in an idle moment, you were struck by his observation: "With

282

people of only moderate ability modesty is mere honesty; but with those who possess great talent it is hypocrisy." Be honest now, you took yourself to task. Were your glorious gardens the handiwork of only moderate ability? Decidedly not. Mediocrity could scarce conceive, much less execute, the singular foliage contrast of that springtime setting in which you'd played wine-coloured Japanese maple leaves with a pale green sophora nearby, then harmonized the composition with a drift of red azaleas whose paler and darker reds reflected the paler and darker leaves. It would be hypocritical indeed to pretend that talent hadn't played a part in the subtlety of that arrangement. And it was only one of many. Well, all right, great talent. Yes, honesty compelled you to acknowledge that great talent had fashioned this *coup de maître*. To pretend otherwise would be false modesty of the least attractive sort. We all know certain gardeners—not to mention garden writers—who wallow in this way. It's been said that false modesty is preferable to none, but is this truly so? Is false modesty not a perverted form of vanity, a manoeuvring to garner praise by strategically insinuating that neither one's garden nor one's self are worthy of it? Surely, you said to yourself, a forthright conceit is preferable to base dissimulation.

Just as you were musing thus, perhaps by chance you found yourself surrounded by flatterers and sycophants— none of them gardeners, needless to say—whose honeyed compliments seemed unimpeachable at the time. Their paeans of praise for your plantings, coming in a sudden gush like the thermal winds of a summer evening, no doubt caught you at your most vulnerable. Goaded by the silvery tongues of toadies, in no time at all your honest self-esteem perhaps began to swell into a less wholesome self-admiration. Your gardens grew more glorious by the day—it seemed as though a marvellous serendipity were at work and you could do no wrong, the beauty now almost unendurable. Then it was that self-pride slipped in, stealthy as the serpent slithering into Eden. In your innocence and rapture you were easy prey for the deadliest of the seven deadly sins. And with those vile toadies whispering flatteries in your ear like salacious succubi—oh, how could you withstand?

Alas, poor thing, you gave way to an unseemly self-glorification. Sipping a touch too much nectar of the gods, you wobbled into the maze of immodesty. As the fever worsened, you took to parading around your grounds with uncharacteristic haughtiness, dispensing insights and advice where none was called for. You became adept at botanical name-dropping, cast like pearls before swine, tongue-tangling Latin slipping smoothly from your lips. You fished for compliments shamelessly, all the while pronouncing the vanity of other and lesser talents insufferable. In short, you made yourself ridiculous. But, of course, vanity cannot permit the one thing that could save those it preys upon—it cannot laugh at itself.

Your gardening cronies were aghast. So unlike you, they whispered among themselves. Everyone sensed an imminent tragedy, a disastrous reversal of fortune, bringing down a person of superior attainments. All held their breath, awaiting the fall.

This is why the gods send us November. The glitter fades. Things fall apart. Darkness descends. So that we might pause to examine where we are, what fools we might have made of ourselves, so that we might make whatever acts of contrition seem appropriate, with a firm purpose to do better in the future, then to lie down to sleep.

WEEK 48: PASSAGES

Frost and wind, rain and sleet have now just about completed their work of stripping deciduous trees of their leaves and blackening the hardiest herbaceous plants. But even in tatters the garden retains traces of its faded beauty, at least metaphorically a hint of fragrant roses beneath the mouldy aromas of decomposing foliage. We have entered the season of memory, mould and melancholy. I suppose all gardens are places rooted deeply in the past, landscapes of memory as much as of imagination, and never more poignantly so than at this time of year. Remembrance stalks the November garden like Banquo's ghost.

Thinkers of all stripes have long pondered the concept of the garden as a place of remembering. Philosophers and poets, folksingers, screenplay writers and New Age etherialists—they've all had a kick at the concept that within our consciousness there lingers a tribal memory of Eden. Getting Ourselves Back to the Garden, Paradise Refound, Back to Eden—the clichés run deep as black bindweed roots through the subsoil of our culture. We once lived in a place of bliss; we were banished from that place; our life's work is to rediscover it. The mania for gardening is sufficiently inexplicable, it seems to me, that the dream of recreating Paradise Lost is as cogent an explanation as any other.

Our love of gardens perhaps flourishes because of personal recollections of the gardens we experienced as children. They were places in which we were dazzled and enchanted by profusions of flowers, fluttering butterflies and other fascinating insects, ponds wonderfully full of pollywogs and, if we were lucky, a garter snake with which to terrify the aunties. Children's artwork is full of these images, and it makes some sense that as adults we may endure the labours of gardening, at least in part, in an effort to recreate a personal golden age of childhood.

Mostly these days I'm remembering my parents' gardens, because my father died a year ago this month. I remember him in his final days, a wizened little skeleton curled up in a hospital bed, his brain numbed by a series of strokes, his vacant eyes fixed on nothing as I read him old Irish stories. But far more vividly I picture him in the gardens he and my mother created. They were gardens when in full bloom people from around the district would come to view. Neighbours would stroll by on a Sunday afternoon, perhaps take a photograph or two. Every so often someone would ask if they could have a wedding there.

Though on a large lot, it was no great estate, just a working-class English cottage garden in a Toronto

286

neighbourhood indistinguished with parched lawns and desultory conifers. It had large mixed borders, rose beds and vine-draped trellises in front, fruits and vegetables crammed in back, two homemade greenhouses and scarcely any lawn at all. Though rare at the time, it was the kind of garden you can spot in many neighbourhoods nowadays and know instantly that here flourishes the handiwork not of landscape architects, but of passionate amateurs.

My mother processed the produce, often sitting for hours on the front verandah picking heads and tails off currants or gooseberries. My brothers and I were sometimes conscripted into lending a hand with this tedious work, and I suppose that's one of the reasons none of us boys took any interest in gardening. It seemed to me all work and worry and no fun at all. Already cursed with a head of ridiculously red hair, I secretly wished our place was less conspicuous, that we'd have a lawn and clump of conifers like normal people.

Besides managing the food processing department, my mother was also in charge of planning. She'd pore over nursery catalogues in search of "something unusual." It was thought a high attainment to cultivate ornamentals— usually annuals—that nobody else in the vicinity grew. This was not a great challenge, as most of the neighbours didn't garden at all, but it generated lots of excitement at our place as various weird plants (the only ones I can remember were giant castor beans) got established to astonish passersby. My father did the spade work, in fact all the yard work, squeezed in between his regular night shift on the Toronto subway system and his part-time second job at a nearby greenhouse. Neither knew much about garden design principles; Latin names mystified them entirely.

But gardening consumed their lives. They didn't travel or go to movies or dine out. If circumstances had permitted, I believe they'd have done nothing but garden and been quite content. Gardening was the axis upon which their world turned, and their gardens were places of wonderful productivity and untutored beauty. My mother died twenty years ago, and my father kept on gardening alone, I'm sure in part as a way of keeping her memory close by him. He took over the gooseberry and strawberry jam making, the currant jellies and dried pears that had been her engagement. At eighty years old he was still climbing up into his fruit trees (an orchard ladder being considered an unnecessary luxury) in order to prune or harvest them, and growing far more potatoes and tomatoes than he and the entire neighbourhood could possibly eat. "They all want instant potatoes or pizzas nowadays," he sometimes complained to me when neighbours declined another bushel-load of his free produce. After half a century of it, the growing had taken on a life of its own, whether it still made any sense or not.

The last time I toured his garden with him, I was painfully aware that the muscular little Irishman, always so full of vigour and mischief, was suddenly old and frail. He

288

showed me his iris bed, once a thing of exceptional beauty but now overcrowded and weedy, the soil plainly depleted. "They need to all be lifted and the bed dug over to make anything of them," he told me; but we both knew, without saying, that it would not happen, that the iris bed, the whole garden into which he and my mother had poured so much of their lives, would soon be gone and so would he.

Almost overnight his strength deserted him. Reluctantly we settled him into a nursing home for his few final years and the old place was sold off. After helping my brother clean the yard up a bit, I stood there for a final time one bleak late winter afternoon. A cold wind whistled through the derelict old greenhouses and sang in the wires that once held grape vines and raspberry canes heavy with fruit. I've never gone back.

But in a way I see that garden still, as it was in its prime, because over the years my parents shipped out packets of seeds, cuttings, bulbs and roots of their favourite plants for us to propagate as well. Most of what they sent—clumps of Solomon's seal, old-fashioned daylilies, coral bells, fiercely orange tiger lilies—were tough, hardy customers, like my parents themselves. Among their favourite plants was a collection of herbaceous hibiscus with showy dinner-plate blooms in pinks and reds. I have a photo of my dad standing in his garden, a leprechaun beaming proudly at the camera from beneath his giant flowering hibiscus. They grow and flower far less fulsomely for us, but when their few blooms do appear in September, I see him under them and my

289

mother, sitting in her rocker on the veranda, her fingers methodically plucking heads and tails from currants.

The mournful pensiveness of the November garden seems to me composed of melancholy at the passing of seasons and the loss of loved ones, the approach of inescapable death, but also of a thrilling exhilaration at remembrances of significant people and of beautiful things that, with luck, we will experience again.

$\mathcal{D}$ECEMBER

WEEK 49: BIRCH BARKING

Pale winter sunshine came slanting across the yard this afternoon, illuminating a clump of golden-leafed bamboos over near the creek. Choice throughout the year, evergreen bamboos seem to shimmer with particular beauty in winter. We have three different types growing, each of them alluring, and each embodying, as they do in Chinese symbology, attributes we might well wish for ourselves: durability, longevity and graceful strength. This time of year especially, they are a triumph of the garden, and I fully understand the enthusiasms of growers belonging to the various chapters of the American Bamboo Society, about whose activities I receive regular notice from a neighbour. I would be pleased to go on at length about these gentle giants of the grass family, but won't—in part because winter hardiness greatly limits bamboos for most

Canadian gardens and, in part, because alongside the alluringly illuminated golden bamboos stands our version of that quintessentially Canadian coppice: a birch grove.

I have admired birches and their near-relatives in many parts of the country. As a transplanted English schoolboy, I was entranced by tales of noble woodlands Indians and dreamed of some day fashioning my own birch bark canoe. Years later I inscribed a love poem to my bride-to-be on a scroll of white bark cut tenderly from a birch growing in the wilds of Ontario. I'm sure I was inspired in part by one of my favourite real poems, Robert Frost's familiar "Birches" with its charming metaphors of birch trees bent by winter storms. Though not exactly born to birches, I felt drawn to them in a way I had not been, for example, to bamboo. Here was a tree of graceful beauty and rugged hardiness, of unspoiled and lonesome places, in the whispering of whose leaves we might hear the call of the wild.

Nothing would do but that we have a grove of birches, and so in an open corner of the lawn we planted three clustered European white birches and, a little ways apart, a weeping purple birch. I've mentioned them already, back in January, as having been all but annihilated by our killer snow storm. "All but" is the dangling modifier here. For well over a decade our birch grove has staggered from one dismaying "all but" to the next but never quite succumbed. Nor has it yet—I thought the snow storm had finished them off, but no, they've bounced back again, their shattered trunks now sporting multiple shoots like an electrified Afro haircut.

Considering the rugged conditions they endure in the wild, I think it's understandable that we initially thought of birches as very tough customers, well adapted to the rough-and-tumble of life in the great outdoors. Such proved not entirely the case in our little grove. First off, the deer stripped away whatever leaves they could get at, which was most, as the lovable ungulates balanced on their hind legs, wobbling around like tipsy ballerinas. So I fenced in the stripped-down saplings with wire cages. These prevented repeat defoliation, but considerably diminished the aspect of our carefree country copse.

I had, of course, secured the saplings with stout yellow cedar stakes, which worked admirably up to a point. The birches, however, eventually surpassed that point and, once above it, showed a disconcerting propensity to waver. Admittedly, a formidable wall of mature native conifers towering on the southeast of the grove may have compounded the problem, forcing the birches to reach sideways in search of sunlight. But their grasp exceeded their reach and they began to wobble more than weep. I then attached long supplementary stakes, lashing them high up on the contorted trunks in an elevated effort to encourage vertical growth. Combined with the encircling wire cages, the stakes and ropes further degraded the natural carefree look of the grove.

Eventually the trees struggled up into an ungainly adolescence. They began to bear lovely winter catkins and their wayward trunks, by now several inches thick, developed the papery peeling white bark of your classic birch grove. With their foliage well beyond the reach of the deer, I removed the wire cages that we might better appreciate the bark. Within days the exposed lower trunks were gouged and stripped by deer rubbing their antlers against them. Thousands of trees all about, and they have to rub their wretched antlers on our four scrawny birches. In the rubbing process, they'd pushed two of the smaller trees half over. With a dark heart towards deer, I painted the wounds, restaked the wobbly stems and recaged the grove. I ran high guy wires from stouter trees to help support the weaker ones. By this point, the grove as a whole, with its lashings and upliftings, was beginning to resemble something Madonna might have done to herself for publicity purposes.

The following spring our young trees proved highly attractive to a pair of yellow-bellied sapsuckers nesting in the neighbourhood. These old feathered friends had previously demolished several of our mountain ashes and played bloody mischief among the apple and cherry trees. The sapsuckers took to perforating the birch bark and slurping up the sap, leaving great running sores behind. Again, you'd have to ask, with thousands of healthy trees all about, why are these confounded sapsuckers picking on our lurching birches?

Whenever I'd spot a sapsucker at work, I'd drop whatever I was doing and run screaming across the lawn after the bird. The trees were by now pouring sap so badly from the drill holes, I had to repeatedly get out the ladder, remove the wire cages, climb up and paint over the holes, climb back down and replace the cages. By the time I'd put the ladder away the sapsuckers would have returned. Eventually they took to drilling higher up on the trunks than I could conveniently reach. By then the lovely white boles, splotched and smeared with sapsucker holes, oozing sap and pruning paint, looked more like a postmodernist installation than a grove of trees.

Finally, after many seasons of travail we achieved the poetic moment immortalized by Frost, when birches are bent to the ground by ice storms, graceful as young girls down on their hands and knees, their long hair flung forward on the ground to dry in the sun. Our purple pendula, always the weakest of the bunch, was the first to attempt this poetic bending-down. A soggy snowfall brought her to her knees. Her exhausted stake snapped off, her wire cage collapsed like fallen socks around her ankles. Her ropes and guy wires lay splayed in all directions like burst garter belts. Her poor contorted trunk, rubbed by antlers, pecked by birds and smeared with paint, lay prostrate on the grass, not quite so winsomely as Frost's young girls. More like a poor charwoman, old before her time, worn out from the unfair blows of fate, no longer possessing the strength to stand.

This was a poignant moment indeed, reminding me how blessed we gardeners are, in exchange for our labours, with these prescient opportunities for reflection on the vagaries of life. As I say, the birches have bounced back in their own peculiar way, but for all their Group-of-Seven true-blue Canadianness, they're not at home at our place, not the way that graceful Asian bamboos are. As the poet might have put it, one could do worse than be a grower of birches, though it's hard to imagine quite how.

WEEK 50: THE PERMISSIVE GARDENER

"We didn't want to move, but the garden became too much for us." This can be the sad lament of aged or infirm gardeners who are no longer able to maintain their gardens. Once a source of delight, the garden becomes a burden, now generating stress after so long serving to disperse it. Running out of control, the garden instills worry rather than pleasure, a discomforting reminder of one's declining powers.

This is not my own case yet. I'm in my early fifties—an age at which, if one's health still holds, as mine does, you can revel in the splendid intersection of a still-vigorous body now taking its orders from a mind well tempered by experience. I like that old Chinese axiom that ideally one should spend the first fifty years of life in learning its meaning and the second in wise application of what has been learned. But, wisdom and vigour notwithstanding, Sandy and I have come to recognize that the grand estate we've slaved to create for ourselves over the past three decades is now, although far from complete, already too large to be maintained except by working virtually non-stop at a pace that would exhaust a world-class athlete. Arthritis has begun to creep insidiously into certain overworked joints.

Old bones, broken years ago in reckless youth, now ache painfully after a day of heavy spading.

Thus I was delighted to come across a slender book titled *The Permissive Garden,* written and illustrated by an Englishwoman named Erica Lady Pearce. She gardened for more than fifty years on a windswept hill in Sussex and completed the book shortly before her death in 1985. She dedicated it: "To those who are thinking of changing their houses because they can no longer manage their gardens." Written from the wisdom of experience, her little volume offers a refreshing look at how, rather than having a garden that has become a worry, one can continue enjoying "the secret garden of my old age."

The main thing, she advises, is to cut out unwanted work. "In the permissive garden you must rid yourself of any work that has to be done. Fun to do, yes; better be done, perhaps; but *has* to be done, certainly not, or the garden will become a tyrant." I know many gardeners can relate to that sense of tyranny—the requirement to pull yourself up out of relaxation or other engagement and drag yourself outdoors in filthy weather because some garden chore absolutely *must* be done lest disaster befall you.

It has occurred to Sandy and me over the past year or two that we could, and perhaps should, break down and hire some strapping youth to come in and lend a hand now and then. We've actually hired someone the past few years to help get the winter's firewood split, confirming my suspicion that it's always easiest to find people capable of doing the jobs you most enjoy doing yourself. The long and short of it is I don't really want some callow youth crashing around in the mixed borders and interrupting every twenty seconds to ask whether this just-uprooted plant is a weed or not. I've been that callow youth myself and have nothing against him at all; indeed, I love him dearly, but at a distance, en passant, and decidedly not in the garden.

Erica Lady Pearce is with me on this, arguing that it's unwise to become dependent upon outside help because it may suddenly become unavailable, making matters worse than ever. Instead she advocates retooling the garden (rationalizing and downsizing I suppose we'd have to call it if we listened to certain voices) through both a change of attitude and some practical alterations that help ensure the labours you'll still be doing is work you want to do, not have to do.

The first, and crucial, step is to realize that we garden for ourselves, not for other people. We may have had a marvellous show garden in our time, but that time is past, and good riddance. We are now set free to garden for no one's approval or admiration but our own, which means we can have a garden as idiosyncratic as we want. This is one of the grand latitudes of age.

Emancipated, we begin reducing the workload by eliminating features that require repeated attention. Grass, for example. The fundamental problem with grass is that something always has to be done with it. The same area paved over with flagstones or concrete, perhaps leaving certain gaps for plantings, becomes relatively hassle-free. Plantings in pots, tubs and urns are also problematic as they require endless watering and watching and should, in Lady P's words, "be resisted on principle." I foresee an enormous glut of pots in the second-hand shops a few years from now as all the poor souls seduced by the current vogue for container gardening hit the wall of watering. The same goes for vigorous climbers that involve a lot of pruning and tying. Working on a wobbly ladder to get after things like the irrepressible runners of a wisteria can be both time-consuming and dangerous. Better not to have the vine. Our several wisterias—a sullen bunch from the outset—have scarcely bloomed, but already I'm plotting their removal on the grounds of reduced workload. Absurdly, we've also just put in about fifteen new clematis vines whose pruning, tying and incessant disentangling will probably polish me off within the decade. Hedges that demand repeated shearing—don't get me started on hedges again!—may have to be sacrificed for a trouble-free fence or wall.

The garden hardscape can also be restructured with an eye to minimizing exertions. The compost heap and toolshed should be within easy reach. In a hillside garden, it's far easier dragging rubbish downhill than up. Where possible, steps should be avoided for ease of wheelbarrowing—something I would have appreciated knowing before constructing my monumental stone steps, but far be it from me to complain at this late date. Raised beds, of course, reduce stooping and bending. Many of the other innovations recently conceived for wheelchair gardeners are applicable here, and long-overdue manuals on the subject are now available.

Having just got our own gardens to a more-or-less passable state through heavy reliance upon vast plantings of hardy perennials, we've since come to recognize that the secret garden of old age works best if it's planted in mostly trees and shrubs rather than labour-intensive annuals and perennials. Lady Pearce concurs, noting that although shrubs and trees entail an initial expense, they are still "cheaper than moving house." And avoid most ground covers, she warns. "In my experience almost anything that is strong enough to overcome weeds is also strong enough to overcome shrubs." After protracted battles with St. John's wort and periwinkles, both major and minor, Lady Pearce banished all ground covers other than London pride and dianthus. There's no question she's overreacting here, but that's allowed, indeed encouraged, in the permissive garden.

Lastly, she writes, the key to trouble-free gardening is mulch. Her method was to pile up among her shrubs a six-inch-deep layer of bracken cut from a neighbouring common. Only an inveterate gardener would describe scything bracken, bundling it by hand and dragging the bundles by rope back to the garden as labour-saving activity. She also spread scrap pieces of paper and cardboard under plants. Thereafter, all twigs, cuttings, leaves and spent flowers are thrown on top of the mulch to contribute

to it. No need to haul anything away, except prickly bits
like holly or rose clippings that are hazardous to walk on.
She would throw weeds either onto paved areas or into
wire-mesh cages placed around the garden for that purpose. Once dead, the weeds too would be added to the
mulch layer. Mulch, of course, further reduces labour by
suppressing weeds, retaining ground moisture and allows
the gardener to walk on the beds even in wet weather. I'm
already a fanatical mulcher myself for these reasons. Trouble is, our principle mulch material is grass clippings caught
from the lawns we should be downsizing and eliminating, so I can see a conflict of interest brewing there already.
Still, the principles hold, and these various labour-saving
schemes will, as Rosemary Verey writes in her foreword to
Lady Pearce's lovely little book, ease "growing old gracefully in your garden and still enjoying the beauties of it in a
permissive manner."

WEEK 51: WINTER SOLSTICE

"God gave us memory," wrote J.M. Barrie, "that we might
have roses in December." I think that's a splendid senti-
ment, one with which we may all agree in our dotage, if
only we can remember it. Yes, I can picture it clearly: sitting feebly in the sunroom at some dreary nursing home,
fussed over by good-hearted but overworked staff, our
principal delight the tender memories of days long gone
and never to come again. I imagine it similar to remembering on a cold and dreary day like today, the darkest of

the year, how marvellous it was at summer solstice, so long gone, but really only the flutter of an eyelash ago. I remember Celia Thaxter waxing enthusiastically about the very soul of summer "like the spirit of romance, sweet as a youth's tender dreams." That's what we'll be recalling in our dotage, with luck, unless we're among the truly blessed who live in their gardens to a grand old age and at last topple over and pass away directly into the sweet embrace of earth.

The only flaw in this poignant "remembering the roses" scenario is that so many gardeners have such notoriously deficient memories, I'm not at all confident we'll be able to remember much of anything by the time recollection is all we have left. Everywhere you look across the gardens of the nation, you see alarming manifestations of memory impairment. Take the matter of vanishing implements, for example. How is it that a person can enter their garden, trowel firmly in hand, only to emerge twenty minutes later with absolutely no idea of where the trowel has gotten to? A full-scale search proves futile, as does questioning the absent-minded miscreant.

Where were you using it last?

I don't quite remember; somewhere in the garden.

Can you remember what you were doing?

Trowelling, I suppose, but I must have gotten distracted.

The case is hopeless; the trowel's gone for good. Secateurs, spades, even wheelbarrows—there seems to be no limit to a gardener's capacity to forget where they've left something. An excessive number of sheds and storage areas—another symptom we've already discussed—can often compound the problem. I spent significant portions of three afternoons this past summer wandering from woodshed to toolshed to potting shed to the old goat barn, trying to discover where in blazes I'd stored the soaker hoses the previous fall. I knew I'd seen them somewhere, I could visualize them clearly, but I'd be damned if I could recall just where.

Whenever I can't lay my hand on a missing tool, I choose not to blame my own forgetfulness, but rather to inwardly accuse someone else. Perhaps the single most important role filled by a gardening companion is this one: that they can be conveniently blamed for pilfering an implement whose whereabouts you've forgotten. Colleagues, neighbours and former friends are extremely useful too and can be credibly blamed for borrowing and failing to return the most unlikely missing items. But then the devilish question arises: Who was it that borrowed the post hole digger, anyway? Of course, you can't remember.

It would be extremely useful, whenever a recently acquired plant dies unexpectedly, to retain in memory where you purchased it, so that you could return it with a mournful countenance and a reasonable expectation of a complimentary replacement. But can you remember?

Not exactly.

Do you recall where you might have put the sales slip?

Not just at the moment.

Many's the gardener whose condition has advanced to the point where they don't even recall having introduced certain plants. "Hello, what's this?" they'll exclaim one day, perhaps encountering a shrub whose presence in the garden is entirely unaccountable—as though certain plants were, like feral cats, given to sneaking into gardens under cover of darkness.

Though less apt to reveal surprise additions, the vegetable patch has its own way of playing mind games with you. Crop rotation is a very fertile field, for example. In the best of all possible worlds, one would record what was planted where each year so that you'd minimize disease and pest problems by never planting related crops in the same bed without a decent interval. Needless to say, there was insufficient opportunity to get this crucial mapping work done at the time, while you could still remember what was growing where. Or if you did manage, in an uncustomary burst of efficiency to get the layout meticulously recorded, you now can't remember where you put it. This is why you so frequently see certain persons out in their gardens in springtime, staring vacantly at the bare earth, perhaps scratching themselves where they wouldn't if they knew you were watching, trying mightily to recall what was growing where a year ago. Same thing with trying to remember the name of an especially productive variety you grew last year. You know you should have written the name down somewhere. Maybe you did write it down. Somewhere.

In its fullest blossoming, memory loss can produce a tragicomedy in the garden that would be hilarious were it not so pitiable. The absent-minded gardener simply cannot remember what he or she is about. She takes a few determined steps down a path. Stops. Looks around, trying to recall where she's going and why. Then doubles back the other way to do something else which in turn flits in and out of mind faster than a toad's tongue. Eventually the poor soul's reduced to simply standing in the garden, staring out blankly into an unfathomable universe. If this condition should strike you yourself, and you're observed in its disquieting grip, I find the best escape is fake mysticism. Rather than confess you're becalmed because you can't remember what you're supposed to be doing, you smile knowingly to indicate you were in ecstatic rapture over the enchantments of plants.

Plant names, of course, are another omnipresent pitfall.

"What's that plant over there?" one of several visitors asked me some time ago.

"Oh, that," I glanced down nonchalantly, but completely flummoxed inwardly, "is a potentilla."

"Isn't it a goom?" one of the others suggested.

"A goom?" I echoed, inwardly flailing like a drowning swimmer, not remembering anything ever called a goom, but feeling a perfect fool for not even knowing my own plants. "It's either Miss Wilmott or Mrs. Bradshaw, I forget which," I said with a blithe indifference aimed at implying that I was far too artistically *outré* to worry myself over such trifles.

"I knew it!" exulted my tormentor. "It's a goom!"

These conversations are best terminated as quickly as good manners allow, especially if they involve another person as absent-minded as yourself. Two or more gardeners wracking their brains for elusive names can be a disheartening sight. "Oh, it's on the tip of my tongue!" one will exclaim. "I know the name as well as my own!" These remarks are accompanied with much finger snapping, head shaking and other peculiar gestures aimed at bringing the elusive name to mind. Chronic sufferers take to sticking identification tags all over their gardens, creating an overall effect less of information than desperation. Fancy nameplates done in ceramics or bronze may strike a tonier tone than plastic tags, but the sorry message is the same: Lest We Forget.

Of course there are a few people who flounce about with razor-sharp minds able to bring up obscure plant names with prodigious speed and accuracy. Generally speaking, these are not the sort of people one wants to cultivate, even if you could remember their names. Nor should one succumb to feelings of inadequacy in their presence. Rather, I take comfort in that old line from Elbert Hubbard: "A retentive memory is a good thing, but the ability to forget is the true token of greatness." This attitude serves us admirably in the short term, but it's no help at all when it comes to remembering roses in December and I dread to think how it will serve us in the dark hours of the nursing home.

WEEK 52: YEAR'S END

As I assume I've made clear over the course of our year together, I am not a master gardener. But almost everyone I meet nowadays is.

"How do you do?" These people greet you with an earthy handshake. But before you can tell them how you do, they announce straight off: "I'm a master gardener, you know." You didn't know, but you might have guessed by their air of robust confidence. "I took The Course," they tell you, pronouncing "The Course" with a reverential tone others might reserve for "The Holy Grail" or "The Ninth Insight."

It's tricky finding an appropriate response to these disclosures. To say "That's nice" seems somehow insufficient, given the weight of the occasion. I'm often tempted to reply, "Oh, so am I!" But this wouldn't be truthful, and I fear I'd soon be caught out by a trick question concerning sexual preferences among sempervivums. Instead I normally reply, "Wonderful!" with what I hope sounds like enthusiasm. This is the same response I employ when somebody tells me they keep fourteen cats or have thirty-nine grandchildren. And it is wonderful, in its own way, to have hordes of master gardeners roaming the planet in search of people who are not master gardeners but might enjoy meeting one.

I have come to the conclusion that the fundamental difference between master gardeners and garden-variety

307

gardeners has nothing to do with gardening per se, but everything to do with time management. Ordinary gardeners—as I'm sure we've achieved consensus over the course of our year together—never seem to have a spare moment; they're always bustling about the yard desperately trying to keep up. Master gardeners, by comparison, not only have matters well in hand on their estates, but also have scads of surplus time for taking The Course and various post-course courses, seminars, lectures, workshops and other instructional wonders. And it's plainly the case that the more courses they take the more time they free up for taking more courses.

The situation gives rise to extremely delicate questions concerning how ordinary gardeners and master gardeners should relate to one another. I believe it is only the admirable good-heartedness of both groups that prevents sectarian unpleasantness from breaking out. Master gardeners seem to be extraordinarily well schooled in not adopting a condescending or patronizing tone. They may see at a glance what is amiss in an everyday garden they happen to be visiting, but they are sensitive enough not to lecture or harangue the poor wretch responsible. They deliver constructive criticism, for the ultimate good of both gardener and garden, with utmost discretion and never so much as a hint of haughtiness.

For their part, run-of-the-mill growers, upon encountering the breezy expertise of a master gardener, might be tempted to Envy, for who wouldn't feel envious of these accomplished characters? But, although they themselves have never taken The Course, chiefly from lack of time, everyday growers are astute enough to beware of Envy and its foul companion, Spitefulness, knowing that these are evil spirits which, if allowed to linger in a garden, quickly devour the joy in it.

The long and short of it is that all gardeners, whether masters or not, are far more intimately bound together by their commonalities than divided by their differences. And never more so than now as we each sit musing on the year's dark and final hours. Our thoughts naturally turn to reviewing the seasons just past, perhaps casting back a full year as I'm doing now, to the killer snowstorm that caused us to ponder at the outset whether gardening begins in disaster but ends in triumph or the other way around. Silly, in hindsight, to even pose the question. Because by now, if we've not had our spirits soured by spiteful envy or outlandish vanity, we're almost certainly singing canticles for whatever it was led us into the entranced life of gardening. It is an invitation not issued to everyone, this call to join the company of our green-fingered forebears.

No matter what other cards destiny may deal us, all of us who garden live a life of high privilege. Even on bad days I feel inclined to at least mumble a few token words of gratitude for all the good food that comes out of the vegetable patch during the year—the wholesome crunch of living spinach salads, the unimpeachable sweetness of fresh-picked peas and corn. I remember at one point last summer we were exulting, night after night, in desserts concocted of our own fresh-picked figs, peaches and strawberries—dishes of sublime, sensuous succulence. Even the most curmudgeonly among us would admit that, in a world where millions go hungry and millions more stuff themselves on refined rubbish, an abundance of fresh wholesome produce is a luxury that warrants a bit of benediction.

And to be surrounded by beautiful plants! I think back to walks around the springtime garden, peering into open crocuses, the saffron sheen of their petals and the brilliant yellow stigmata at their centres. We had a young tree peony flower for the first time this year—I haven't mentioned it yet—a single huge blossom of creamy white petals with a hint of the palest pink streaked through them. Looking into the heart of the enormous flower one morning I discovered a large spider living there—she was cream-coloured with faint pink striping, a brilliant duplication of her flowery house. For moments like those you give thanks.

The gardening life is one of virtues—quiet contemplation, delight in beauty, the tranquility of the moment—that are peculiarly close to those of the religious life. I like the notion of the gardener as pilgrim, one on a purposeful venture full of unexpected excitements, high drama, strange turnings in lovely landscapes. A journey of discovery, of learning as we go, knowing that we'll never learn enough. As well a pilgrimage of dirt and disappointment, sudden deaths and regretful diggings-out. For the enchantments of the journey, the chance to live in touch with the earth, to find ourselves within its seasonal turnings—for these we pause and give thanks. With luck, along the path of pilgrimage we come to truly appreciate the extraordinary beauty of each ordinary day. We learn to value it as a precious and perfect thing, to know that our allotted number of days is finite and will run out as swiftly as this year now gone. That the time may soon enough arrive when we'll look back with a keen longing to experience just one more of those extraordinary ordinary days.

So I sit now on my little island in the dark of midwinter, as I did a short year ago, dreaming old dreams of things that have gone before and seeing fresh visions of a new year dawning.

Also by DES KENNEDY

· · ·

FICTION

The Garden Club

Flame of Separation

· · ·

NON-FICTION

The Passionate Gardener

Living Things We Love to Hate

Crazy about Gardening

ABOUT THE AUTHOR

NOMINATED THREE TIMES for the Stephen Leacock Memorial Medal for Humour, Des Kennedy is an accomplished novelist and satirist as well as a garden writer. He has lived for the past thirty-six years with his partner, Sandy, in their hand-hewn home on one of British Columbia's Gulf Islands. The author of countless magazine pieces and five previous books, Kennedy has also made numerous TV and radio appearances and written for and narrated documentary films. A popular speaker on the gardening circuit, Kennedy has been active in the environmental scene for many years and was a founding director of a community land trust on his home island.